Akbar: An Eastern Romance

P. A. S. van Limburg Brouwer

Alpha Editions

This edition published in 2024

ISBN : 9789366388496

Design and Setting By
Alpha Editions
www.alphaedis.com
Email - info@alphaedis.com

As per information held with us this book is in Public Domain.
This book is a reproduction of an important historical work. Alpha Editions uses the best technology to reproduce historical work in the same manner it was first published to preserve its original nature. Any marks or number seen are left intentionally to preserve its true form.

Contents

Introductory Life of Akbar..- 1 -
Biographical Notice of the Author...- 16 -
The Author's Preface. ....- 18 -
Chapter I. The Hermit. ....- 20 -
Chapter II. Iravati...- 30 -
Chapter III. Agra. ....- 41 -
Chapter IV. Akbar...- 53 -
Chapter V. A New and an Old Acquaintance. ....- 65 -
Chapter VI. Salim. ....- 76 -
Chapter VII. Secret Meetings. ....- 89 -
Chapter VIII. A Tempter..- 100 -
Chapter IX. The Weighing of the Emperor. ....- 112 -
Chapter X. Surprises. ....- 122 -
Chapter XI. "Tauhid-i-Ilahi."1..- 133 -
Chapter XII. Assassination. ....- 143 -
Chapter XIII. Parting. ....- 151 -
Chapter XIV. The Discovery. ....- 161 -
Chapter XV. Amendment. ....- 170 -
Chapter XVI. Faizi's Curse...- 178 -
Chapter XVII. The Tomb..- 185 -

Introductory Life of Akbar.

The object of the Romance which is now presented to English readers, in a translated form, is to convey a generally accurate idea of the court of Akbar, the greatest and best native ruler that ever held sway over Hindustan. The author, Dr. Van Limburg-Brouwer, was an oriental scholar, who strove, by this means, to impart to others the knowledge he had himself acquired, through the study of contemporary writers, of the thoughts and habits of the great Emperor, and of the manners and civilization of those who surrounded him.

If he has attained any measure of success in this attempt, his labours will certainly have been useful, and his work deserves translation. For on Englishmen, more than on any other people, is a knowledge of so important a period of Indian history incumbent. This romance of Akbar is, it is true, but a sketch, and is only intended to excite interest in the subject. But if it has that effect, and leads to further inquiry and research, it will secure the object with which it was written, and will have done useful service.

"Akbar, an Eastern Romance," ("Akbar, een Oostersche Roman,") was first published in Dutch, at the Hague, in 1872, the year before the author's death.[1] A German translation appeared at Leipzig in 1877.[2] A native of Holland might not unnaturally undertake such a work, for the best European contemporary account of the reign of Akbar was written by a Dutchman, Pieter Van den Broeck.[3]

Students of Indian history are looking forward to the publication of the Life of Akbar by Prince Frederick of Schleswig Holstein. A really good biography of so great a ruler will be a work of the highest importance, and the Prince's proved literary skill[4] and thoroughness in research justify the anticipation that his Life of Akbar will be worthy of the subject. The romance by Van Limburg-Brouwer, in its English dress, will answer its purpose if it gives rise to a desire for more full and complete information in a graver form, and thus serves as an *avant courier* to the life of Akbar by Prince Frederick.

The epoch of Akbar is the one of greatest importance to English students of the history of India, for two reasons. It is the period when administration under native rule was best and most efficient, and it is, consequently, the one with which a comparison with British rule should be made. It is also the period of which the most detailed and exact accounts have been written and preserved; so that such a comparison will be reliable and useful.

A brief introductory notice of the great Emperor's life may, perhaps, be acceptable to readers of Van Limburg-Brouwer's historical romance. Akbar was the third Indian sovereign of the House of Timur. Hindustan had been ruled by Afghans for two centuries and a half5 when Baber crossed the Indus and founded the Mughal6 Empire in 1525. Baber died in the Charbagh at Agra, on December 26th, 1530, and his son and successor, Humayun, was defeated and driven out of India by the able and determined Afghan chief, Shir Shah, in 1540. Shir Shah died on the throne, and was succeeded by a son and grandson, while Humayun took refuge with Tahmasp, the Shah of Persia. The restored Afghans kept their power for fifteen years.

The story of Humayun's flight is told by his faithful ewer bearer, named Jauhar, who accompanied him in his exile.7

Jauhar tells us that, in October 1542, a little party of seven or eight horsemen and a few camels was wearily journeying over the sandy wastes of Sind, worn out with fatigue, and famished with thirst. The fugitive Prince Humayun, his wife the youthful Hamida,8 the ewer bearer Jauhar, an officer named Rushen Beg, and a few others, formed the party. Extreme misery had destroyed alike the differences of rank and the power of concealing the true character. When Rushen's horse was worn out, he insisted upon taking one which he had lent to the Queen, a young girl of fifteen within a few days of her confinement. Humayun gave his own horse to his wife, walked some distance, and then got on a baggage camel. A few hours afterwards the forlorn wanderers entered the fort of Amarkot, near Tatta, which is surrounded by a dreary waste of sand-hills. Here, under the shade of an *arka* tree,9 young Hamida gave birth to a prince, who afterwards became the most enlightened thinker, and the ablest administrator of his age. Akbar was born on the 14th of October 1542. Jauhar, by Humayun's order, brought a pod of musk, which the fugitive king broke and distributed among his followers, saying, "This is all the present I can afford to make you on the birth of my son, whose fame, I trust, will one day be expanded all over the world, as the perfume of the musk now fills this room."

The fugitives then fled up the Bolan Pass, and the little Akbar remained for some time in the hands of his turbulent uncles at Kandahar and Kabul, while his parents took refuge at the court of Persia. Then the wheel of fortune turned. Assisted by Bairam Khan, a very able general and a native of Badakshan, Humayun fought his way back into military possession of Lahore and Delhi, and died in 1556, leaving his inheritance, such as it was, to his young son.

At the time of his father's death, Akbar was only in his fifteenth year. He was then in the Punjab, with Bairam Khan, putting down the last efforts of the Afghan faction. Bairam Khan became Regent, and remained in power until 1560, when the young King assumed the sovereignty.

In order to appreciate the full extent of Akbar's achievements, it must be considered that he had to conquer his dominions first, before he could even think of those great administrative improvements which signalized the latter part of his life and immortalized his name. In his first year he possessed the Punjab, and the country round Delhi and Agra; in the third year he acquired Ajmir; in the fourth, Gwalior and Oudh; and in 1572 he conquered Gujrat, Bengal, and Bihar; but it took several years before order could be established in those countries. Orissa was annexed to Akbar's empire in 1578, by Todar Mall, who made a revenue survey of the province in 1582. In 1581 Kabul submitted, and was placed under the rule of Akbar's brother, Mirza Hakim. Kashmir was annexed in 1586,10 Sind in 1592, and in 1594 Kandahar was recovered from the Persians. In 1595 Akbar commenced a long war with the Muhammadan Kings of the Dakhin, ending in the acquisition of Berar. These wars, which were spread over nearly the whole of Akbar's reign, need not further engage our attention. But in contemplating the reforms of this admirable prince, it must be borne in mind that their merit is enhanced by the fact that most of them were effected during troublous times, and at periods when there must have been great pressure on his finances. He was a renowned warrior, skilled in all warlike exercises, and an able and successful general. But it is not these qualities which raise Akbar so far above the common herd of rulers. His greatness consists in his enlightened toleration, in his love of learning, in his justice and magnanimity, and in the success with which he administered a vast empire. The excellence of his instruments is one striking proof of his capacity and genius.

The commencement of Akbar's intellectual revolution dates from the introduction to him of Faizi and Abú-l Fazl, the illustrious sons of Mubarak. Their father, Shaikh Mubarak, traced his descent from an Arabian dervish, of Yemen, who settled in Sind. The Shaikh was a man of genius and great learning, and, having established himself at Agra, gave his two sons excellent educations. Faizi, the eldest, was born in 1545. He first went to court in 1568, at the age of twenty-three, and soon became the Emperor's constant companion and friend. In 1589 he was made Poet Laureate, and he was employed on several diplomatic missions. He was a man of profound learning and original genius. He was loved by the Emperor, who was thrown into the deepest grief at his death, which took place at the age of fifty, on October 5th, 1595. "Shaikh Jío," he exclaimed, "I have brought Hakim Ali with me, will you not speak to me?" Getting no answer, in his grief he threw his turban on the ground, and wept aloud.

Shaikh Abú-l Fazl, called Allami, the younger son of Mubarak, was born on January 14th, 1551, at Agra. He zealously studied under the care of his father; and in his seventeenth year, towards the end of 1574, he was presented to the Emperor Akbar by his brother Faizi.

Owing to the birth of his eldest surviving son Salim, at Sikri, in 1570, Akbar had made that place a royal abode. He built a palace and other splendid edifices there, and it became one of his favourite places of residence. It was called Fathpúr Sikri. Thither Akbar went after his campaign in Bihar in 1574, and there his intimacy with Abú-l Fazl commenced. It was at this time that the memorable Thursday evening discussions began. Akbar's resolution was to rule with even hand men of all creeds in his dominions, and he was annoyed by the intolerance and casuistry of the *Ulamas* or learned men of the predominant religion. He himself said, "I have seen that God bestows the blessings of His gracious providence upon all His creatures without distinction. Ill should I discharge the duties of my station were I to withhold my indulgence from any of those committed to my charge." But he invited the opinions of others on religious points, and hence these discussions arose. Akbar caused a building to be erected in the royal garden of Fathpúr Sikri for the learned men, consisting of four halls, called *aiwán*, where he passed one night in the week in their company. The western hall was set apart for Seyyids, the south for Ulamas, the north for Shaikhs, and the east for nobles and others whose tastes were in unison with those of the Emperor. The building was called *Ibadat-Khana*, and here discussions were carried on, upon all kinds of instructive and useful topics.

Besides Faizi and Abú-l Fazl, there were many learned men in constant attendance on the Emperor. Their father, Shaikh Mubarak, was a poet, and a profound scholar. Mulla Abdul Kadir, called El Badauni, was born at Badaun, in 1540, and studied music, astronomy, and history. He was employed to translate Arabic and Sanscrit works into Persian; but he was a fanatical Muhammadan, and in his "Tarikh-i Badauni," a history brought down to 1595, he always speaks of Faizi and Abú-l Fazl as heretics, and all references to the speculations of Akbar and his friends are couched in bitter and sarcastic terms. He, however, temporized, and did not allow his religion to interfere with his worldly interests. His history contains much original matter. He also translated the great Hindu epic "Mahabharata" in 1582, and the "Ramayana" between 1583 and 1591. Of the former poem he says, "At its puerile absurdities the eighteen thousand creations may well be amazed. But such is my fate, to be employed on such works! Nevertheless, I console myself with the reflection that what is predestined must come to pass." The Khwaja Nizamu-d din Ahmad was another historian of Akbar's court. He also was a good, but not a bitter Musalman. His "Tabakat-i Akbari" is a history of the Muhammadan Kings of Hindustan from Mahmud of Ghazni to the year 1594, which was that of his own death. Other historians of the reign were Shaikh Illahdad Faizi Sirhindi, whose "Akbar-nama" comes down to 1602; Maulana Ahmad, of Tatta, who compiled the "Tarikh-i Alfi," under the Emperor's own superintendence, and Asad Beg, who related the murder of Abú-l Fazl and the death of Akbar, bringing his narrative down to 1608.

The greatest settlement officer and financier of Akbar's court was Todar Mall. There were also poets, musicians, and authors of commentaries who were encouraged by the liberality of the Emperor.

Professors of all creeds were invited to the court of this enlightened sovereign, and cordially welcomed. Among these were Maulana Muhammad, of Yazd, a learned Shiah; Nuruddin Tarkhan, of Jam, in Khurasan, a mathematician and astronomer; Sufi philosophers, fire-worshippers from Gujrat, Brahmans, and the Christian missionaries Aquaviva, Monserrato, and Henriquez.

The Thursday evening meetings at the *Ibadat Khana*, near the tank called *Anúptalao*, in the gardens of Fathpúr Sikri, were commenced in 1574. Akbar was at first annoyed by the intolerance of the Muhammadan Ulamas, and encouraged the telling of stories against them. Quarrels were the consequence. On one occasion Akbar said to Badauni, "In future report to me any one of the assembly whom you find speaking improperly, and I will have him turned out." Badauni said quietly to his neighbour, Asaf Khan, "According to this a good many would be expelled." His Majesty asked what had been said, and when Badauni told him, he was much amused, and repeated it to those who were near him. Decorum was, however, enforced after this, and the more bigoted Muhammadans had to curb their violence. But their feelings were very bitter when they saw their sovereign gradually adopting opinions which they looked upon as more and more heretical, and at last embracing a new religion.

El Badauni says that Akbar, encouraged by his friends Faizi and Abú-l Fazl, gradually lost faith, and that in a few years not a trace of Muhammadan feeling was left in his heart. He was led into free thinking by the large number of learned men of all denominations and sects that came from various countries to his court. Night and day people did nothing but inquire and investigate. Profound points of science, the subtleties of revelation, the curiosities of history, the wonders of nature, were incessantly discussed. His Majesty collected the opinions of every one, retaining whatever he approved, and rejecting what was against his disposition, or ran counter to his wishes. Thus a faith, based on some elementary principles, fixed itself in his heart; and, as the result of all the influences that were brought to bear on him, the conviction gradually established itself in his mind that there were truths in all religions. If some true knowledge was everywhere to be found, why, he thought, should truth be confined to one religion? Thus his speculations became bolder. "Not a day passed," exclaims El Badauni, "but a new fruit of this loathsome tree ripened into existence."

At length Akbar established a new religion, which combined the principal features of Hinduism with the sun-worship of the Parsís.11 The good parts of all religions were recognized, and perfect toleration was established. The new faith was called *Tauhid-i Ilahi*, divine monotheism. A document was prepared and signed by the Ulamas, the draft of which was in the handwriting of Shaikh Mubarak. The Emperor, as *Imam-i Adil* (just leader) and *Mujtahid*, was declared to be infallible, and superior to all doctors in matters of faith.12 Abú-l Fazl was the chief expounder of the new creed.

Had Akbar, as a private individual, avowed the opinions which he formed as an Emperor, his life would not have been worth a day's purchase; but in his exalted station he was enabled to practise as a ruler the doctrines which he held as a philosopher. Or, as Abú-l Fazl puts it: "When a person in private station unravels the warp and woof of the veil of deception, and discovers the beautiful countenance of consistency and truth, he keeps silence from the dread of savage beasts in human form, who would brand him with the epithets of infidel and blasphemer, and probably deprive him of life. But when the season arrives for the revelation of truth, a person is endowed with this degree of knowledge upon whom God bestows the robes of royalty, such as is the Emperor of our time." The disputations came to an end in 1579, and Akbar held the new creed to the end of his life.

Meanwhile Akbar's learned men were engaged in compilations and translations from Arabic and Sanscrit into Persian. The history called "Tarikh-i Alfi" was to be a narrative of the thousand years of Islam from the *Hijrah* to 1592 A.D. Akbar held that Islam would cease to exist in the latter year, having done its work. The "Tarikh-i Alfi" was intended to be its epitaph. It was chiefly written by Maulava Ahmad, of Tatta, but Abú-l Fazl and others assisted. Faizi translated the Sanscrit mathematical work called "Lilawati"; and, as has already been said, Badauni, with the aid of others, prepared translated versions of the two great Hindu epics.

But the most famous literary work of Akbar's reign was the history written by Abú-l Fazl, in three volumes, called the "Akbar-namah." The first volume contains a history of the House of Timur down to the death of Humayun; the second is a record of the reign of Akbar, from 1556 to 1602; and the third is the "Ain-i Akbari," the great Administration Report of Akbar's Empire.

The first book of the "Ain-i Akbari" treats of the Emperor, and of his household and court. Here we are introduced to the royal stables, to the wardrobe, and kitchens, and to the hunting establishment. We are initiated into all the arrangements connected with the treasury and the mint, the armoury,13 and the travelling equipage. In this book, too, we learn the rules of court etiquette, and also the ceremonies instituted by Akbar as the spiritual guide of his people.

The second book gives the details of army administration, the regulations respecting the feasts, marriage rites, education, and amusements. This book ends with a list of the Grandees of the Empire.14 Their rank is shown by their military commands, as *mansabdars* or captains of cavalry. All commands above five thousand belonged to the Shah-zadahs or Emperor's sons. The total number of *mansabs* or military commands was sixty-six. Most of the higher officers were Persians or Afghans, not Hindustani Muhammadans, and out of the four hundred and fifteen mansabdars there were fifty-one Hindus, a large percentage. It was to the policy of Hindu generals that Akbar owed the permanent annexation of Orissa.15

The third book is devoted to regulations for the judicial and executive departments, the survey and assessment, and the rent-roll of the great finance minister. The fourth book treats of the social condition and literary activity of the Hindus; and the fifth contains the moral and epigrammatic sentences of the Emperor.

It is to the third book, containing the details of the revenue system, that the modern administrator will turn with the deepest interest. Early in his reign Akbar remitted or reduced a number of vexatious taxes.16 His able revenue officers then proceeded to introduce a reformed settlement based on the indigenous scheme, as matured by Shir Shah. The greatest among Akbar's fiscal statesmen was Todar Mall, who settled Gujrat, Bengal, and Bihar, and introduced the system of keeping revenue accounts in Persian. Next to him was Nizam Ahmad, the author of the "Tabakat-i Akbari," who spent his life in the Emperor's service.

From time immemorial a share in the produce of land has been the property of the State in all eastern countries. From this source the main part of the revenue has been raised, and the land tax has always formed the most just, the most reliable, and the most popular means of providing for the expenditure of the government. In Muhammadan countries this land tax is called *khiraj*, and is of two kinds, the one *mukasimah*, when a share of the actual produce was taken, and the other *wazifa*, which was due from the land whether there was any produce or not.

In Hindu times, and before the reign of Akbar, the *khiraj* in India was *mukasimah*. The Emperor's officers adopted the system of *wazifa* for good land, and carried the settlement into effect with great precision and accuracy in each province of his dominions. Bengal and part of Bihar, Berar, and part of Gujrat, however, appear to have been assessed according to the value of the crops, the surveys of the land not being complete. Akbar took one-third of the estimated value, and he left the option of payment in kind to the farmers, except in the case of sugar-cane and other expensive crops.

The lands were divided into four classes, with different revenue to be paid by each, namely:—

1. Land cultivated every harvest, and never fallow.

2. Land lying fallow at intervals.

3. Land lying fallow for four years together.

4. Land not cultivated for five years and upwards.

The principle of *wazifa* was only applied to the two first of these classes of land, and to the second only when actually under cultivation. The lands of these two classes were divided into good, middling, and bad. The produce of a *bigah* (5/8 of an acre) of each sort was added together, and a third of that was considered to be the average produce. One-third was the share of the State, as settled by Akbar's assessment. Large remissions were allowed on the two inferior classes of land. The settlements were for ten years. In about 1596 the land revenue derived from the fifteen *subahs* or provinces of Akbar's empire was as follows:—

		Rupees.17
1.	Allahabad	53.10.677
2.	Agra	1.36.56.257
3.	Oudh	50.43.954
4.	Ajmír	71.53.449
5.	Gujrat	1.09.20.057
6.	Bihar	55.47.985
7.	Bengal	1.49.61.482
8.	Delhi	1.50.40.388
9.	Kabul	80.71.024
10.	Lahor	1.39.86.460
11.	Multán	96.00.764
12.	Malwah	60.17.376
13.	Berar	1.73.76.117
14.	Khandeish	75.63.237
15.	Tattah	16.56.284
		14.19.05.511

A later return, referred to by Mr. Thomas, gives Akbar's land revenue at £16,582,440. Under his grandson, Shah Jahan, it increased to £22,000,000, and Aurangzib's land revenue, in 1707, was upwards of £30,000,000.18 On an average about a twentieth is deducted for *jaghírs*, or rent-free lands, and *sayurghals* or assignments for charitable purposes.

The "Ain-i Akbari" of Abú-l Fazl is rendered valuable not only by the varied information it contains, but also by the trustworthiness of the author. Mr. Blochmann says that Abú-l Fazl has been too often accused by European writers of flattery, and of wilful concealment of facts damaging to the reputation of his master. He bears witness that a study of the "Akbar-namah" has convinced him that the charge is absolutely unfounded. Abú-l Fazl's love of truth, and his correctness of information are apparent on every page of his great work.

The last years of the reign of Akbar were clouded with sorrow. His eldest son, Salim, was dissipated, ungrateful, and rebellious, and bore special hatred against his father's noble minister. The two younger sons died early from the effects of drink. "Alas," exclaimed Abú-l Fazl, "that wine should be burdened with suffering, and that its sweet nectar should be a deadly poison!"19

In 1597 Abú-l Fazl left the court, and went for the first time on active service in the Dakhin. He had been absent for more than four years, when the rebellious conduct of Salim, the heir apparent, induced Akbar to recall his trusty minister. His presence was urgently needed. Abú-l Fazl hurriedly set out for Agra, only accompanied by a few men. Salim thought this an excellent opportunity of getting rid of his father's faithful friend, and bribed Rajah Bir Singh, a Bundela chief of Urchah, through whose territory he would have to pass, to waylay him. On the 12th of August 1602, at a distance of a few miles from Narwar, Bir Singh's men came in sight. The minister thought it a disgrace to fly, which he might easily have done. He defended himself bravely, but, pierced by the lance of a trooper, he fell dead on the ground. The assassin sent the head of Abú-l Fazl to his employer; and Akbar, with all the diligence of his officers and troops, was never able to secure and punish the murderer. His own son was the greater criminal of the two, and in his memoirs Salim confesses his guilt with unblushing effrontery.20

Mr. Blochmann thus sums up the career of Abú-l Fazl. "As a writer he is unrivalled. Everywhere in India he is known as the great Munshi. His letters are studied in all Madrasahs, and are perfect models. His influence on his age was immense. He led his sovereign to a true appreciation of his duties, and from the moment that he entered court the problem of successfully ruling over mixed races was carefully considered, and the policy of toleration was the result."

The great Emperor did not long survive his beloved and faithful minister. Akbar died on November 10th, 1605, in his sixty-third year, and was buried in the magnificent tomb at Sikundra, near Agra. There his bones still rest, and his tomb is treated with all honour and respect by the present rulers of the land. A new cloth to cover the actual tomb was presented by the Earl of Northbrook, after his visit to Sikundra in November 1873, when he was Viceroy of India.

Akbar's wives were Sultana Rajmihal Begum, a daughter of his uncle Hindal, by whom he had no children; Sultana Sulimah Begum, a daughter of a daughter of Baber, who was a poetess; Nur Jahan; and the Rajput Princess Jodh Bai, the mother of Salim.

His children were Hasan and Husain, who died in infancy; Salim, his successor; Murad and Danyal, who died of drink in the lifetime of their father, and three daughters.

Akbar is described by his son Salim as a very tall man, with the strength of a lion, which was indicated by the great breadth of his chest. His complexion was rather fair (*color de trigo* is the description of a Spanish missionary who knew him), his eyes and eyebrows dark, his countenance handsome. His beard was close-shaved. His bearing was majestic, and "the qualities of his mind seemed to raise him above the denizens of this lower world."[21] The Emperor Akbar combined the thoughtful philosophy of Marcus Aurelius, the toleration of Julian, the enterprise and daring of his own grandsire Baber, with the administrative genius of a Monro or a Thomason. We might search through the dynasties of the East and West for many centuries back, and fail to discover so grand and noble a character as that of Akbar. No sovereign has come nearer to the ideal of a father of his people.[22]

Akbar was the contemporary of Queen Elizabeth. He began to reign two years before her, and outlived her for two years, but he was nine years younger than the great Queen. He was succeeded by his son Salim, under the name of Jahangir, who reigned from 1605 to 1627.

The native sources whence the story of Akbar's glorious reign are derived, have already been indicated. To a considerable extent they are accessible in an English form. The translation of the "Ain-i Akbari," by Gladwin, was published in 1800, and that of the historian Ferishta, by General Briggs, in 1829. Elphinstone gives a brief account of Akbar's reign in his history of India. In 1873 Blochmann's admirable translation of the two first books of the "Ain-i Akbari" was printed at Calcutta, for the Asiatic Society of Bengal. The work also contains many extracts from El Badauni and the "Akbar-namah," and a perfect mine of accurate and well arranged information from other sources.

In Volumes V. and VI. of the great work edited by Professor Dowson,[23] the history of Akbar's reign is very fully supplied by extracts from the "Tabakat-i Akbari," the "Akbar-namah," the "Tarikh-i Badauni," the "Tarikh-i Alfi," the work of Shaikh Nurul Hakk, and that of Asad Beg. Mr. Edward Thomas, F.R.S., has published a most valuable little book on the revenue system of Akbar and his three immediate successors.[24]

The slight notices of Akbar by contemporary or nearly contemporary Europeans are derived from reports of the Jesuit missionaries, from those of the Dutch at Surat, and from Hakluyt's Voyages. As early as 1578 the Emperor had received a Christian missionary named Antonio Cabral, at Fathpúr Sikri, had heard him argue with the Mullas, and had been induced to write to Goa, requesting that two members of the Society of Jesus might be sent to him with Christian books. In 1579 Rudolf Aquaviva[25] and Antonio Monserrat were accordingly despatched, with Francisco Henriquez as interpreter. They were well received, and again in 1591 three brethren visited Akbar's court at Lahore. Finally a detachment of missionaries was sent to Lahore, at Akbar's request, in 1594, consisting of Geronimo Xavier (a nephew of St. Francis), Emanuel Pineiro, a Portuguese, mentioned by Captain Hawkins,[26] and Benedek Goes,[27] the famous traveller, who went with Akbar on his summer trip to Kashmir. Xavier and Goes also accompanied the Emperor in his Dakhin campaign; and when Goes set out on his perilous overland journey to China, that liberal monarch praised his zeal and contributed to his expenses. This was in 1602. Xavier celebrated Christmas with great solemnity at Lahore, and wrote a life of Christ in Persian, which Akbar read with much interest. Accounts of the visits of these missionaries to Akbar's court, and of their journeys, are to be found in the Jesuit Histories.[28]

But the most valuable European account of the reign of Akbar was written by Pieter van den Broek, the chief of the Dutch factory at Surat in 1620. It was published, in Latin, by Johan de Laet, and forms the tenth chapter of his "De Imperio Magni Mogolis" (Leyden, 1631). De Laet calls it "a fragment of Indian history which we have received from some of our countrymen, and translated from Dutch into Latin."[29] Mr. Lethbridge has supplied an English version in the "Calcutta Review" for July 1873.[30] Ralph Fitch is the only English traveller who has written an account of a visit to the court of Akbar.[31] Accompanied by Mr. John Newbery, a jeweller named William Leedes, and James Story, a painter, he reached the court at Agra with a letter of introduction from Queen Elizabeth, in the year 1585. Thence Newbery started to return overland. Leedes entered the service of Akbar, settling at Fathpúr; and Fitch went on to Bengal, eventually returning home.

Abú-l Fazl tells us, casually, that, through the negligence of the local officers, some of the cities and marts of Gujrat were frequented by Europeans. Two centuries and a half after his master's death, these intruders held undisputed sovereignty not only over the whole of Akbar's empire, but over all India, a vast dominion which had never before been united under one rule. They approached from the sea, the base of their operations is their ships, and not, as in the case of Akbar's grandsire, the mountains of the north-west frontier.

If the balance of administrative merit is in favour of the English, and this is not established, it in no way detracts from the glory of the great Emperor. Yet we may claim that the islanders who now occupy the place of Akbar are not unworthy to succeed him. The work that is before us is more prosaic than was the duty of the puissant sovereign. The charm of one central glory, round which all that was great and good in India could congregate; the fascination of one ruling spirit, combining irresistible power with virtue and beneficence; the pomp and circumstance of a brilliant court—all these are gone for ever. We have instead the united thought and energy of many sound heads and brave hearts, working without ostentation, and achieving objects of a magnitude and endurance such as no single brain of any despot, how great soever, could even conceive.

"The old order changeth, yielding place to new,

And God fulfils Himself in many ways."

---

1 "Akbar: een Oostersche Roman," door Mr. P. A. S. Van Limburg-Brouwer. 's Gravenhage: Martinus Nijhoff, 1872. 8vo. pp. 358.

2 "Akbar. Ein Indischer Roman. Deutsche autorisirte ausgabe aus dem Niederlandischen des Dr. V. Limburg Brouwer," von Lina Schneider (Wilhelm Berg). Leipzig: Heinrich Killinger, 1877. Small 8vo. pp. 346.

3 Published by J. de Laet in his "De Imperio Magni Mogolis." Leyden: 1631.

4 Prince Frederick has visited India three times. He made an extensive tour in 1863–64, and again in 1867–69. After his first visit he published a narrative of his travels, in three volumes, "Altes und Neues aus den Landern des Ostens, von Onomander." Hamburg: 1859.

5 Mahmud of Ghazni, the first Muhammadan invader of India, reigned from A.D. 997 to A.D. 1030. His dynasty lasted until 1183. The Ghori dynasty lasted from A.D. 1192 to 1289. The Khilzi dynasty, from 1289 to 1321. The dynasty founded by Tuglak Shah, from 1321 to 1393. Then followed the inroad of Timur and subsequent anarchy; and the Afghan Lodi dynasty lasted from 1450 to the invasion of Baber in 1526.

6 "Mogul" is the old form. Dowson and Thomas have "Mughal"; Blochmann and Hunter, "Mughul."

7 Jauhar wrote his "Tazkiratu-l Wákiat" thirty years after the death of Humayun. It was translated by Major Stewart, and printed for the Oriental Translation Fund in 1832.

8 Humayun met this young lady, when on a visit to his brother Hindal's mother. She was a daughter of a Seyyid, a native of Jami in Khurasan.

9 *Calotropis gigantea* (*Asclepiadaceæ*). It is a shrub from six to ten feet high, generally found in waste ground or among ruins. An acrid, milky juice flows from every part of the plant when wounded, which is used by native doctors for cutaneous diseases. The bark fibre is spun into fine thread.

10 Kashmir was ruled by Hindu princes until the beginning of the fourteenth century, when it was conquered by the Muhammadans. Owing to distractions in the reigning family, Akbar sent an army into Kashmir in 1586. The king then submitted, and was enrolled among the Delhi nobles.

11 Akbar was also much interested in the gospels as explained to him by Christian missionaries; and, as Colonel Yule says, he never lost a certain hankering after Christianity, or ceased to display an affectionate reverence for the Christian emblems which he had received from his Jesuit teachers.— See "Cathay and the Way thither," ii. p. 532, note.

12 This was in 1579. See "Blochmann," i. p. 185; "Elliot," v. p. 531.

13 For a plate of Indian arms and accoutrements in the time of Akbar see the very interesting work by the Hon. Wilbraham Egerton, M.P., published by order of the Secretary of State for India in Council, "A Handbook of Indian Arms," p. 23. (Wm. H. Allen & Co., 1879.)

14 Mr. Blochmann has supplemented this list with biographical notices of Akbar's nobles, of which there are four hundred and fifteen. These notices are chiefly taken from the "Tabakat-i Akbari," the work of El Badaoni, the "Akbar-namah," the "Tuzuk-i Jahangiri," and a manuscript called "Maásir ul Umará" in the collection of the Asiatic Society of Bengal.—Blochmann's "Ain-i Abkari," i. pp. 308 to 526.

15 See Hunter's "Orissa," ii. p. 5.

16 Namely the poll tax (*jiziah*), the port and ferry dues (*mirbahri*), the pilgrim tax (*kar*), the tax on cattle (*gau shumari*), tax on trees (*sar darakhti*), offerings on appointments (*peshkash*), trade licenses, fees to darogahs, tahsildars, treasurers, and landlords, fees on hiring or letting, for bags on cash payments, on the verification of coins, and market dues.

17 Akbar's returns are in dams, forty dams making one rupee.

18 In 1877 the whole land revenue of India, including the Madras Presidency and Burma, was £19,857,152. Of this sum £3,993,196 came from Madras,

and £835,376 from Burma, which provinces were not included in the empire of Akbar; nor was a great part of Bombay (probably about half) under Akbar's revenue system. In Bombay land revenue (including Sind) in 1877 was £3,344,664; and half this sum £1,672,332. For a rough comparison these three sums (namely the amount of land revenue from Madras, Burma, and half Bombay) must be deducted from the land revenue of 1877, and £807,102 (the revenue of Kabul) from the land revenue of Akbar. This leaves £15,775,338 as Akbar's land revenue, and £13,356,248 as the land revenue obtained by our Government in 1877 from the same provinces.

19 Many Muhammadan princes died of *delirium tremens* before the introduction of tobacco, which took place towards the end of Akbar's reign. Asad Beg says that he first saw tobacco at Bijapur. He brought a pipe and a stock of tobacco to Agra, and presented it to the Emperor, who made a trial. The custom of smoking spread rapidly among the nobles, but Akbar never adopted it himself.—"Dowson," vi. 165.

20 "Memoirs of Jehanghir."

21 "Memoirs of Jehanghir," written by himself, and translated by Major David Price for the Oriental Translation Fund, 1829. When I was at Madrid Don Pascual de Gayangos gave me a copy of a very interesting Spanish manuscript by an anonymous missionary (probably Aquaviva) who describes the personal appearance and habits of Akbar. It was left at the Asiatic Society, before Mr. Vaux's time, and was mislaid. Don Pascual has also mislaid the original, so that the loss is irremediable.

22 Colonel Yule compares Kublai Khan with Akbar ("Marco Polo," i. p. 340), and Mr. Talboys Wheeler has drawn a parallel between Akbar and Asoka ("History of India," iv. p. 136).

23 "History of India, as told by its own Historians—the Muhammadan Period; being posthumous papers by Sir H. M. Elliot, K.C.B., edited and continued by Professor Dowson."

24 "The Revenue Resources of the Mughal Empire in India, A.D. 1593 to 1707," by Edward Thomas, F.R.S., pp. 54. Trübner: 1871.

25 Rudolf Aquaviva was born in 1551. He was a nephew of Claudio Aquaviva, the fourth General of the Jesuits, and a grandson of Giovanni Antonio Aquaviva, Duke of Atri, in Naples. The Dukes of Atri were as famous for their patronage of letters as for their deeds of arms. The missionary, Aquaviva, after his return from Agra, was sent to Salsette, where he was murdered by the natives in 1583, aged only thirty-two. Akbar, on hearing of his death, sent an embassy of condolence to the Portuguese Viceroy, and to the Jesuit Fathers at Goa.

26 See my "Hawkins' Voyages" (Hakluyt Society), pages 396 and 403. Pineiro wrote an account of his travels.

27 See Colonel Yule's "Cathay and the Way thither," ii. pp. 529–591, for the journey of Benedek Goes. The narrative is taken from a work entitled "De Christiana expeditione apud Sinas, suscepta ab Societate Jesu, ex P. Matthaei Ricii commentariis, auctore P. Nicolao Trigantio." 1615.

28 See the "Histoire de la Compagnie de Jésus composée sur les documents inédits et authentiques par J. Crétineau-Joly" (6 vols. 8vo. Paris: 1844), ii. p. 510–12; also "Ranke Histoire de la Papauté," iv. p. 159. Colonel Yule refers to the work of Jarric.

29 Johan de Laet was born at Antwerp in the end of the sixteenth century and died in 1649. He was a Director of the Dutch West India Company, had an extensive acquaintance with learned men, and had special opportunities of collecting geographical and historical information, of which he diligently availed himself. His chief work was the "Novus Orbis seu descriptionis Indiae Occidentalis" (folio 1633). He wrote works on England, France, Spain, Portugal, Holland, and Italy, which form part of the collection known under the name of "Les Petites Republiques," printed by the Elzevirs at Leyden. De Laet also had a learned controversy with Grotius on the origin of the American races. He edited Pliny and Vitruvius.

30 Fragments of Indian History, "Calcutta Review," July 1873, No. cxiii. pp. 170–200. De Laet is quoted by Blochmann, and also by Mr. Thomas and Dr. Hunter.

31 Fitch's interesting account of this visit to the court of Akbar was published by Hakluyt.—See "Hakluyt Voyages" (2nd ed.), ii. pp. 375–399. Besides the narrative of Fitch, there are letters from Newbery, and the letter from Queen Elizabeth to Akbar.

Biographical Notice of the Author.

The author of the romance of Akbar, Dr. P. A. S. van Limburg-Brouwer, was the son of the Professor of Greek at Groningen. He was born at Liege in 1832, and was a Doctor of Law, residing chiefly at the Hague, and devoting himself to eastern and other studies. He held an appointment in the office of the Royal Archives, and was for a short time a member of the States General for the district of Trenthe.

With reference to his eastern studies, we find them bearing fruit in the periodical literature of Holland during the last ten years of his life. In 1863 Van Limburg-Brouwer contributed an essay on the Ramayana, to the "Gids," a magazine published at Amsterdam.[1] In 1866 a historical sketch from his pen, entitled the "Java Reformers," appeared in the same periodical.[2] In 1867 he contributed three articles, entitled, "The Adventures of an Indian Nobleman"; "The Book of Kings: an Essay of Indian History"; and "The Vedanta: an Essay on Indian Orthodoxy."[3] In 1868 he published articles entitled "Eastern Atheism," and "A Cure for Beauty."[4] His metaphysical drama, "The Moon of Knowledge," saw the light in 1869.[5] In the following year he seems to have given his attention to Arabian lore, and published two articles entitled "Poetry of the Desert," and the "Kabbala."[6] Towards the end of his life Van Limburg-Brouwer commenced the study of Chinese, and among the results of his labours in this field of research was his article on "The Sage of the Celestial Empire, and his School."[7] He was a man of extensive and varied learning, endowed with a rich and fertile imagination, and with great powers of expression. In his romance of Akbar, his most carefully drawn character, and that on which he seems to have bestowed most thought, is the Hindu girl Iravati. In her he endeavoured to portray his conception of the class of devoted loving women of whom Damayanti is the type; and Siddha Rama is evidently intended to be the Nala of a later age. But he has bestowed equal care on his treatment of the more difficult part of his subject, and has brought considerable ability and much study and research to the task of presenting to his readers a vivid and at the same time a life-like picture of that remarkable prince round whom the action of the story centres, and of the two brothers who were his devoted friends.

Akbar is the work on which Van Limburg-Brouwer's literary fame will mainly rest. It was only published in 1872, the year before the author's death. He died at the Hague, in his forty-first year, on the 13th of February 1873.[8]

---

1 "Het Ramayana," Gids, 1863.

2 "Javas Hervormers: een Historische Schets," 1866.

3 "De Avantoren van een Indisch Edelman," Gids, 1867. "Het Boek der Koningen: eene proeve van Indische Geschiedenis," Gids, No. 6, 1867. "Vedanta: eene proeve van Indische regtzinnigheid," Gids, No. 12, 1867.

4 "Oostersch Atheisme," Gids, 1868. "Eene Schoonheidskuur," Gids, No. 8, 1868.

5 "De Maan der Kennis," Theologisch-Metaphysisch Drama, Gids, No. 70, 1869.

6 "Poesie der Woestijn," Gids, No. 21, 1870. "De Kabbala," Gids, No. 7, 1870.

7 "De Wijze van het Hemelsch Rijk en zijne school."

8 An obituary notice of Dr. van Limburg-Brouwer ("Ter Nagedachtenis van Mr. P. A. S. van Limburg-Brouwer") was written by Dr. H. Kern, the Professor of Sanscrit at Leyden, and published in the "Nederlandsche Spectator," 1873.

The Author's Preface.

The grand figure of the Emperor Akbar, the ruler of India during the last half of the sixteenth century (1556–1605), for many reasons appeared to me to be of such importance that I could not resist the temptation of making him the chief person in a romantic sketch which I now venture to offer to public notice.

Some readers may desire to be able to distinguish accurately between what is, and what is not historical. For their benefit I give the following explanation. To real history, besides Akbar himself, belong his son Salim, the Wazir Abú-l Fazl, and his brother Faizi, Abdul Kadir Badaoni, Rudolf Aquaviva the Jesuit, and a few others of less note. Parviz belongs to history, but he bore another name. Nandigupta is not a historical personage, but rather the type of a character often met with in the history of India, and especially of Kashmir. Gorakh and his Thugs are also types. Iravati was not a real person, but the image of a Hindu woman as she is often met with in the ancient dramas and legends of India. Many of the sayings and speeches placed in the mouths of the characters in the romance are historical. For reasons which may be easily understood, the events in the narrative are made to deviate slightly from historical truth. In the days of Akbar, for instance, Kashmir was no longer ruled by Hindu Princes, although the people were entirely Indian. Again; the attempt of Salim, concerning which many particulars are given, was not made during an expedition against Kashmir, but against the Dakhin. Faizi was older than Abú-l Fazl, and died before his brother's murder. Fathpúr lies at a greater distance from Agra than would appear in the following pages. In the characters and acts of the people there are also some slight and unimportant deviations from historical fact.

The attempt has been made to follow the oriental forms, especially in the conversations, so far as was possible without slavish imitation. The poems, which are here and there woven into the narrative, have been translated by me from the originals.

It is scarcely necessary to give here an exact list of the sources which have aided in the composition of this work; nor is there much to impart, on this subject, that would be new to the historian. He knows well that the principal authorities for the life of Akbar, for his institutions and ideas, are the writings of Abú-l Fazl and Abdul Kadir, whence eastern as well as western writers have drawn their information. The reports of the Jesuits of that period, though often prejudiced, yet in many points supplement and illustrate the works of native historians. It is also necessary to add that various modern histories and books of travel have been used.

For what is purely Indian in this romance, Sanscrit literature, with its many legends, dramas, and romances, has been made use of. For the philosophical ideas of Akbar the best authority is his principal opponent, Abdul Kadir. The Vedas, from which the Emperor borrowed many of his ideas, have also been consulted.

One source of information merits special mention, as it is but little known. That is, the reports on the country and people made by merchants of our East India Company, who, shortly after Akbar's reign, were established at Surat and Agra. Their letters are still preserved in our colonial archives.

How accurate soever one may strive to be, yet in an attempt of this kind there must always be the possibility of errors, especially in the descriptions of places. If here and there mistakes have crept into the text, the writer asks pardon in anticipation, and will be grateful for any corrections.

THE HAGUE,
October, 1872.

Chapter I.
The Hermit.

The last rays of the setting sun shot through the sky in crimson light, and were reflected back by the snows of Badari-natha[1] and the sharp peaks of the Himálaya, while a soft south wind wafted to the mountain tops the perfume of trees and flowers which all day had hung over the valleys. For centuries and centuries had the rays of the same sun lit up the same heights, and the perfume of flowers had risen to the mountains, with no change and no disturbance; while far in the distance men fought and struggled, mighty kingdoms rose and fell, and thoughtful minds vainly sought the aim and reason of the existence of the universe.

Towards the end of the sixteenth century of our era, when Jelalu-dín-Muhammad, surnamed Akbar the Great, had raised the empire of the Moghuls to the highest point of power and glory, the lofty Himálaya, once the scarcely accessible abode of the Devas,[2] still remained wild and inhospitable. These solitudes were scarcely ever trodden by human foot, and seldom even did the cry of some passing bird of prey, or the hum of dancing insects, break the intense and almost audible silence.

Still the place was not so entirely deserted as a careless observer might imagine. Nearly hidden in the long grass a tiger lay stretched out, his coat flecked with black, dreaming in philosophical rest, sometimes gazing upwards at the snow-crowned peaks, and then half closing his eyes before the still vivid light. He looked down on the lovely green valleys far below, stretching away until they met other mountains rising into the clear sky, losing themselves and seeming to melt and blend into the brilliant colours of the horizon. Of what did he think? sometimes gazing upwards, sometimes looking down into the depths below, perhaps in misty remembrance of the times when, in another form, he reigned—a mighty rajah over luxurious Kashmir, with vassals bowing before him and lovely women vieing with one another for the honour of his notice. Or was, indeed, the royal beast nothing more than a gigantic cat? a monster of the jungle? and not the lost soul of some former proud and haughty ruler. He was now, in truth, the king of the wilderness, where no rival dared to challenge his rights. That he well knew his power, could be seen in the proud glance he cast around him. But, suddenly waking from these day-dreams, he sprang to his feet and listened. A noise, the sound of men's voices, had fallen on his quick ear.

Though still at some little distance, a group of riders was descending by the only accessible path in the mountains towards the valley. A young and handsome man, whose proud carriage and rich clothing showed that he was of noble birth, accompanied by another, older in years and more gravely clad, and followed by two servants, formed the party. The youth was mounted on a white Arab, small but powerfully built, and of great speed. The older man rode a larger horse of dark colour, while the servants bestrode rough but strong mountain ponies. The youth wore a blue silk jacket ornamented with golden buttons, wide trousers and red shoes, and a light cap with a long feather fastened by a diamond. A short sabre hung at his side, and a jewelled dagger was stuck into his richly ornamented girdle. In his right hand he held a long spear. He was tall and well formed, and his complexion was fair, being scarcely tanned by the sun's rays. His eyes and hair were dark, and a brown moustache betokened, unmistakeably, that he sprang from the Aryan race. His companion was a powerful, broad-shouldered man of dark complexion, yet showing by his finely cut features that Aryan blood also flowed through his veins. A thick curling beard nearly hid his face, which was shaded by a white turban. His person was enveloped in a long robe of dark but fine material, which reached nearly to his feet, and was secured round his waist by a golden belt. He, also, was armed with sabre and spear, and from his shoulder hung a small round shield. The only clothing of the servants was a cloak thrown round their dusky limbs, and many bright copper rings on their wrists and ancles clanked against each other as they rode along. Short spears and small shields were their only weapons.

It was easy to discover from their conversation who these travellers were, whence they came, and the reason of their journey. The young nobleman, Siddha[3] Rama[4], was the son of the First Minister of Kashmir, entrusted by his father with important letters to the court of the Emperor Akbar at Agra, where he was to take command of a division of Rajput cavalry belonging to the imperial army. He was accompanied by Kulluka,[5] his tutor, a Brahman of high descent, a man of learning and a warrior, one who knew as well how to instruct his pupil in the arts of war and martial exercises, as in the sacred language with its classic and holy writings.

But before reaching Agra they had to visit a hermit in the mountains, and then to make their way to Allahabad, where Siddha's uncle, in the Emperor's name, commanded the fort at the junction of the Ganges and Jamuna. There too was Iravati, his daughter, and the betrothed of Siddha, counting the days to their coming and the meeting with her future husband.

"But, honoured Kulluka," said Siddha, after having ridden for a time silently by the side of his tutor, "you, who know the way, tell me that we are close to the abode of Gurupada.[6] It may be so, but I can see nothing that is at all like a cell. Is it possible that the holy man has departed?"

"A little more patience," answered the Brahman, "and we shall soon come to the turning, whence you will see the little wood in the valley where Gurupada has built his solitary dwelling. But it seems to me you might speak with more respect of one so venerable. You will, however, learn that when you meet him."

"I intended no harm and no disrespect," rejoined Siddha. "But what is that?" cried he, suddenly pointing with his spear towards the tall grass on the mountain side, which was waving gently, though unstirred by the wind.

Before his calmer companion could restrain him, the impatient hunter had turned his horse into the long grass, and was hurrying towards the spot where the movement had been seen. But before either Kulluka or the servants could hasten after him, they saw him draw rein and remain motionless, gazing before him.

All movement in the grass had ceased, not one blade stirred, and not a sound was to be heard. Then again the grass moved and bent, but much farther off, betraying the presence of a large glossy tiger bounding away.

Siddha put spurs to his horse, and the next moment lay full length on the ground. A hole, thickly covered with vegetation, had thrown horse and rider. But both instantly recovered their footing.

"It is nothing, Vatsa,"[7] he said to his servant, who had flung himself from his pony and hurried to his master. "I have fallen softly enough; nor, it is to be hoped, has any harm come to my horse."

On examination they found that the noble grey was as uninjured as his headlong rider; but no sign of the tiger was any longer visible.

There was nothing left to be done but to spring into the saddle and continue the interrupted journey.

Siddha rode silently by the side of his guru, not a little ashamed of his foolish adventure, but the latter broke the silence by saying, "That was but a childish trick, dear lad."

"Yes," replied Siddha, in a shamefaced tone, "I must have indeed appeared ridiculous, rolling over in such a way."

"But," continued Kulluka, "that you could not help."

"No one can see concealed holes."

"What I mean is something quite different."

"What then?"

"That you will soon learn, if what I suspect is the case."

The smile that played round Kulluka's mouth at these words only increased Siddha's curiosity; but his questions were interrupted by their reaching a turn in the road where, spread out before them, bathed in golden sunshine, lay another part of the valley.

"See there," said Kulluka, pointing with his lance to a thick clump of trees below them, near which, like a silver thread, flowed a little stream; "there lives Gurupada!" And, without more words, the riders descended a steep declivity, following a path partly formed by nature and partly by the labour of men, that led towards the plain.

Under the dense shade of trees stood a low building roofed with reeds, and built with slight bamboos overgrown with creepers, more like some resort of pleasure than the poor cell of a holy man passing his life in penance. Behind was the dark jungle, in front an emerald lake, reflecting back a hundred different tints, and bordered by blue and white lotus flowers. The clear silver stream entered at one end and, flowing out at the other side, continued its course to the lower valleys just seen in the haze of the distance. Far away the ranges of mountains rose like rocky giants to the heavens, their summits never trodden by the foot of man.

For a moment our travellers remained still, lost in admiration of a view at once so magnificent and so lovely. But quickly remembering that they had reached the end of their journey, they dismounted and entrusted the horses to their servants, while Kulluka advanced to the dwelling, meaning to give notice of their arrival. But he might have saved himself the trouble, for he had scarcely reached the door when the hermit appeared in the threshold, followed by a servant who, at a sign from his master, took charge of the visitors' horses.

Extraordinary was the impression which the sight of this recluse made on Siddha. In his own country, among his mountains and forests, he had seen penitents, self-denying holy men, wandering mendicants, in numbers and of all kinds—some in foul and sordid rags, with long bamboo staves in their hands and rosaries at their sides, some with a cloth made of the bark of trees, others with no clothing, shaven, and covered with ashes, their foreheads and breasts smeared with white chalk: all supported by the strength of a boundless fanaticism. No wonder that the young man, used to the most polished civilisation, should have looked with the deepest contempt on such people; and in spite of his respect for his tutor, who had always named the hermit of Badrinath with veneration, he had expected but little from the man who now stood ready at his door to receive them. All the greater was the impression now made upon him by the tall and stately figure advancing to them, with dignity but at the same time with an air of friendly welcome.

He was an old man, in a dazzling white garment, with a few fine locks on the otherwise bald head, and a heavy silvery beard, but not in the least bent by the weight of years. His friendly though proud expression showed plainly that he had been accustomed to give, rather than to receive and obey, commands.

"You are welcome friends," he said, taking his two visitors by the hand, who bent respectfully before him. "Welcome to my solitude. It is indeed a pleasure to hear again of"—here he seemed to hesitate, but proceeded in a firm voice, "of you and my country and people."

Before either Kulluka and Siddha could reply, their attention was drawn to a low growl close to them, and in another instant, from behind the building, a magnificent tiger appeared with slow and stately tread, and drew near the three men, waving its heavy tail from side to side. Instantly Siddha drew back a step, and laid his hand on the dagger in his belt.

"Leave that plaything in its place," said Gurupada, laughing. "Do not injure Hara."8 Then, turning to the tiger, he called him in a commanding tone, and instantly the powerful animal laid himself down at his master's feet.

"Did I not tell you?" said Kulluka to Siddha, pointing to the tiger. "Do you now understand why it was a foolish trick you played?"

"Pardon, honoured lord, pardon!" said Siddha, turning with clasped hands to Gurupada, understanding that it was the tiger of the hermit that he had given chase to. "Indeed I did not know."

"I understand," interrupted Gurupada, "you have been hunting Hara. That has happened before, but has not always ended so well for the hunter as for my four-footed friend here. For he can become angry, though he has never harmed those who leave him alone. I have had him, as Kulluka knows, ever since he was a small cub, and we are now well accustomed to each other. Is it not so, Hara?" he said, bending towards the tiger, that, half raising itself up, rubbed its broad head against its master's hand. "And my friends," continued he, "are also his. See now!" And Siddha, drawing near, laid his hand gently on its shoulder, on which the tiger, looking alternately at both, laid down at Siddha's feet, and leant its head against his hand. This time the young man did not step back, but stroked the animal's head; nor was he startled when, yawning, it opened its mighty jaws, showing rows of white sharp teeth.

"That is right," said Gurupada, as Hara returned to him. "I have seen many older than you who would not have remained so calm. But now let us think of other things. Travellers, after so long a journey through a wilderness where there is not much to be found, must need refreshment. Follow me." And, going before them, the hermit entered his dwelling.

The interior contained nothing beyond necessaries, but all in most perfect order, and arranged with elegance.

After the guests had rested themselves with him, on fine mats spread on the floor, the servant, who had taken charge of the horses, brought in some dishes of food.

The simple and easy tone in which the otherwise dignified hermit spoke, showed that he was a man of the world, and soon gave confidence to the Minister's son. Siddha answered Gurupada's questions respecting his father, his betrothed Iravati, and his life in Kashmir, with frankness mingled with respect. To his astonishment the hermit appeared to know all that had happened in earlier days in Kashmir, and showed himself acquainted with circumstances that must have been a secret to all excepting those who had access to the most private parts of the royal palace. Without doubt, in earlier years, Gurupada must have been a trusted councillor of one of the princes. But Siddha dared venture no indiscreet questions touching the hermit's former rank. He remarked that Gurupada's conversation was cheerful, and that he appeared perfectly content with his present station. Yet at times, in talking over political events in the north, a dark cloud momentarily crossed his noble countenance, as though the strong will of the philosopher could not hinder a passing emotion from being visible.

It had become late, and night was drawing on, the moon throwing her silvery light over the landscape which was visible through the open bamboos.

"Now," said Gurupada, rising, "pardon me, noble Siddha, if with your tutor and my friend I withdraw from the pleasure of your company. I have much to say to him which for the present must be a secret, and in which you probably would have but little interest. If you wish to refresh yourself there is the lake, and to a bath in the open air you are doubtless well accustomed."

The two elder men left the room together, and for long after Siddha saw them arm-in-arm, walking up and down, deep in earnest converse. When they returned it was time to go to rest, and the travellers were well pleased to stretch their weary limbs on the sleeping-places prepared for them.

Early the next morning, after a fresh bath and hearty breakfast, our travellers were ready to continue their journey. While the horses were being saddled, Gurupada drew Siddha on one side, out of hearing of Kulluka, and said—

"Holy hermits, when young men visit them, are not accustomed to let them depart without some instruction and advice. You expect, perhaps, the same from me; but you are mistaken. I can add nothing to what Kulluka, your wise and learned guru has doubtless already taught you. The world you are going to seek, and life itself, must teach you what remains. Still, one word, to which I will add a request. Do not fear, when you enter the luxurious and magnificent court at Agra, to take your part in all lawful diversions and amusements; and thus you will learn to distinguish the real from the unreal.

Think always of what doubtless your tutor has often taught you, keep your conscience pure, and take good care that no deed of yours shall ever give cause of shame either to others or to yourself. But should it happen that, in spite of your earnest striving to keep these precepts, the repose of your conscience should be disturbed, and you wish for some friend to whom you could open your heart, think then of an old friend of your father and your tutor, and come to the Hermit of Badrinath. Will you promise me this?"

"I promise it," answered Siddha, simply, but with manly earnestness, as he folded his arms respectfully on his breast. With greater friendliness than before, Gurupada took him by both hands, and pressed them heartily.

The horses were soon brought forward, and the riders, after taking leave of the hermit, sprang into their saddles, and, followed by the servants, took their way from the jungle to the mountain path.

More than once Siddha looked back, casting a glance to where the figure of the wise man was still visible between the trunks of the tall trees, standing at the threshold of his dwelling, with the tiger by his side, and then rode silently by his companion, buried in thought.

Suddenly, as though waking from a day-dream, he drew in his horse with such force as almost to throw it upon its haunches.

"Kulluka," he exclaimed, "I never saw such a man as Gurupada." But at the same time he coloured to the ears, thinking, but too late, that this exclamation might not be very pleasing to his friend and teacher.

But he had needlessly alarmed himself. Kulluka's countenance expressed unfeigned pleasure at the admiration of his pupil for his old friend.

"Indeed," he said, "it gives me great pleasure that you should so think of him, and it speaks well for you."

"But," Siddha said, after a moment of silence, "who then is Gurupada?"

"Well," was the answer, "that you have seen for yourself—a hermit of the Himálaya."

"Yes," replied Siddha, impatiently, "that I know well; but what was he first, before he came here and tamed tigers?"

"He attempted to tame men," answered Kulluka, "but in that he did not always succeed. But why did you not ask him yourself who he was?"

"Would that have been discreet,—should you have approved of that?"

"Certainly not, and you acted rightly in not violating the rights of hospitality by indiscreet curiosity, even if it arose from real interest and for that you deserve that your curiosity should be set at rest. Gurupada gave me permission to recount his former life and tell you his name. So listen!

"He was once a king."

"How now," said Siddha, a little disturbed, "are you going to tell me a tale from Somadeva,9 like those I heard so often from you when I was a little boy?"

"Listen or not, as you will, to my tale," answered Kulluka, calmly. "He was, I say, once a king, who, supported by good councillors, governed his kingdom with wisdom and prudence. He had no children, only a younger brother, a young man of great ability, to whom he was warmly attached, and whom he had chosen as his successor when death should take him, or when the weight of affairs of state should become too heavy for him to bear. But the brother was ambitious, and, in spite of some good qualities, he had not patience to wait his time. He allowed himself to be led away by parties in the state inimical to the existing government. First he intrigued secretly, and in the end he took up arms against his brother and lawful prince. But he and his followers were defeated, and brought prisoners to the capital. However, this did not put an end to the insurrection. Disturbances still continued, and the only means that remained to the king to suppress them was by the death of his ambitious and dangerous brother, however dearly he loved him, and by subjecting his followers to the same fate. But by so doing his throne would be founded on the blood of his brother and others; which might call endless feuds into life, to which there could be no other end but the utter exhaustion of the kingdom. Yet hardly anyone doubted that the king would, in the end, have recourse to this now unavoidable measure. Suddenly, a rumour spread that he had disappeared from the palace, and in all probability, though not certainly, had fallen a victim to treachery. Since that time he has never been heard of, and his brother, released from prison, ascended the throne as the lawful heir, and has reigned ever since, wisely retaining his brother's councillors at his side. Though not ruling with equal wisdom, yet his reign has been fortunate, and peace has been restored to his country."

Here, for a moment, Kulluka broke off his tale to look at his companion and pupil, but his countenance showed neither astonishment nor special interest.

"What you tell me," he said, "is simply the history of our present king and his predecessor and elder brother Nandigupta,10 which is known to all, to me as well as to every other Kashmiri."

"Certainly," replied Kulluka, "the history of which I remind you is well known. What is not known to every one, only to a few, is that King Nandigupta did not fall through treachery, is not dead, nor was he driven away. Of his own accord, and without the knowledge of his brother, nor of any but a few most trusty friends, he took refuge in a distant retreat, where by spreading a report that he had been slain, he saved his brother from a shameful death and his country from probable destruction."

"And so Nandigupta still lives," cried Siddha, "and he is——"

"As you doubtless have already guessed," answered Kulluka, "the hermit we have just left; but you must hold his secret sacred. The secret of his kingdom and his race is entrusted to your honour. The son of his most faithful servant and friend should know it, and will know well how to guard it."

"Why," asked Siddha, half dissatisfied, "did you not tell me this while we were still there? I might then have thanked the prince for all the benefits which, in the days of his greatness, my father and all our race received at his hands. But, it is true, you had no right to speak as long as he himself did not do so. But I still have an opportunity; for Gurupada, if he will be so called, made me promise to seek him if ever I should find myself in circumstances of difficulty and need good advice."

"And you have done well in giving your promise," said Kulluka. "Keep your word. Gurupada is better and wiser than any of us."

But Siddha scarcely heard. He was again immersed in thought. The meeting with the hermit, and the discovery of his secret, made a deep impression on him: that in the beginning of his journey he should have met with a princely philosopher, who, possessing almost unlimited power, and living in luxury, had willingly sacrificed all for love of his brother and his country; and who, happy in the consciousness of having done well, showed himself cheerful and contented with his simple life in the wilderness, with no other companions than a faithful servant and a beast of prey. Now he was on his road to the court of the fortunate and far-famed ruler of a great empire, who ruled his people more by wisdom than by the power of the sword; who had at his disposal enormous revenues; and who might call himself the ally of mighty princes in most distant countries, and protector of all known religions in the world.

The good Siddha, who had been accustomed to pride himself somewhat on his nobility and consequence, suddenly felt how small he was in comparison with two such men. It was indeed difficult to decide which was the greater of the two, and he wisely determined to suspend his judgment until he should have seen the Emperor Akbar himself.

This decision brought him back to the next goal of their journey, a visit to Allahabad, where his dearly loved bride—the beautiful Iravati—awaited his coming. His countenance, which for some minutes had been grave and earnest, brightened up, and striking spurs into his horse, as a long flat piece of country stretched out before them, he cried, joyfully, "Come, now for a gallop!" and darting forward, Kulluka saw brandishing his light spear, and shouting the name that carried off the victory in his thoughts—"Iravati!"

"Forward! forward, then!" muttered the Brahman to himself, setting his horse to a gallop, "until the end is reached; for me it is almost done, but for him the journey of life is only beginning. Oh that he may always find it smooth as this! but he also must meet with rocks and slippery precipices, and perhaps also—abysses. But may they only," he added, smiling to himself, as he thought of the adventure of the preceding evening, "be harmless precipices."

---

1 Badari-natha is a place sacred to Vishnu in the Himálayas. The Badari-natha peaks, in British Gurwhal, form a group of 6 summits from 22,000 to 23,400 feet above the sea. The town of Badari-natha is 55 miles N.E. of Srinagar, on the right bank of the Vishnu-ganga, a feeder of the Alakananda. The temple of Badari-natha is situated in the highest part of the town, and below it a tank, supplied from a sulphureous thermal spring, is frequented by thousands of pilgrims. The temple is 10,294 feet above the sea.

2 *Deva*, in Sanscrit, is a god, a divinity.

3 *Siddha*, in Sanscrit, means perfected, hence an adept. *Siddhanta*, a final conclusion, or any scientific work. The *Siddhas* are a class of semi-divine beings, who dwell in the regions of the sky.

4 *Rama* is a name in common use. Rama was the hero of the Ramayana epic, and the form taken by Vishnu in two of his Avataras.

5 Sanscrit name. Kulluka Bhatta was the famous commentator whose gloss was used by Sir W. Jones in making his translation of Manu.

6 *Guru*, a teacher. *Pada*, a word.

7 A common Sanscrit name.

8 *Hara* is the name of a branch of the Chuhan Rajpúts. It is also a name of Siva.

9 The most popular of the collections of old Hindu tales was the *Kathâ-Sarit-Sâgara*, or, "Ocean of the Streams of Narrative." It originated in the desire of a queen of Kashmir to provide amusement and instruction for her grandson. Somadeva, the Prime Minister, produced, in consequence, this collection of tales in verse.

10 *Nandi* is the bull of Siva usually placed in front of temples. *Gupta* is a concealed ascetic. The *Guptas* were a dynasty of kings reigning at Magadha.

Chapter II.
Iravati.

A young girl was seated on a balcony, all overgrown with trees and plants, in the great castle of Allahabad—palace and fortress in one. Her head rested on her hand as, musing, she gazed on the landscape stretched out before her on both sides of the two rivers that met here, and were now glittering in the light of an unclouded morning sun. To the left the rocky heights and sandy shores of the Jamuna; to the right the valley of the Granges; everywhere thick masses of mango-trees, in which numberless parrots and other bright-plumaged birds made their homes. Here and there small islands raised themselves above the surface of the water, and in the background there were rocky hills crowned with pagodas. Judging only by her dress, it would not have been supposed that the girl, sunk in a day-dream, was of exalted rank. She wore a simple white robe, with a narrow border of dark red, clasped by a golden girdle; a golden band held back her thick black locks, in which a single flower formed her only ornament, and that was all. But what need had the slight graceful figure, the fine-cut face, with its great dark eyes shaded by long silken lashes, for other ornament than that given by nature, and by Rama the god of love? And assuredly no offshoot of degenerate stem, no daughter of low degree, could have arrayed herself with so much elegance, and at the same time with such simplicity.

But the longing eyes did not, as of yore, rest with delight on the magnificent scene around. To-day, as yesterday and many days before, she gazed on the far-off mountains, in the direction from which the long-expected one must come; but long had she watched in vain. Where did he tarry? What could keep him? And did he think of her, or was it only occasionally that his thoughts wandered to her, who for days and months had devoted every thought to him and to him alone?

Then a heavy step was heard behind, in the room which opened on the verandah, and, preceded by a servant who flung back the curtain hanging before the door, a short, thick-set man of middle age approached, in a close-fitting garment that came down to his feet. A short sword with a richly ornamented hilt, stuck in his belt, was the only token of his rank.

"Noble lady," said the servant, respectfully waking his mistress from her day-dream, "Salhana the governor, your father, comes to visit you."

"He is welcome," answered the girl, accustomed from infancy to be addressed with respect; and rising, she advanced to meet her father.

"Iravati,"[1] said he, looking at her with his black, penetrating eyes, which gave the only expression to his pale countenance, "some time ago I told you that

I expected Siddha Rama, from Kashmir, your cousin and betrothed, with Kulluka his tutor. They have just arrived, and are now in the neighbouring gallery. We will go there to receive them."

On hearing these tidings, for one moment Iravati seemed to forget all the calm reserve to which she had schooled herself, and would have hurried past her father to welcome him whom she had so long waited for; but Salhana delayed her by a slight motion of his hand.

"First one word," he said. "It is known to me that the professors of Islam, under whom we live, disapprove most highly of free intercourse between unmarried youths and young girls, and that many of our Hindus have adapted themselves to the opinions of our governors; but for my part, as you know, I am a follower of our old customs, however much I wish to see observed all fitting forms, and so I give you permission, as in early days in our own country, freely to speak with your cousin and bridegroom, but only allow our most trusted friends to know it, otherwise my influence here, where I govern, and your good name, may suffer. Now come." And going before her, he led the way to the open verandah looking down on the river, where their two visitors stood awaiting their appearance.

"You are welcome, my lords and friends," said Salhana, with dignity; "and I thank you for granting my request, and coming straight to my dwelling, instead of taking up your abode in the town, as many do." These words sounded cordial, though the tone in which they were pronounced was as expressionless as his stiff countenance.

Some might have remarked this, but not Siddha, who, barely greeting his stately uncle or giving Kulluka time to receive the reverent greeting of Iravati, flung himself on his knees before her, and pressed a burning kiss on the hand she held out to him.

"Welcome," she said, signing to him to rise, (and how sweet sounded that gentle voice!) "welcome, friend. How long we have watched for your approach, looking towards yonder mountains, and almost doubting if you would ever come!"

"You did not believe, beloved," cried Siddha, almost indignantly, "that I would have delayed my arrival in Allahabad for one moment longer than was necessary. If I could have leapt over rivers and mountains to have been sooner with you, and had my horse had more wings than Vishnu's Garuda,2 I should not, indeed, have spared him."

"I believe you willingly," said Iravati, with a friendly smile, "and indeed I meant no reproach to you or to our trusty friend Kulluka, and we must rejoice all the more at being together, as I hear from my father that it is only for a very short time."

"Indeed," said Salhana, after a few words with Kulluka, interrupting the conversation of the two lovers, "our friends must leave us early to-morrow; but I did not expect otherwise. Yet, noble Siddha, I must shorten by a few minutes your interview with your bride, as I wish to speak a few words with you, and at once, for my time is precious, and before our mid-day meal I have many things to do. Will it please you to follow me?"

This request was not to be refused, and unwillingly and with many a longing look towards Iravati, Siddha followed his courteous but imperious uncle to the garden on the other side of the palace. There, under the thick shade of trees, Salhana seated himself on a carpet, signing to his nephew to take a place by his side.

"And so you are going," he began, "to seek your fortune in the immediate service of the great Emperor. In truth you may hold yourself fortunate that you have a father who knows how to give you so favourable an opportunity, and also, if I may add it without presumption, an uncle who, by the accident of his position, may be able to afford you help in case of need."

"For that I am very grateful," answered Siddha, "and I hope never to forget that you, perhaps more than my father, have aided to make easy to me the first step on the ladder, not only because it may be that I shall have opportunities of distinguishing myself, but that I shall be able to achieve more here than in our own beautiful but far-away country; and at the same time I shall see the Emperor living in all the splendour of his court, of which I have heard so much at home."

"Certainly," said Salhana, "but a word of counsel; beware of exaggerated expectations, not as regards the magnificence of palaces and courts, of which in the north we can hardly form an idea, but of the Emperor himself; it is better to begin without highly wrought expectations."

"How," asked Siddha, in astonishment; "in truth does not Akbar deserve his name? is he not, as my father and my tutor have always represented him, a great man as well as a mighty prince?"

"That I did not say," was the answer; "but our great men can have their faults, which may threaten to become dangerous for others. Listen," continued the governor, looking round to see there was no one within earshot, and sinking his voice to a whisper: "whenever a man attains such power as Akbar, through his own courage and prudence, then is the longing to attain more not easily satisfied. The Emperor, who has subdued states and people to his rule, can hardly bear that your and my fatherland should remain so entirely independent. You know, moreover, do you not, how every now and then, although it was kept secret from most, divisions have broken out in Kashmir between our king and his two sons, in the same way as in earlier days between him and his brother Nandigupta?"

"No, I did not know it," said Siddha; "this is the first time it has come to my ears."

"Well," rejoined the other, "you should inquire about it when the opportunity offers. I can tell you somewhat of it at once, but do not speak of it to Kulluka; for that, I think, might not be well. The divisions between the king and his two sons were stirred up—you understand by whom. If open feuds once broke out, and the country was divided into parties, then a pretence for declaring war on us would easily be found, and the Emperor would invade our country with a strong army, guided through the mountain passes by his spies, and so our country would be incorporated in his empire. This does not prevent my acknowledging with admiration his wonderful conquests, but the same ambition which has made his people great may be the cause of the destruction of our independence."

"But how," asked Siddha, after a moment's thought,—"if this is so, how can you remain the servant of a man who has sworn the destruction of our country?"

"And why not?" said Salhana, in his turn surprised. "Is it not well that one of us, without harming the Emperor, but, on the contrary, serving him in many important affairs, should keep an eye on his plans and actions. It is well that you yourself, under my recommendation and protection, should come still more closely in contact with our ruler. Certainly you will be less suspicious than I, but still in this respect you can be of great service."

"But," asked Siddha, doubtfully, after a moment's thought, "is that honourable?"

"Young man," answered Salhana, in a dignified tone, although his countenance expressed no anger, "let me remark to you that a man of my age and experience should know well what is honourable and what is not; and you, only just commencing your part in life, should not attempt to give counsel on such a subject."

"Forgive me, uncle," answered Siddha, "you know that I am still so little acquainted with the principles of state affairs, that I cannot understand them at once; and, also, Kulluka, my guru,3 has always impressed on me to follow the right path, and never to act ambiguously towards anyone, and——"

"Kulluka, my best friend," interrupted the other, "is an excellent man, for whom I have the greatest respect; but he is a man of learning, not of facts; a man of theory, not of what is practical. See, now, your country and people, who are dear to you, are threatened by a prince whom you look upon with admiration, and would willingly serve in all but that one thing. You should hold it as a duty to work against him in this, as far as possible. The opportunity is now opened to you, not entirely, but in a certain measure. Should you now spurn this opportunity, because of an exaggerated idea of political honour? And does he himself act with honour in accepting your services and mine while at the same time he has designs on our king and country? and if not, what claim has he on such special loyalty on our side? Moreover, go, if you will, to Akbar, and say to his face, if you dare, that you see through his plans and will oppose them; and before the day is over, my good friend, you will be fettered in a dungeon, or on your way banished to the furthest bounds of the Dakhin or Bengal, if worse does not befall you. Such opposition would be of no service to us; far otherwise would it be to make good use of favourable opportunities. By doing so, there would be no harm done to the prince, while, on the other hand, we may perchance save our fatherland from destruction."

Not convinced, but still not knowing how to refute such reasoning, Siddha vainly sought for an answer, and remained silent, waiting for what his uncle might have further to say. But he appeared to consider the interview at an end, and made a movement to rise, when, in the path leading to the place where they were seated, a figure appeared, just such a one as would attract Siddha's attention and draw his thoughts from the preceding conversation. He was tall, brown, and closely shaven all but a single long lock of hair; his right arm and breast were naked excepting for the sacred cord of the Brahmans; a narrow white garment was thrown round his emaciated limbs. His sunken dull eyes and hollow cheeks spoke of long fasts and severe penances. Although not easily alarmed by man or beast, and accustomed to strange appearances, yet for a moment Siddha started back. Many a tiger had he slain in the jungle, and without fear killed many a deadly snake, yet he could not overcome a feeling of horror at this sudden appearance.

"Gorakh[4] the Yogi,"[5] explained Salhana, "priest of the Durga[6] temple, yonder on the hills. Meet him with respect; he deserves it, and has more to impart to you than you suspect."

Gliding rather than walking, the priest approached the two men who had stood up to receive him, and, raising his clasped hands to his forehead, he said, in a slow, drawling voice, "Om, Om![7] You, the favoured of the Lord of the World, and of Durga his glorious consort. Om!"

"I greet you well, most honoured Gorakh," answered Salhana to this curious salutation; "you see here my nephew Siddha Rama, from Kashmir, of whom I have already spoken to you."

"He is welcome," was Gorakh's reply; "and may he, above the strife of disunion, know how to lay the foundation that leads to the endless blessings of union, wherein you, my friend, begin more and more to recognise the true part of salvation. Yet," continued he, after a moment of dignified silence, "the experience of life must teach him the way, as it has done for you and me. We must allow the time needed for the scholar. In truth, I know him, and know that he will belong to us." And here he turned to Siddha: "It is but lately that I met you."

"Pardon me, honoured lord," was the reply; "that I cannot recall."

"You could not," was the answer, "for at that moment I was invisible to human eye."

Too well acquainted with the extraordinary claims to the power of rendering themselves invisible asserted by the Yogis, Siddha contented himself with listening in silence to the priest, who, to his astonishment, continued:—

"It was on that evening when you gave chase to the hermit's tiger;—but we will speak to each other later. Now the noble Salhana wishes to converse with me, so for the present farewell, and may Durga's mighty consort bless you." And murmuring in a low tone his "Om, Om!" the priest of Durga and Salhana left him in the garden, his uncle crying to him, "We shall meet again soon."

The last communication of the Yogi was well calculated to excite Siddha's astonishment. How could the man know what had happened to him yonder in the mountains, where, excepting his own companion, he had seen no human being? But here the sight of his servant at a little distance, wandering through the trees, brought to his mind the way by which the riddle might be unravelled.

"Vatsa," said he, beckoning to the man, "have either you or Kulluka's servant just spoken with a priest?"

"No, my lord," answered Vatsa, "we have not even seen one."

"No!" said Siddha, now really astonished. "Good; you can go." And turning away, he murmured to himself, half disturbed and half alarmed, "I will speak to Kulluka about this." But how could a priest or anyone else occupy his thoughts when, having gone but a little way, he caught sight of the white robe and slight figure of Iravati, seated under the thick shade of a mango, close to a pool of lotuses, while the air was filled with the sweet music of a sparkling fountain, and cooled by its falling waters. Flowers lay scattered around, and in her hand was a half-finished wreath. Hearing footsteps approaching, and catching sight of Siddha, she flung the wreath away, and hastened to meet her lover, raising her clasped hands to her forehead. Siddha seized them in his own, and, leading her back, flung himself on the moss at her side.

"What a cruel man your father is," said he, "to part us so soon, when we had scarcely exchanged two words!"

"Well," answered Iravati, "you must thank him for allowing us to talk together, since it is long since this was allowed to those who are betrothed to each other."

"From my heart I will be grateful to him," said Siddha, "and more highly prize the happy moments spent with you. But you do not seem quite to share in my joy; tell me the reason."

"Ah!" sighed Iravati; "how can our meeting be unclouded happiness, when we are to part again so soon? Perhaps, and even probably, these are the only short moments in which, for a long time, we shall speak freely one to another; and to-morrow you depart for the luxurious, turbulent city, where a simple girl like me may easily be forgotten."

"Forgotten!" cried Siddha; "have I deserved such suspicion from you? and what is the absence of a few months! Returns not"—asked he, in the words of Amaru, as, taking her hand in his, he drew her nearer to him—"Returns not he who departs? Why, then, beloved, art thou sad? Do not my heart and word remain yours, even though we part?"8

"Ah," answered Iravati, "if poets could comfort us! But tell me, Siddha, have you never made any verses on me?"

"I wish that I could," was the modest reply; "and indeed I have tried, but what I wrote was never worthy of you. Still, there is another art in which I am more accomplished than in poetry, and my attempt in that line you shall see." And drawing from his girdle a small locket, set with jewels, he showed a miniature, in which she recognised her own image.

"Siddha!" she exclaimed, joyfully; "but I am not so beautiful as that."

"Not so beautiful!" repeated he. "No; but a hundred times more beautiful than my pencil or that of any other could represent."

And he was right, for according to Indian taste he had exaggerated the eyes and mouth, when their regularity was one of the beauties of Iravati's face.

"But why," said he, as she suddenly drew herself up and quickly escaped from his arms, "why are you now going to leave me?"

"Wait a moment," she replied; "in an instant I will be back."

With the swiftness of a gazelle he saw her taking her way through the trees to the palace, ascending the broad marble steps as though she scarcely touched them, and in a few moments return, holding in her hand an object which, in the distance, he could not distinguish, but as she drew nearer, and, with a blush, held it out to him, with an exclamation of admiration, he recognised his own portrait. But this, in truth, was an idealized likeness.

"My dearest!" he said, in ecstasy; and before she could draw back he had thrown his arms round her, and pressed a burning kiss on her lips.

"See," said she, gently disengaging herself; "my father should be well pleased with us, for we have done just like the princes and princesses in our old national legends, and have drawn each other's portraits."

"Not exactly so," added Siddha, "for they drew their own likenesses, and then exchanged with one another. But I think our way is much the best; theirs appears to me extravagant vanity, in our way of looking at it, or utterly aimless."

"Fie!" said Iravati, reproachfully; "do you make such remarks on the writings of the ancients? Who knows if you will not next criticise our holy books!"

"And why not," asked he, "if they here or there make mistakes, or show a want of taste, or——"

"But you are not, I hope, an unbeliever?"

"An unbeliever in what?"

"In the law of the Holy Veda, for example."

"Come, dear one," interrupted Siddha, laughing, "do not let us employ the few moments allowed us as many of our countrymen do, who can hardly meet each other without at once discussing theological and philosophical questions."

"You are right," she answered, "and I know of a game that is far prettier, and one that you also know." And bending over the brink of the tank, she gathered a dark-blue lotus, and picking up a long leaf that lay on the ground, and weaving it into a kind of boat, she placed the lotus in it and let it float on the surface of the water, which was gently stirred by the falling fountain. "The lotus is my Siddha," said she, half to herself; "let us see if he will remain faithful to me."

"No," said Siddha, in his turn reproachfully, "that is a foolish game, and one that you should not play."

Iravati hardly listened to him, but watched with breathless attention the waving leaf that was dancing on the rippling water. "Faithful, faithful!" she cried; but then a sigh from the south wind caught the frail vessel. It turned over and floated bottom upwards, while the lotus disappeared. "Alas!" cried Iravati, as she let her head sink in her breast; "my forebodings, then, have not deceived me."

"Fie! I say now in my turn," said Siddha; "a noble, well educated lady to hold to such follies, that are only to be excused in ignorant peasant girls. And so you place more faith in the leaf of a tree than in the word of honour of a nobleman who has pledged you his troth, as you have to him?"

"Ah! Siddha," sighed Iravati, "you must forgive me if I do seem rather childish; and does not my uneasiness show you how much I love you? However great my faith in your word is, I cannot help thinking with anxiety of the city to which you go; and who knows what temptation awaits you there? But I confess that I was wrong, and," continued she, leaning her head on his shoulder, "I know that Siddha is mine, now and always, and no other woman lives who can rob me of his heart."

Putting his arm around her, Siddha gazed at her in silence; but his look said more than the warmest assurance could have done. A jingling of bangles made them look up, and Iravati said, "Our interview, my friend, is ended; there comes Nipunika, my servant, to warn us." And a moment after, the servant appeared, her brown ancles and arms clasped with golden bangles, and announced to her mistress that the Governor requested her to return to her apartments, and begged his nephew to join him and Kulluka at their meal. Giving him her hand for a moment, Iravati, accompanied by Nipunika, returned to the palace. Siddha followed to seek his uncle and his travelling companion. The meal was not wanting in magnificence and luxury, and was served in one of the smaller apartments, from the open verandah of which there was a magnificent view of the country around. There were cushions of silk with richly embroidered borders, on which the guests took their places; gold and silver vessels; choice meats and wines; numbers of servants of all nations, and in every costume; in a word, everything that was conformable to the rank of Salhana, governor of the fortress, and, for the moment, the man of the highest rank of all the inhabitants of the royal palace. But merriment was wanting to the courtly feast, and confidential intercourse was not possible. All was formal, stately, and stiff, and the conversation meaningless and polite, and only sustained by the three men because silence would have been uncourteous. How different, thought Siddha, was their simple meal with the hermit of the mountain; and it seemed that Kulluka was of the same opinion, for, stealing a glance at his guru, he saw a smile on his face, unobserved by Salhana. At last their repast came to an end, but the remainder of the day brought no pleasure to Siddha. He wandered for some time under the balcony of the apartments which Nipunika, whom he met, pointed out as those of her mistress. But Iravati did not show herself, and when, towards evening, she appeared in the presence of her father and his guests, it was only to take leave of him with the same formality that had attended their meeting in the morning.

At dawn next morning they were to recommence their journey, to avoid the heat of mid-day, and the travellers withdrew early to their apartments. Needful as rest was, the younger man was not inclined at once to seek it. Taking off his arms, instead of throwing himself on his bed, he stood for some time at the open window, from which there was a view of the whole fortress, and all the thickets of trees, half-hidden in the dimness of night. Behind them rose hills, with here and there temples and other sacred buildings. His mind was not alone occupied with Iravati's image, but also with the conversation with his uncle, and the strange meeting with the mysterious priest, who, by some artifice or accident, had become acquainted with his adventure with the tiger, though how, he could not guess. But to what did all this tend? What did the man want? And Salhana the governor; could he trust him? and were his instructions to be followed, and all that had happened this morning kept secret from Kulluka? or would it not be better to consult him about it?

An unexpected appearance made Siddha for an instant lose the thread of his thoughts, though they were at once brought back to him. On the nearest wall, where the low breastwork stood sharply out against the light that still lingered in the sky, two figures suddenly showed themselves above the parapet, who, though he could not distinguish their features, he recognised as his uncle the governor, and Gorakh the priest of Durga. Again the two were together, and at so late an hour. But the most wonderful part of this apparition was the entirely changed bearing of both. There was no trace of their former stiffness and stateliness, and one gesticulated more violently than the other, carried away by their engrossing conversation, as they walked up and down, now towards the castle, and now towards the hills. This continued until they were suddenly disturbed by the appearance of other figures, which, one by one, moved along the outer wall, their emaciated forms entirely naked with the exception of a white cord round their necks, which here in the half light was visible in contrast with their dark skins. On their approach Salhana disappeared, probably through some stairs leading to the palace, invisible from where Siddha was. The priest, immediately regaining his dignity, and pointing with his right hand towards one of the temples, placed himself at the head of the band, and led the way along the wall to the dark wood lying at the foot of the rocks. A long row of figures followed him, and Siddha had long ceased to count them ere the last disappeared in the jungle.

In spite of himself a slight feeling of horror had seized on him as he saw their strange forms pass by, and associated them with the name of the goddess to whose service Gorakh was dedicated, and to whose temple they appeared bound. Could it be true that the sect still existed, of which he had so often heard, but believed to be either rooted out or to have died out—that mysterious league of demons in human form that had so long been the plague and terror of Hindustan, the most terrible product that religious fanaticism had ever brought to life? And with the leader of such a band was it possible that his uncle, the servant of the Emperor, should be allied! It was indeed not to be believed, and laughing at his foolish fancies, Siddha left the window, and hastily throwing off his clothes, flung himself on the bed prepared for him. But it was long before he could sleep, for the conflicting images of Iravati, Salhana, Gorakh, and his naked followers, kept passing through his head; and before he fell asleep he had come to the determination not to speak to Kulluka of what he had that day seen and heard. That his uncle was mixed up with secret affairs was clear to him; still for a statesman that was not unnatural, and there was nothing to make him suspect they were criminal, though their discovery might be injurious to Salhana, and perhaps to his nearest relatives. He would not, he felt, be justified in betraying what confidential conversation and a pure accident had made him acquainted with. Kulluka himself would certainly condemn such a course of action.

---

1 Iravati is the Sanscrit name of the river Ravi or Hydrastes. Iravat was a son of Arjuna.

2 Vishnu, the god, rides on a mythical bird called Garuda.

3 A spiritual teacher or guide.

4 *Goraksh* or *Gorakh*, a cow-herd.

5 *Yogi*, a follower of the *Yoga* philosophy. An ascetic.

6 *Durga*, a goddess, the wife of Siva, and destroyer of evil beings and oppressors. Also called *Kali*.

7 The mystic monosyllable to be uttered before any prayer. It is supposed to consist of three letters, *a u m*, combined, being types of the three Vedas, or of the three great divinities, Brahma, Vishnu, Siva.

8 From the hundred love sentences of the Amaru-Sataka, a poem written by a king named Amaru.

Chapter III.
Agra.

The call of trumpets sounding gaily awoke Siddha from his morning sleep, and, on springing up and looking out of the window, he saw the great court before the castle filled with horsemen, half of whom were occupied in unsaddling their horses, while the others were mounting and forming in line. These, with whom our travellers were to continue their journey, were on the point of starting for Agra, to relieve the soldiers just arrived; and amongst them Siddha saw his servant waiting with his grey charger. It took him but a few minutes to finish his preparations for the journey, and he was in the saddle some moments before Kulluka and the Governor appeared. But in the meantime, before the cavalcade moved off, Siddha found an opportunity to ride round the corner of the bastion to the balcony towards which, the day before, he had so often and so vainly looked. This time it was not in vain, for between the plants that covered the balcony he caught sight of a well-known figure, dressed in white, who at his approach waved a handkerchief in the gentle breeze; and as he drew nearer, she let it slowly fall; but he, quickly turning his horse, caught it on the point of his lance. It was one of the brightly coloured tissues of Kashmir, fine as a spider's web, well calculated to be the despair of all the weavers in the world, and as easily drawn through a finger-ring as bound into a turban. He quickly pressed to his lips this parting gift so precious to him; then, binding it to the hilt of his sabre, he waved a farewell, and in a few bounds had rejoined his travelling companions. Salhana accompanied his guests for a short distance, and then took leave, telling his nephew that he hoped before long to see him again, as in a few days he thought of visiting Agra himself. Our travellers continued their way, in company with the commanding officer of the detachment.

The journey lasted for more than one day, generally by or near the banks of the Jamuna, and led through sandy plains, where stones were more frequently met with than trees, though sometimes they came to lovely hills clad in green. At length the evening of their last halt came, at a short distance from Agra, and on the following morning a short ride took them to the city of the Emperor, the view of which more than repaid them for the weariness of their journey.

In a semicircle on the opposite shore of the river, lay, between garden and fortification, the long row of palaces and mosques, which made, at this time and for long after, Agra, or Akbarabad, one of the most beautiful as well as one of the most magnificent cities in the world. In the middle, standing above all, as brooking no rivalry, stood the palace of the Emperor.[1] The central building, which from the delicate joining of its red, smooth-polished sandstones, seemed hewn from a cloud of granite glittering in the sunshine, was surrounded on all sides by small pleasure-houses and thick clumps of trees. This building, from its colossal size, with its numerous cupolas, and slight towers, with their delicate tracery visible against the blue sky, could not fail to strike the beholder with wonder and admiration. Around the central palace were the pleasure-houses of the great courtiers, of rich noblemen and prosperous citizens, and mosques with their cupolas and minarets, while here and there a few solitary temples were the only witnesses of a civilisation whose ascendancy belonged to the past.

The beauty of the view made the travellers draw rein, and gaze on it with delight. One man alone, a mighty conqueror and deep-thinking reformer, had, as though by magic, called this splendour and beauty to life, as it were, from the barren plain. A feeling of anxiety crept over Siddha as he thought how soon he would meet him, and perhaps exchange a few words, formal though they might be.

On reaching the other side of the river, they took leave of the officer who had been their travelling companion, and, with their servant, made their way to a house that had been hired for them by a friend of Kulluka. It was simply but tastefully and comfortably arranged, with cheerful views of the gardens around, and of the river that lay glittering in the morning sun.

"Come, this will do," said Kulluka, as he entered; "and I see the camels with our baggage have arrived. We must not be idle, but dress ourselves, and at once go to wait on Abú-l Fazl the Minister. Now for a bath, and meantime Vatsa can unpack."

Half an hour later both were ready for the visit, Siddha in a dress of cloth-of-gold, reaching to the knees, and opening a little at the throat, showing a pearl necklace. On his head was a turban ornamented with a feather. Kulluka was also dressed with elegance and with less severe simplicity than hitherto. They were armed with sabre and dagger, but more for show than use.

It was not far to the palace of the Minister, and passing through the courtyard, they gave their names to a servant, who immediately showed them into one of the inner apartments, to await the coming of the Wazir; but their patience was not put to proof. The curtain that separated their apartment from others was soon drawn aside, and Abú-l Fazl entered. He was a man of middle height, rather inclined to corpulence, and about fifty years of age. He was dressed in a costly garment of yellow flowered silk, wore no beard, and his smooth countenance, in spite of a look of weariness, expressed manly strength and a strong resolute will, though this was tempered by kindly dark eyes.[2]

"It gives me great pleasure to see you here so soon," said he, after the usual greetings, which on the part of Kulluka and Siddha were full of respect. "Our young friend shows himself no laggard in entering the Emperor's service—thanks, I suppose, to your inciting, O wise Kulluka."

"It would indeed have been a bad beginning," was the reply, "if he had delayed a moment longer than was necessary in assuming the position which your favour and the Emperor's had assigned him."

"No favour, my friend," interrupted Abú-l Fazl, "but a wise choice, I hope. We do not consider it needful to give all appointments to our own noblemen, but hold them out also as prizes to the native nobility of countries that are allied with us. And you know that our Rajputs would see with displeasure their commanders chosen from any but their own countrymen. And what could give me greater pleasure than to call the son of an old and tried friend to a post that his father wished to see him fill!"

"Nevertheless, my lord," said Siddha, as the Minister finished, "allow me to look upon it as a favour, and to thank you most heartily both for my father and for myself, and I hope to prove myself not unworthy of your goodness."

"Above all, be faithful," said Abú-l Fazl, gravely. "Perhaps this recommendation appears needless to you; but when you have been here longer you will discover that treachery lurks in every corner, and even the best may sometimes be led away and become faithless. To-morrow, meantime, your commander will give you the necessary instructions for your service, and he will warn you to be careful with your Rajputs, for you know that many of them, although their position is lowly, are noble as you yourself, and you cannot treat them as though they were common soldiers. Now, doubtless, you wish to see more of the city than you have yet done, and I will not keep you. But wait a moment," he continued, as Siddha rose to take his leave; "a guide would be welcome to you, and I think I can give you a good one." Clapping his hands, he asked the servant who appeared, "Is my nephew Parviz in the house?"

"I have just seen him in the courtyard," answered the servant.

"Say that I wish to see him."

In a few minutes a young man appeared, of about Siddha's age, richly dressed, and with ornaments of pearls and jewels. His face was pleasing, but, in spite of a black moustache, somewhat feminine.

"Parviz," said Abú-l Fazl, "you see here our two visitors from Kashmir, of whose coming I spoke to you; the noble Siddha I hope you will soon call your friend; and now will you serve him as guide, for this is his first visit to our city?"

"Willingly, uncle," answered Parviz, as he greeted Siddha with friendliness; "it will be as much a pleasure as an honour."

"Then go," said the Minister; "Kulluka will perhaps remain a little longer with me, to talk over the affairs of Kashmir. But, gentlemen," said he, more to Siddha than to the Brahman, "do not forget to visit my brother Faizi to-day; he might take it amiss if you put off doing so until to-morrow, although he would not grudge me the preference." And making them a friendly sign of farewell, the two young men left the palace together.

"Come," said Parviz, "luckily it is not so very hot, and we can go at once to see—what to our visitors to Agra is the greatest of all the sights—the Palace of the Emperor—that is if the walk is not too far for you, after your long ride of this morning."

"Oh," answered Siddha, quickly becoming familiar with his new friend, "I care as little for heat as for cold—we are well accustomed to both amongst our mountains; nor do we think much of fatigue. But I am sorry to give you the trouble of showing me what you must often have seen before."

"Though not so indifferent to weather," said Parviz, jestingly, "as you who come from wild mountains and forests, still I can manage a short walk, and, even if it is hot, all inconvenience will be forgotten in the pleasure of your companionship."

They soon became more familiar, and confided to each other their various affairs and concerns. Parviz, among other things, told Siddha that he had no taste for military service, and that his uncle thought him unfitted for it, and therefore destined him for some civil employment. Thus talking they came to a fine broad street that formed one of the principal approaches to the royal palace. This street ended in a gateway in the form of a triumphal arch. Passing through it they entered a large *maidan* overshadowed with plane-trees. Six other streets equally broad opened on this space, under similar arches; in the middle stood a colossal stone elephant, the trunk of which formed a fountain, throwing up jets of water. Three sides of the place were shut in by marble colonnades, behind which arose gradually the different stories of the building. Though this view was not so striking or picturesque as that from the river, yet the extraordinary extent of palace, with its various buildings and fortifications, was more apparent.

"You understand," said Parviz, "that it is impossible to visit all we see at once; even if we were proof against fatigue, we should not have the time. But let us take a glance around, so that you may be able to form an idea of the whole, and later you will become acquainted with it all."

As they entered one of the verandahs Parviz spoke to the guard, who at once called a servant to guide them to those apartments that were accessible to visitors of their rank. Following him, they passed through long rows of rooms, each furnished with more splendour than the last, and all built in the light Moorish style, with charming views of the gardens around, with their fountains and luxuriant growth of flowers of all kinds. Here were marble walls, inlaid with flowers in delicate Mosaics; there, from all corners, tiny fountains filled the air with coolness; everywhere curtains and hangings of silk, embroidered with gold and silver; and heavy carpets, and soft silken cushions.

"In the other wing," said Parviz, "are things still more beautiful; but they are not shown, for there are the women's apartments. I have had just a glance at one or two before they were finished, and while they were uninhabited. The great audience hall, is it open?" he said, turning to the guide.

"No, my lord," was the answer; "but in a few days."

"It does not signify," interrupted Parviz. "Soon," continued he to Siddha, "there will be a public audience given, and we can then see it. As to the apartments of the Emperor, in all probability you will soon become well acquainted with them."

They then took their way through high, broad galleries, filled with servants and soldiers, and then through the pleasure-grounds, while Parviz pointed out to his companion the various halls and buildings, telling him to what purposes they were destined. Here was the imperial library, with its richly bound manuscripts; yonder the work-room of the goldsmith and jeweller, and laboratories of the perfumers, the store-houses and kitchens, and also the arsenal of the fortress, and stables for the horses, elephants, and camels, kept for the use of the Emperor.

Siddha had considered himself well acquainted with palaces, but the conviction now crept over him that, until this moment, he had never seen one. The extent of the stables struck him with astonishment, appearing like a village from the compound round which they were built.

"What a number of noble animals there must be there!" he remarked.

"Yes," answered Parviz, "there are at least a hundred elephants here; and I scarcely know how many are kept for the Emperor in other places, but according to report he has as many again, and equal numbers of horses and hunting-leopards."

"But," asked Siddha, "what can any one, even though he be the great Akbar, do with such profusion?"

"Not much for himself," was the answer. "Less perhaps than you imagine. Born in a wilderness, while his father wandered in banishment, and brought up in a camp, he places no value on all this excessive luxury; but he is convinced, I believe, that a prince like him, in these countries and among such people as he governs, has as great need of a striking magnificence as of a fine army and experienced statesmen. We all—Persians, Mughals, Arabs, or Hindus, your people as well as ours—are accustomed to feel greater respect for a monarch the more outward show he makes. But you must not think that with all this show there is also great prodigality. On the contrary, I can assure you nothing is lost or wasted, and in the smallest affairs of this great court there is the same strict order as in the different departments of government, which can perhaps everywhere in the kingdom of the Great Mughal be held up as an example of what intelligent administration should be. My uncle Abú-l Fazl is busied in describing all this exactly in his great work on the institutions and the government of the Emperor,3 in which he allows me to help him occasionally. But there are some things in which Akbar may be called prodigal, especially in aiding those who are in trouble and difficulties, and who have some claim on his liberality; and also in the advancement of science and art. As regards these, his treasurer has some trouble in keeping him within bounds. But now," continued Parviz, after a moment's silence, "it is about time to be returning; the sun commences to burn, and I must confess to a little fatigue. If we loiter here longer I shall be inclined to repose on one of these seats, and await the coolness of the evening; but in this way we should lose our meal."

"So let us turn back," answered Siddha; "and I thank you heartily for your company."

Taking a by-path on the other side of the garden and building, Parviz guided his friend back to his lodging, and there taking leave, he said, "To-morrow probably you will be too busy with your appointment to see more of our town; but the day after, or later, I shall gladly be at your orders, only let me know if I am to come for you."

The two young men took leave of each other, and Siddha sought, in a cool apartment, the mid-day rest, which he found far from unwelcome. When evening fell, he, with his elder friend, took their way to Faizi, brother of the Minister. A comfortable and tastefully built bungalow, surrounded by thickly growing trees, was the habitation of Abú-l Fazl's younger brother. They were immediately admitted, and presently a servant appeared, to lead them to Faizi's own apartment. There, close to a verandah that ran round the greater part of the building, sat a man, in the prime of life, bending over a table covered with papers. Around him, on the ground, were scattered many others. He rose to meet his visitors without any formality, and holding out his hand with a simple welcome, signed to them to seat themselves with him on the cushions before the verandah.4

What principally distinguished Faizi from his elder brother was the frank, joyous expression of his smoothly shaven countenance, and a peculiar easiness of manner, mixed with the courtly forms of a man of the world. His calm and tranquil look was more characteristic of a quiet thinker than of a man of warlike experience, although as a warrior he had not failed in many a brave deed, and as ambassador had aided in setting at rest many an intricate question.

"I knew well," he said, as a servant offered wine and refreshments, "that you would not let the day pass, worthy Kulluka, without giving me, as well as my brother, the pleasure of seeing you and making acquaintance with your young friend, who, before long, I hope to call mine. And what do you think of our new city?" he asked Siddha. "You must already have seen something of it."

"Your nephew Parviz, noble lord," answered Siddha, "was so kind as to show me a part of the palace this morning; but to tell the truth, I cannot at this moment form an opinion of it. I am now simply overcome with astonishment at so much magnificence and such a profusion of splendid works of art. I had imagined much, but my imagination fell far short of the reality."

"That I can easily believe," rejoined Faizi: "it happens to everyone on their first arrival here. However much one may have heard or read of Akbar's palace beforehand, one is overcome with astonishment on really seeing it. But tell me, Kulluka, how things go in the north; I am anxious to hear news of your Kashmir."

Kulluka willingly replied, keeping to general affairs, and without then alluding to the divisions that were beginning to arise; and soon Siddha also took a lively share in the conversation. Never before had he found himself so quickly at his ease with a stranger as he did with the celebrated Faizi, the great Emperor's friend and councillor, and of whose learning and knowledge he had heard so much. The conversation soon passed from the subjects of the day to various topics, especially those relating to literature.

"You admire our palaces," said Faizi, turning to Siddha, "and say they far out-do your expectations; but it was quite the contrary with me when I first made acquaintance with your simple, classical, and sacred literature. Our faithful were not very learned; Mullahs had assured me they were nothing but a confused and tasteless collection of monstrosities, as pernicious to our civilisation as dangerous to our belief in Allah and His Prophet. I say nothing about this last accusation; but as to what concerns the cultivation of taste and knowledge, I find far more aid in your poets and thinkers than in ours. How splendid is your heroic poetry, how fine your lyrics, and sparkling your dramas! what noble, elevated feelings, yet, at the same time, what purity and humanity, and what a breadth and depth of thought was there in your philosophers of old! But why should I remind you of all this, which you naturally know and understand far better than I do, who with great difficulty have learnt to understand your language, which is so entirely different from our Persian or Arabic."

"After all," said Siddha, "Sanscrit does not come so naturally to us Hindus, who generally speak Hindustani. Ask Kulluka if he did not find difficulties in teaching it to me."

"Even," remarked Kulluka, "even if in the beginning Faizi found the same difficulties in learning Sanscrit that others have done, his translation of our Kashmiri chronicles, and his rendering of Nala and Damayanti,5 can well make us forget that the language is not his native one."

"What splendid poetry, is it not?" continued Faizi, who did not let the conversation easily drop when it once touched on Hindu literature; "and how far short any translation must fall when compared with the original, so simple and yet so exalted, with its unsurpassed women! Think of the noble, pure Damayanti, proof against all the trials and slights of her unworthy husband! My translations have been undertaken to please Akbar, who naturally cannot find time to learn a strange language, and yet is desirous of reading everything. Now he has given me the task of translating the Evangelists."

"Of what?" asked Kulluka.

"Of the holy books used by the people of the West, who are called Christians, after the founder of their religion, of whom you must have heard. There is much worth reading in those books, and I find many exalted and profound ideas in them, mixed with matter of less consequence, as is also the case with your philosophies; but on the whole there is not much that is new to those who are acquainted with your philosophical writings. But what always strikes me particularly," he continued, again turning the conversation to the praise of ancient India, "are your proverbs. How insipid ours appear when compared with them! Even if I had only learnt this one of you, it would have been enough to give me fresh courage for working at my manuscript,—

"The treasure that never fades is never robbed, but grows

The more it is expended; that treasure is called knowledge."

"Is that right?" said he, turning to Siddha; "or have I made some fault in the pronunciation?"

For a moment Siddha hesitated, but glancing at Kulluka, who smiled and nodded to him, he replied, with confidence, "Not quite right, my lord; but the mistake is a very slight one." And repeating the word in fault, he showed how it should be pronounced.

"Now I am fortunate," cried Faizi, joyfully; "but do repeat one of the sayings from Bhartrihari;6 no doubt you know many."

Siddha thought for a moment, and then recited:—

"Every one who lives was born, but only those are truly born

Who, dying, leave a name to their descendants."

"Oh," laughed Faizi, "in your Kashmir you have learnt other things than Sanscrit,—you are also learned in the art of flattery, my friend."

"Flattery?" asked Siddha. "Should not your name and that of your brother Abú-l Fazl—that have penetrated from Persia to the furthest districts of Hindustan—should not your names be preserved by coming generations?"

"My brother's name," he answered; "yes, that will not lightly be forgotten: preserved, perhaps, not so much through his deeds as through his immortal work, the 'Akbar Nama,'[7] in which he describes the history of our great Emperor's reign. That is indeed a book, my friend, in comparison with which all my writings sink to nothing. But I have remarked to him that he raises Akbar too much to the clouds; for after all, he, as a man, has his faults, like others, and perhaps in the future he may be accused of flattery of princes and of prejudice. But he would not listen to me, nor in the least diminish his praise of the Emperor. 'If I,' he answered me, 'may not say all that I in truth think of the man, who is more than my prince—he is my benefactor and truest friend,—rather than not say what I think, I would throw my book away.' As you can understand, against all that there was no reasoning; and one can see also that to Akbar, although he says nothing, the praise of a friend whose opinion he prizes so highly is very welcome."

"Noble Faizi," said Siddha, interrupting a short silence, "may I ask you a question?"

"Certainly," was the reply; "and I hope to be able to answer it frankly."

"Well, then, when we spoke of Abú-l Fazl, a warning he gave me this morning crossed my mind. He warned me against treachery that here surrounds the Emperor. Do you, whose opinion is of such great weight, believe that there can be people here so foolish and so criminal as to league themselves against so great and beneficent a prince as Akbar; can it really be?"

"Oh!" cried Faizi; "my brother sees treachery everywhere; but after all, that is but natural to a Minister, and still more to the first, the great Wazir. However, you may make yourself easy; people here are not so base, nor are they so foolish, as to engage in a game in which their heads are the stakes, and the chances ten to one against them."

"Faizi," said Kulluka, gravely and half reproachfully, "your hopeful views prove your good heart; but do you not think that they may be sometimes dangerous to young people, and lead them, as for example might be the case with our inexperienced friend here, into imprudence?"

"I do not see that he is inclined to want of caution," was the reply; "and I only mean that it is better that he should not begin with his head full of imaginations of court and state intrigues, but enter life with confidence and courage. We all began so, and dangers never harmed us. If he begins with too much suspicion, he will end by trusting no one, not even my brother or myself."

"That could never be," cried Siddha, quickly, as he looked confidently into Faizi's friendly face. "As little as I could ever suspect secret enmity from you, so little could you expect faithlessness and treachery from one who prizes your friendship and good opinion as highly as I do."

"Remember what you have said," Kulluka remarked, gravely; "and think, too, that no one has the power of foreseeing all the events and circumstances that may end in influencing him, short-sighted as he is, to give up his free will."

"See," said Faizi, in his usual joyous tone, "here we are again in philosophy. You know well it is my favourite subject, although I have not made so much progress in it as Kulluka maintains. Let us call for lights—night begins to close in—and we will have some discussion touching Sankhya and Vedanta,[8] in which he is so strong. What a pity that we cannot ask Akbar to join us! he finds more pleasure in the driest philosophical discussion than in the most sparkling banquets."

"Nothing should I like better, honoured Faizi," answered Kulluka, "than to pass an hour with you deep in such subjects, as in past days; but now I am afraid we must go, Siddha must take over his command early to-morrow morning, and I have much to settle to-night in readiness for my departure, which is fixed for the day after to-morrow. Will you, then, excuse us if we take our leave, and thank you for your reception—as kind and friendly as ever it was in days gone by?"

"Indeed I will excuse you, my worthy friend," answered Faizi, as he called to a servant to show them out. "Siddha," he said, as he took leave, "we were speaking of imprudences; be on your guard against them. But a young man like you may happen to fall into them as well at your court as at ours; and if you ever find yourself in any difficulty, come straight to Faizi, who may be able to keep you out of the fire." And without waiting for either answer or thanks, he turned back to his own apartments.

Who could have asked for more, on his entry into life, than was given to Siddha! Neither councillors nor support failed him. For important affairs there was the hermit of the mountain; for more trifling difficulties the wise and influential Faizi. The favour of the First Minister had already been granted him, and that of the Emperor himself was promised him.

1 Akbar's palace, in the fort of Agra, is built entirely of red sandstone. It is a square building, 249 feet by 260 feet. In the centre is a courtyard, 71 feet by 72 feet, on either side of which are two halls facing one another. Every feature round this court is of pure Hindu architecture. There are no arches, but the horizontal style of construction everywhere. General Cunningham, as Mr. Fergusson thinks erroneously, ascribes this palace to Jahangir. He describes it in his "Reports," vol. iv. p. 124, and gives a plan (Plate xiii.).

2 Abú-l Fazl (called Allami) was a son of Shaikh Mubarak, son of Shaikh Khizr, who came from Sind. Mubarak was one of the most learned men of his day, and inclined to be a free-thinker. Abú-l Fazl, his second son, was born on January 14th, 1551. He was a devoted student, and his range of reading was very extensive. His elder brother, Faizi, had been invited to the court of Akbar in the twelfth year of that sovereign's reign, and by his means Abú-l Fazl was introduced in 1568, when in his seventeenth year. His abilities were immediately recognised, and every year he grew in favour and power. He was made Prime Minister and Mansabdar of four thousand, discharging his duties with distinguished abilities and success. Both brothers inherited the liberal opinions of their father, and carried them to greater extremes. Hence orthodox Muslims reviled them as apostates and free-thinkers. In them Akbar found congenial minds, with feelings and opinions similar to but more decided than his own. The murder of Abú-l Fazl on August 12th, 1602, is noted further on. He was the author of the "Akbar-namah" (2 vols.), a history of his master's reign down to 1602, and of the "A'ín-i-Akbari."

3 The "A'ín-i-Akbari."

4 Faizi was the elder brother of the minister Abú-l Fazl. He was the most popular poet of his time, and a great favourite and constant companion of Akbar, who gave him the title of the Prince of Poets. Our author, for the purposes of his story, makes Faizi, the younger brother.

5 The story of Nala and Damayanti is a beautiful episode in the "Mahabharata," which was translated into Persian by Faizi, and into English by Dean Milman. Nala, King of Nishadha, had been chosen by the lovely Princess Damayanti for her husband, but the vindictive demon Kali was the enemy of Nala, and was determined to effect his ruin. He perverted the king's mind by urging him to play at dice with his brother Pushkara. Nala lost his kingdom and all he had, but refused to play for his wife; and the royal pair wandered away destitute from the palace. Nala, still instigated by the demon, deserted his weary, sleeping wife, and left her exposed in the forest. She at

length found a hospitable refuge. Nala engaged himself as a charioteer, and was eventually restored to his faithful wife. Freed from the power of Kali, and fortified with a preternatural amount of skill in gaming, he finally won back his kingdom.

Our author, in writing the story of Siddha and Iravati, evidently had in his mind the classic tale of Nala and Damayanti.

6 A brother of King Vikramaditya. He wrote a Sanscrit poem called "Bhatti Kavya," relating the adventures of Rama, in twenty-two cantos.—See Colebrooke's "Miscellaneous Essays," ii. 115.

7 History of the reign of Akbar.

8 The Sankhya system of philosophy was founded by Kapila. Its aim was rest, or exemption from transmigration, to be attained by looking steadily at the whole united universe, and recognising that man, and all which is created, is transitory, but that beyond the transitory is the eternal. The doctrine of Kapila is taught in six *Sutras* or lectures. His main position is that absolute prevention of all three sorts of pain is the highest purpose of the soul. The three sorts of pain are evil proceeding from self, from eternal beings, and from divine causes. Deliverance from these evils is attainable by knowledge of the twenty-five true principles of existence.

The Vedanta philosophy is intended to give the end and ultimate aim of the Vedas.

Chapter IV.
Akbar.

Early next morning, on the great *maidan* of the fortress, our young soldier took over the command of his detachment from the chief mansabdar[1] of the Rajputs. The officer above him exacted a strict observance of discipline; but to that Kulluka's pupil was well accustomed, and he himself saw the necessity for it. This mansabdar, too,—who presented him with the white feather and other symbols of his rank,—in spite of the severity of his disposition, was a man of cultivation and courteous, friendly manners. Siddha was equally pleased with the appearance of his men, clad in the same splendid array as their leaders. They were splendid riders, with soldier-like bearing, and countenances sparkling with life and courage.

At the request of the commander, Siddha put his troopers through some evolutions, which gave him the opportunity of showing off his own admirable riding and the training of his horse. Had Kulluka been present at these exercises he would have seen with satisfaction the approbation with which his pupil was regarded by his superiors. After some evolutions with all the troops assembled, the bugle signalled that the exercises for the day were over, and commanded the retreat. Siddha, giving his horse to Vatsa, who was in waiting, turned his footsteps towards one of the gardens of the palace, to which officers of his rank had access. But before he had reached the court he saw a young woman approaching him by one of the side-paths, who, from her attire, appeared to be a servant belonging to some great house. As she drew near she hesitated for a moment, and then said, "Are you not, my lord, the noble Siddha, just arrived from Kashmir?"

"You are right," he answered; "you seem to know me."

"Not personally," said the servant; "but the noble lady who sent me gave me your description. She requests a few minutes' conversation with you, if you will have the kindness to grant them to her."

"But," asked Siddha, "who is your mistress?"

"Excuse me, my lord," was the answer, "if I withhold her name for the present; doubtless she will herself enlighten you, if you honour her with a visit, and, if you will, she expects you this evening. Come at about ten, by that mosque." And she pointed to a beautiful building on a height, whose gilded cupolas and marble minarets were sparkling in the sunshine.

Siddha hesitated and sought for an answer. An adventure—and he thought of Iravati. A plot—and he remembered the warning of Abú-l Fazl.

"Well?" asked the maid, mockingly. "A soldier like you, and not know what to do when an illustrious lady asks for a short conversation! You are not afraid, I hope."

"Afraid!" cried Siddha, while a flush of anger mounted to his face. "What gives you the right—but," continued he, restraining himself, "my irresolution may appear strange, but the reasons are no concern of yours. Meet me at the appointed time at the mosque."

"It is well," replied the woman; and greeting him, she returned the way she had come.

For a moment Siddha thought of attempting to follow her unseen, and so to discover with whom he had to do; but a moment's consideration convinced him she certainly would be on her guard. Dissatisfied with the whole affair, and with himself, he continued his walk, and soon reached the garden.

Rich and magnificent as it was, there was more to fatigue than satisfy the eye. Straight paths, one resembling another, paved with smooth polished stones, were shaded by trees; and there were tanks bordered with marble, from the centres of which fountains of various forms arose. The groups of trees in all directions threw thick, cool shade, inviting the passers-by to repose. After having wandered for some time without meeting any one, Siddha saw a middle-aged and powerfully-built man seated under the shade of one of these trees. There was something in the man's appearance that immediately excited his attention, though he could scarcely have given a reason. The stranger was distinguished from the courtiers he had met, by something that words can hardly convey. The expression of his face, closely shaven, like others, was calm and frank; neither handsome nor the contrary, his attire was rich yet simple; and excepting the elaborately worked hilt of his sword, his only ornament was a diamond of extraordinary size that glittered in the folds of his turban. But what neither ornaments nor beauty of feature could give, was the peculiar expression and bearing that Siddha had remarked in Gurupada the hermit, but which was still more marked in this man, and bespoke him a ruler. Still, in the unknown he did not suspect more than a courtier or a great warrior attached to some prince who was in attendance at Akbar's court. With a silent greeting he was about to pass by, when the stranger addressed him by name, and without rising or further introduction, asked if he had made acquaintance with his Rajputs. Somewhat surprised that everyone should know who he was, Siddha replied in the affirmative, and the other proceeded in explanation.

"By the heron's feathers I recognised your rank, and knowing all your fellow-officers personally, and knowing also that you were expected to take up your appointment, I had no difficulty in guessing who you were. And how do you like your appointment? Sit down by me."

"I should indeed be ungrateful," said Siddha, accepting the invitation, which sounded more like a command, and scarcely noticing that the stranger treated him as an inferior,—"I should indeed be ungrateful to my benefactor and the Emperor if I did not highly prize the noble occupation in which they have placed me."

"The Emperor!" repeated the other; "well, yes. But tell me, do you come to serve him, or simply to enjoy the privileges that your rank gives you at his court?"

"A hard question, noble lord," answered Siddha, frankly, "and one I have never put to myself; but still I can answer without difficulty, that, above all, I should desire faithfully to serve the Emperor, as far as honour and duty allow. My having entered into his service of my own free will testifies to this."

"Prudently answered," remarked the stranger; "but now the question is, what do you understand by honour and duty?—those are difficult words to explain."

"For some," replied Siddha; "but I do not find them so. I take them in their strongest meaning. Honour and duty would forbid me to undertake anything against my country, even if Akbar himself should give the orders; and in that case to give up all the privileges secured to me by his favour."

"And you would do well," replied the other, approvingly; "but what reasons have you for imagining that the Emperor would ever require from you what would be to the prejudice of yourself and your countrymen?"

For a moment Siddha hesitated, as the conversation with his uncle crossed his mind. But quickly recovering himself, and looking in the stranger's open face, he asked, with no further introduction, "Is not Akbar ambitious?"

"Young man," exclaimed the stranger, in a tone and with a look that made Siddha involuntarily shrink from his side, "until now you have contented yourself with prudent remarks; but, at the court of Akbar himself, so to express yourself to a perfect stranger appears to me rather rash."

"It may appear so," answered Siddha, without embarrassment. "I do not know you, that is true; but to know your name or rank is indifferent to me. I see you and hear your voice, and know that it would be impossible for you to betray or harm a young and inexperienced man, who has trusted you and spoken frankly."

These simple words caused a look of pleasure to cross the stranger's countenance, not of flattered vanity, but a nobler and purer feeling of satisfaction. Flattery was not strange to him, nor was he insensible to it. But these were words from the heart, spoken in ignorance of who he was, and praising in him that which he prized above everything.

He said, laying his hand on Siddha's shoulder, while his voice sounded gentler, "What you have said is true. You trust me, you say, though you do not know me; do the same when the time comes that you know me well. But now for Akbar. He is ambitious: in that you are right. I know him, and all is not so well as I could wish, and I agree that he is ambitious; but then, in what way? Do you really believe that his only desire is to add more and more kingdoms and peoples to his empire, which already is far too extended? Should he not be content with what he already has? I think the small kingdom of Agra and Delhi were his sole inheritance. Little if anything else was left him by Humayun,2 his unfortunate and sorely tried father; and at present his dominions extend from the borders of Persia to the furthest extremes of Bengal, and to the districts of the Dakhin and Golkonda. Then why do you imagine to yourself new conquests, and especially that of your far-distant Kashmir, which would not repay the many sacrifices that would be necessary to attain it. Still, reasons might arise which would force a prince no longer to respect the independence of neighbouring states; that is, if they should threaten to become dangerous for the peace and prosperity of his own people. And in such a case he must act, although he would gladly leave his sword in the scabbard; and although the peace and liberty of surrounding nations are as dear to him as those of his own dominions. Still all this does not prevent the descendant of Baber and Timur3 from being ambitious; and from his earliest manhood his ambition has been not only to found a great and mighty empire, but, above all, to ensure the happiness, prosperity, and cultivation of the people that the great Power has entrusted to him. He has striven to improve their condition, and to calm the jealousies and divisions of the different races, to put an end to religious disputes, and to bridle the tyranny and oppression of the powerful and selfish nobles. He has tried to benefit the industrious classes of Bengal, and striven to increase prosperity everywhere, to encourage science and art, and to raise his subjects to a state of cultivation and enlightenment for which many have shown great aptitude. Say, if you will, frankly, that this is too much for one mortal to accomplish, and I shall not contradict you; but the striving after an ideal should not be condemned even if it is unattainable. And, in truth, Akbar's own ideal will never be fulfilled. How many years of thought and toil has he devoted to this goal; and how far, alas! is he now from attaining it!"

With respect and awe Siddha listened, as, carried away with his subject, the stranger rose to his feet, lifting his hand toward heaven; but as he finished, dejectedly he sank back, bending his head on that breast which contained a warm and noble heart. For a moment Siddha felt inclined to rise to his feet, not doubting but that he saw before him the Emperor himself; but then the idea that so great a man should so confide in a young, unknown stranger appeared too absurd to be reality. As he was about to attempt, by roundabout questions, to find out with whom he was speaking, approaching footsteps interrupted the conversation, and presently a man appeared, short and bent, clad in grave garments, and with what was rare at court, a thick black beard.

"Abdul Kadir,"4 said the stranger, more to himself than to Siddha, while a dark cloud crossed his countenance. Notwithstanding, he greeted the new comer with courtesy, at the same time making him a sign that he wished to remain unknown.

With a defiant glance Abdul Kadir looked at Siddha, who had stepped on one side, from head to foot, and then turned his back on him, without saying a word. That the blood rose to the cheeks of our Indian nobleman at such treatment was not surprising; but as he was about to demand an explanation of the insult, the stranger restrained him, and said, "Do not, noble Siddha, allow the treatment of my friend here to arouse your anger. It is not personally meant, of that I am sure; but he cannot bear the sight of you Hindus, as he imagines that you damage his faith. Is it not so?" he asked, turning to Abdul Kadir.

"You are right," he answered. "I have, indeed, no personal enmity to you, young man," he continued, turning to Siddha. "I do not know you, but to fight and strive against you, root and branch, is to me a holy duty; and I do strive against you, and hate you with an irreconcilable hatred. Still, as men, there are many among you whom I respect and honour. You injure our faith, and even make the Emperor himself averse to it. You deny Allah and mock His Prophet, and seek to drive us, the faithful, away, and to become masters of offices and employments, that you may put your false gods and false doctrines in the place of the God without whom there is no god, and of those who, in truth, acknowledge Him. Therefore, and for that reason alone, I hate you and yours, and will strive against you and yours till the death. You are either atheists or idolaters; in either case you lead the people astray, and tempt the prince. Enough that you are nothing but unbelieving——"

A severe, penetrating glance from the stranger held back on the lips of the speaker the word that was about to follow. Had it been spoken, Siddha, in spite of all his endeavours, would scarcely have been able to restrain his anger.

"Unbelieving, then," continued Abdul Kadir; "and that for a true son of the Prophet is more than enough. But what can it concern you, if I, who here have nothing to say, nor am of the slightest importance, am not one with your race? The favour of the Emperor is assured to you, who can and does do anything as it best pleases him. He has freed you from the burthen justly laid on you by the true believers for your denial of the true faith. He calls you to all employments, places you at the head of his armies, chooses amongst you his councillors and friends. What would you have more? Leave me, then, leave us, our just wrath. We cannot harm you; but it may be that the anger of heaven will one day fall on your heads, and perhaps on his, also, who showered favours on you, instead of chastising you with the rod and the sword, which for this purpose Allah himself placed in his hand."

"It appears to me," coldly said the stranger, after this hot outbreak, "it appears to me that our conversation so carried on is neither profitable nor agreeable. Doubtless, friend Siddha, you have more to say in reply to Abdul Kadir, and I myself am far from agreeing with him. But if I do not mistake, this time he sought us not for the sake of a fruitless dispute, but to talk over an important affair, and on this I will willingly listen to him. Excuse me, therefore, if for the present I say farewell, hoping that we may meet again before long. Abdul Kadir," he said, as with a respectful greeting Siddha took his leave, "what do you want with me?"

"Sire," was the answer,—for it was indeed Akbar himself with whom Siddha had been conversing,—"my duty as a subject as well as a friend, though one of little importance, obliges me to seek your Majesty."

"I know it," interrupted Akbar; "you are not self-seeking, you care not for protection or favours. And yet I would that you did; then, perhaps, I might be able to content you, in which now I seldom or never succeed. But I suspect that it is on religious subjects you wish to speak to me. The exaggerated words you have just used have told me what was coming; at any rate, be so good as to use a little moderation."

"In truth," answered Abdul Kadir, "the faith, the one pure, true faith, is what now leads me here. For that I request a few minutes' conversation,—and," continued he, with a stern look, "earnest and grave conversation."

"I will do my best," replied Akbar, courteously; "and will promise not to laugh, if you will keep within bounds."

"That will depend on your opinion," remarked the other; "but I will do my best to treat the subject calmly. To warn you, and most earnestly to warn you, is imperative on all who mean well to Shah Akbar, and yet know what has come to my ears. As you well know, there has long been deep discontent among us true Muhammadans, caused by state offices being placed in the hands of men lukewarm like Abú-l Fazl, or atheist like Faizi. But what you do not know is that a party has arisen in the midst of your kingdom, and in the neighbourhood even of your court, which has irrevocably sworn to work for your fall and destruction, because you have refused to give ear to the claims which they, as the representatives of the ancient and only true friends of the House of Timur, have a just right to demand. Lately I had the opportunity of being present at an assembly of our Mullahs, and what I there heard was enough to make me shudder when I thought what such influential men among the Muhammadan population might accomplish, even against

Akbar, if supported by ambitious nobles and discontented generals, of whom many may be found in the court of Agra, as well as throughout Hindustan."

"But," asked Akbar, impatiently, "what do your Mullahs and their followers want? Have they not the fullest liberty to think and speak as they will, and to make as many proselytes as they can? Have I ever laid as much as a straw in their path?"

"Certainly not," replied his companion; "but does not that also call to heaven? Of what value to them is the liberty which is shared by unbelievers? Here, in your court, in the army, and in every kind of employment, are they offended by the defiling presence of the *kafirs*. And where is the vindication of the true faith, to which, above all men on earth, the Emperor is called, as the representative of Allah?"

"Yes," cried Akbar; "here is again the old story, your people alone are entrusted with the truth, and before that all must give way, even I; and he who will not bend must break. But why should you alone be in possession of the truth?"

"Because the Prophet, blessed be his name, "has himself declared it to us, and because——"

"Because," interrupted Akbar, "because he, and no one else, is good. Yes; we have the Padres, who come from the West, from the land of the Franks: brave, honourable men, as yourselves. They also have a Prophet, who, if I mistake not, they honour as their God. I do not clearly understand it; but, in any case, their faith is older than that of Muhammad. Then there are the Jews, who are not content with this or that, but hold by Moses alone; and then what do you say to our Brahmans? They have ancient books which merit the greatest reverence,—so venerable that they themselves can scarcely understand them; so ancient, that Moses with his Thora, Christ with his Evangelist, and Muhammad with his Koran are all new in comparison. And now I ask you, from your conscience, how can I, a simple man, who has heard somewhat of all this, but not a hundredth part of the whole,—how can I make myself judge amongst these various faiths, and decide, for example, whether that of Christ or Muhammad is the true one?"

"But you were brought up in the teaching of Islam."

"No very satisfactory foundation for any one's faith. A sure foundation should rest on conviction brought about by one's own inquiries, and should hardly depend on the will of one's father. But the question now is not what I personally believe—that concerns no one—but how I, as prince and ruler over the kingdom of the Mughals, should conduct myself towards the professors of the various religious sects who alike are subject to my rule, and who alike have a claim to my protection. And this question, best of friends, believe me, you will never answer as long as you only look at it from one side and not the other."

"But, then, the dangers that threaten your kingdom and throne?"

"I have others to think of," replied the Emperor, with a contemptuous smile, "than those with which the anger of your religious fanatics threaten me."

"Others!" said Abdul Kadir, looking earnestly at the Prince. "Just so; you mean the kind of dangers caused by strangers. But what of those dangers, at present secret, but which may become open, and may find support in your own house, encouraged by those of your own race? If your son———"

"My son Salim!" exclaimed Akbar; "and yet," he continued, "that is not impossible. Among the reigning houses around us, how many, through family feuds, have been subjected to our rule? And so you mean that Salim himself is ready to join these malcontents against me? for that appears to me what your words point to."

"It is so, Sire," answered Abdul Kadir; "at least, I mean that his religious zeal might induce him to do so; but I do not say that this is the case already."

"One thing is certain," rejoined Akbar, "if this should ever take place, religious zeal will not be Salim's inducement. He cares far more for fine wines and beautiful women than for the Koran and the Prophet. But that is no reason that I should not thank you for the warning. If you had begun with it at first, many useless words might have been spared. If in the future you should have any more such communications to make, we will thank you for them. We must be a little on our guard, and keep a look-out on our people here. But, for the present, farewell."

And, with a somewhat ironical smile on his lips, the Emperor left Abdul Kadir to think over the impression that his words might have made.

"By Allah," muttered the follower of the Prophet between his teeth, "I have done a fine thing by naming Salim. I had only intended to disturb him, and so to render him more pliant to our will; instead of which I have simply warned him, and instead of helping, we shall now find him still harder to deal with. Now he knows or suspects that some of us league ourselves together with his son against him. You are looked upon as a wise man, Abdul Kadir, and yet you have acted like a fool. Ah! if the zeal that fills my soul for our holy faith would but preserve to me the calm that seldom or never forsakes Akbar! What an advantage that gives him over us!"

That the composure Akbar showed was as real as the other believed might well have been doubted by any one who had seen him returning to the palace, buried in thought, and with his eyes fixed on the ground.

In one of his private apartments a man awaited him, whose presence, if Abdul Kadir had but known it, would have given him fresh grounds for a violent outbreak. This was Kulluka the Brahman. He sat in thought, not noticing the splendour around him, nor the lovely view over the smiling gardens. Still, this was not the first time he had seen it.

Presently one of the Imperial Guard came to arouse him from his thoughts, and to conduct him to the Emperor.

"It is indeed a pleasure to see you here again," said Akbar, affectionately returning the Brahman's greeting, "and I hope you bring me good news from Kashmir."

"Alas, Sire," answered Kulluka, "I wish that I did, or that I could hide from your Majesty, as from others, all the causes of uneasiness. But the confidence you have placed in me, as well as the good of my country, oblige me to keep nothing hidden that I know."

"I understand," said Akbar; "the old story over again. Party feuds and disputes: sons against their fathers; brothers intriguing against each other, as in old days."

"But too true," replied Kulluka. "After Nandigupta, the lawful king, had disappeared from the stage, leaving all in his brother's hands, we believed that order would be established, and for some time it was so; and the people were content with the government, although not enthusiastic for it. At any rate, there was no thought of further changes, but now that is no longer the case. The spirit of faction begins to stir up discontent, and fresh revolutions appear ready to break out. The worst of all is that we cannot discover where this plot has its origin. The king's sons, who sooner or later threaten to rise against him, certainly do not act from their own inspiration; but whence, then, does it come? That is what we cannot discover."

"That may be as it will," said the Emperor, decisively. "Whether or not they act independently, the old game seems about to begin again. And what, if it cannot be stopped in time, will be the unavoidable consequence? That, as before, the different parties will take arms, and civil war will destroy your country. On all sides bands will be formed, who, the less they find within the boundaries of Kashmir, so much the more will they carry fire and sword among my people to repay themselves for what they have lost at home. And now I say, without circumlocution, and once for all, that I will not tolerate it. My kingdom and my people shall be respected; and if force is required, whatever trouble or treasure it may cost, I will again assemble my armies and march to the north to re-establish the peace that is necessary to the prosperity of my subjects. Better to tear down and destroy the whole robber's nest than allow it to remain, to the injury of my people."

In spite of his respect for the Emperor, these proud, defiant words could not but excite Kulluka's anger, and, though he gave no reply, the dark colour mounted to his bronzed cheek.

"Forgive me, worthy Kulluka," said Akbar, "if what I have said angers you. But you should know, as well as I myself, that in so speaking I do not mean the good men among your people, such as yourself, your present prince, and his ministers, but the miserable intriguers that will draw down upon you the greatest misfortune, while they threaten us with the consequences of their turbulence. To guard against this is my duty, and I well know how to fulfil it. Do all you can to make my intervention unnecessary, and you may rest assured that I shall be the last to wish to force it on you."

"I place the fullest confidence in your words," said Kulluka, "and if I could not suppress a feeling of anger, it was certainly caused as much by the accursed plots laid for our country and prince as by the threats, for which, I must confess, there is some occasion. But does treachery alone seek a home in Kashmir? Is it so impossible that it should also be present at your court, and that among your own courtiers and relations there may be found those who conspire against us and against your rule?"

"How now, what do you mean by that?"

"I went, perhaps, too far, and spoke rashly; still, I have my suspicions, and though I trust they may prove idle, yet I cannot put them from me. Salim——"

"What, again Salim? Is he also involved in this?"

"With what else he is concerned I do not know; but some slight indications have caused me to warn your Majesty. If they are groundless, so much the better, but to be on one's guard can in no case do harm."

"And that I shall be. For the present, however, all rests on supposition and assumed possibility. We must neither judge nor act rashly; but be assured that nothing you have told me shall escape my closest inquiry. When we meet again the hour for action may have come. But before you go, I must tell you something that will be personally interesting to you—I have just seen and spoken with your pupil."

"How, Siddha?" exclaimed Kulluka, with astonishment. "And who presented him to you?"

"No one," answered Akbar; "I met him in the park, and guessing who he was, spoke to him. You know, occasionally I like thus to converse."

"And did he not know that he spoke with the mighty Emperor?"

"Naturally not; nor did he guess it. Do not tell him; I will myself enlighten him one day. You want to know what I think of him? Well, then, I am content with him. He is a fine, honourable young man, in whom I can trust. Perhaps somewhat imprudent in what——"

"He has not said what was not fitting to the Emperor?"

"Well," said Akbar, laughing, "if he had known to whom he was talking. But do not be disturbed. When I made him see that he spoke a little too freely he blamed himself in a manner that I could not but accept. Enough: I have said he pleased me, and you know that I am not wont to decide so favourably respecting those I see for the first time. Let him only take care that the first good impression continues. But now other affairs call me, and I will not detain you."

With a respectful greeting, Kulluka left the apartment. Akbar looked after him with affection. A man so far separated by rank and station, religion and nationality, was yet bound to him both by respect and friendship, and by a faith that could not fail where he had once given his word.

"On him, at least, I can reckon," said the Emperor to himself; "in him is no deceit." And he was right; but how many stood far nearer to him, and of whom he could not say the same!

---

1 A military title and rank, regulated by the supposed number of horse the holder of the title could, if required, bring into the field, varying from ten to ten thousand.

2 Humayun succeeded his father Baber in 1530. He was driven out of India by the talented Afghan chief Shir Shah, and his son Akbar was born in Sind during the flight. Humayun passed fifteen years in exile in Persia. He recovered Delhi and Agra after the death of Shir Shah, and died six months afterwards in 1556. Akbar then ascended the throne.

3 Akbar was the grandson of Baber, who was born in 1482, and died 1530. Baber was the great-grandson of Timur.

4 Mulla Abdul Kadir Muluk Shah of Badaun was born at that place in 1540. He studied music, astronomy, and history, and owing to his beautiful voice he was appointed Court Imám for Wednesdays. He was introduced early in life to Akbar, and was employed to translate Arabic and Sanskrit works into Persian. He was a fanatical Muhammadan and looked upon Abú-l Fazl as a heretic, though he served under him. But all references to the minister, in the works of Badauni, are couched in bitter and sarcastic terms. He wrote a work called "Tarikh-i-Badauni," which is a history from the time of the

Ghaznevides to 1595, the fortieth year of Akbar's reign. The prevalent tone, in writing of Akbar his benefactor, is one of censure and disparagement. El Badauni also translated the "Ramayana," part of the "Mahabharata," and a history of Kashmir into Persian. He died in 1615.

Chapter V.
A New and an Old Acquaintance.

Siddha reached the Mosque at the appointed time, and had not waited long before he saw the servant approach and sign to him to follow her. She led him through different side-paths until they reached a high garden wall, in which there was a small door. She opened this, and carefully shut it again, after they had entered. A path thickly bordered with cactuses and other plants led him to a kind of terrace with orange-trees and fountains, on which the back part of a small but tasteful house opened; the rest of it being hidden by thickly growing trees. Siddha's guide led him up a flight of marble steps and through a gallery to an apartment open to the fresh air, and having left him she disappeared behind the hangings. On a divan was carelessly stretched a young woman richly clad in the Persian style. No sooner did she become aware of her visitor's presence than she arose and came forward to meet and welcome him. At the first moment Siddha could hardly have told whether she was beautiful or not. Her features were not regular; but her soft blue eyes, overshadowed with silken lashes, had an indescribably sweet and friendly expression; and though she was not tall, her figure, which her closely-fitting robe showed to perfection, was most perfectly proportioned. But what particularly struck Siddha was the whiteness of her neck and bosom, round which a pearl necklace hung; and the rosy tint of her cheeks, which he had never seen in other women.

"Noble lord," she said,—and if the impression she had already made on Siddha had been unfavourable, the sweetness of her voice would at once have won him to her,—"I thank you for so speedily fulfilling my request. Perhaps it seems a little indiscreet; but when you hear the reasons, I trust you will not think harshly of me."

"To refuse such an invitation," answered Siddha, "would indeed have been uncourteous; though I confess I did not await the time with the impatience I should have done, noble lady, had I known whom I should meet."

Acknowledging this compliment with a slight inclination of her head, she continued,—"My excuse is, that no personal reason made me take this step, but the affairs of another, of a friend of mine, whom I love with all my heart. Some time ago she was forced to fly from Agra to escape the snares laid for her by powerful persons here, and sought a refuge in your country, in Kashmir. Now I have a communication to make to her which may be of great importance; but until now I could think of no means of sending safely to her, as I do not trust any of the messengers at my disposal. Then I heard accidentally, it does not signify how, that you with your former tutor had arrived in Agra, and that the guru would shortly return. I at once saw that I could not do better than trust in the honour of a nobleman whose name was well known to me, and so determined on begging you to ask your friend to undertake the delivery of my letter, in which I inform my friend of many things that are only of importance to her; and I trust my request will not inconvenience you or the worthy Kulluka."

At these words, Siddha's first feeling was one of relief. So, then, the whole affair merely consisted in taking charge of an apparently innocent letter, and which, at any rate, did not concern him. But with his satisfaction was mingled a certain degree of disappointment, and that there should be no shadow of an adventure in this affair was not flattering to his vanity. He hastened to assure her he would gladly charge his tutor with the letter, who would willingly undertake to convey it.

At a sign from the lady the servant appeared, bringing her a paper folded in the form of a letter, and fastened with a silken cord, bearing a seal. "The direction, as you see," she said, as the servant left the room, "is not to my friend, but to some one whom perhaps you know."

"Certainly," answered Siddha, "we have often hunted together."

"He will deliver the letter, and so your friend Kulluka will not know who the real recipient is; for I think it is better that as few as possible should share the secret. I hope," she continued, after a moment's silence, "that my friend will profit by what I tell her. Indeed I pity her greatly in her banishment, though at times I almost envy her the opportunity she enjoys of visiting your beautiful country, of which I have read such glowing descriptions. But tell me frankly, are not these descriptions a little exaggerated—at least, they are rather poetical?"

"Indeed," answered Siddha, "though my tutor has always warned me against exaggeration as outstepping the bounds of reality and good taste, still I must say the descriptions you mention fall far beneath the truth. Here nature has her beauties. Charming are the borders of your Jamuna, and with the magnificence and luxury of your palaces there is nothing in our northern land that can be compared; but the beauty of our mountains, woods, and valleys, can hardly be imagined by you, accustomed to less-favoured lands." And led away by recollections of his native land, and by the interest shown by his new and really beautiful listener, our Siddha lost himself in descriptions of Hindustan's world-famed paradise. His eloquence, as well as his good looks, increased the admiration with which his hearer regarded the handsome and powerful youth.

"But I detain you too long," she said, at last rising, "and am taking advantage of your kindness. Still, one more request: let our interview, for the sake of my friend, remain a secret between you and me. This short meeting can be of no importance."

"For you, certainly not," said Siddha; "but for me more than you seem to think."

"I see," she replied, laughing, "that you Hindus are as well versed as our people in the art of paying compliments. But let us leave that. There still remains something that I should say. I should show myself indeed unworthy of your confidence, if, knowing who you are, I should myself remain unknown; and, under the promise of secrecy, I see no reason for withholding my name and rank, lowly as it is. My name is Rezia; my father, an Armenian, came here for commerce, and early married me to a merchant of this town, who was already far advanced in years. Some time ago he went to Persia on his affairs, and perhaps further; but it is long since I have heard anything of him. In the meantime I live here, as you see, solitary and quiet, enjoying the pleasure of a peaceful life. So now you know who you have had the trouble of visiting, although we may never meet again."

"And why, noble Rezia, should that not be?" asked Siddha. "I see no reason against it, and possibly I may have things to tell you of the country where your friend now is, that might interest you."

"Well," answered Rezia, "I will not refuse your friendship; and if some evening you should have an idle hour, I would gladly hear tidings of my letter, and that its charge occasioned no trouble. At any rate, I am sure it has a good chance. No doubt you will meet my servant, and have only to tell her when you will visit me in my solitary dwelling."

"For the opportunity of seeing you again, I shall indeed be grateful," said Siddha, as he carefully placed the letter entrusted to him in his girdle, and prepared for the moment to say farewell.

When he reached his home he stood for some time in the verandah, busied with thought, gazing on the river that flowed softly below him. Those were the same waters that would bathe the walls of Allahabad fortress, and reflect back the lovely features of Iravati; true, might it not be that the waves would take a greeting to his loving betrothed, and whisper words of love and faith? And he snatched Iravati's portrait from the wall, and pressing his lips to her image, he seated himself in the gallery; and as he gazed on her, lovelier than ever seemed the features of the noble and beautiful Hindu girl. But as his eyes wandered over the palace and gardens bordering the river, another's figure appeared before him—the graceful form, the blue eyes, and sweet voice of Rezia the Armenian. What was she to him? Nothing, certainly; but what harm was there even if he found her charming? He had never promised

Iravati that for her sake every other woman should appear to him both ugly and unpleasing.

"Hallo!" was heard next morning in the courtyard of Siddha's dwelling. "Is your master awake? Go and see if a visit from me will disturb him."

Before Vatsa could obey the command, Siddha, who was preparing to go out, recognised the cheerful voice of Parviz, Abú-l Fazl's nephew; and hastened to meet and beg him to come in.

"Are you on service now?" he asked.

"Not for a couple of days."

"That is well. Then perhaps you will come with me for an expedition?"

"Very willingly. Where shall we go?"

"To Fathpúr Sikri,1 the country residence of the Emperor, the place everyone visits when they first make an expedition in the neighbourhood."

"I submit myself entirely to your friendly guidance," answered Siddha; "but excuse me if I leave you for a few moments to say farewell to Kulluka, who is on the point of starting."

He found his tutor in all the hurry of departure, and, as he said farewell, entrusted him with the letter, which Kulluka took without any questions. And before long Siddha and Parviz were mounted and, followed by their servants, on their way out of the town. Their journey was nothing but a pleasant ride, their road lying as it did through an avenue overshadowed with fine trees, with beautiful views on each side, over fields and shady groves.

"See," said Parviz, after they had ridden for some time; "such avenues the Emperor has had planted almost everywhere; and in places where formerly no green leaf was to be seen, and men died of heat, now these shady roads are to be found. Is not this a great and useful work? Certainly every traveller has good cause of gratitude to Akbar."

"Yes, indeed, the Emperor does great things," answered Siddha—and his thoughts turned to the extraordinary man with whom, yesterday, he had talked of Akbar. And he described to Parviz his strange meeting, and asked if he knew who the person he described could be?

"No, I know him not," said Parviz, with difficulty suppressing a smile; "but perhaps you will meet him again."

"Very likely," answered Siddha, "But, tell me, how is it that here there are so many people without beards? I always supposed that your Muhammadans thought a great deal of their beards."

"So they do; but Akbar thinks quite differently. A little moustache, like yours and mine, he can put up with, but would rather see nothing at all on one's face. The wisest men have their whims, and this may be one. Or he may do it with intention to vex the faithful, and to show them how little he thinks of their opinions and customs. But, whatever the reason, so it is; and, unimportant and childish as it seems, this has given rise to much talk and much that is disagreeable. Now we are approaching the dwelling of one of the chiefs of the village of this district, who I know very well, through my uncle the Minister. Shall we rest with him for a few moments while our horses are watered? My bay is much in want of it, for he was waiting saddled long before I was ready."

Agreeing to this proposal they dismounted in the inner court of a farmhouse built of stone and wood, and surrounded by tamarinds and acacias. The proprietor himself soon appeared—a middle-aged, respectable-looking Hindu, with a magisterial air. After the usual greetings, and while fresh fruit and ice-cold water was brought for their refreshment, the conversation naturally turned to agriculture and the great prosperity of the district, although but lately brought under cultivation.

"Partly, of course," said the chief of the village, "we owe the fortunate condition in which we find ourselves to our own labour and exertion; but we owe great thanks to the Emperor, whose wise and beneficent system of ruling first gave us the opportunity of using our own strength."

"I have heard of his system," remarked Siddha; "still, to tell you the truth, I am scarcely master of it."

"Yet it is very simple," replied the Hindu, "and, to one like you, very easy to comprehend. The system rests principally on a wise division of the land, and a just settlement of the taxes on land, and, above all, on the certainty of law and justice, possessed equally by proprietor and tenant. Everything used to depend on arbitrary decisions, and no one knew what he might keep or what he would be obliged to pay; and we chiefs of the villages had to decide what the yearly taxation of the fields should be. Now that is all changed: the fields are correctly measured, their boundaries fixed, and the taxation regulated with reference to their productiveness, according to which they are placed in classes, and rented for a certain number of years.2 And what, perhaps, is the most important of all, the taxes are payable either in money or in kind; and no Government officer can decide as he will, when disputes arise, but by the law alone. The consequence of all this is, that the cultivator, proprietor, or farmer can tell beforehand what land will cost, what he will have to pay, and what will remain his own property. Is it any wonder, then, that he now, understanding his affairs, applies all his energies to them, and becomes prosperous, whereas before he was content if he could but earn his daily rice. You see the fruits of the system around you, and can form your own opinion; but you could do so far better if you had known the former condition of the country as I do."

"The same system in any country would lead to the same results," answered Siddha. "What a blessing for a state to possess a prince like Akbar!"

"We must also be grateful to his councillors," said the magistrate, "particularly to Todar Mal,3 the treasurer, who worked out the system; and to Abú-l Fazl, the great Wazir, who put the last touch to the work, and repressed with severity the extortions of the Government officers. If in the beginning these measures appeared to diminish the revenues of the state, in the long run it has been quite the contrary; but had the revenues been lessened, still they would have been far more productive, because the payments are certain and punctual."

"But, worthy sir," asked Siddha, "is there not danger of these excellent regulations falling to the ground if a less wise prince should ascend the throne?"

"I do not believe it," was the reply. "No despot could easily take from our community such rights when it had once obtained them. You know that our people almost entirely govern themselves by their magistrates, and are thus, to a certain extent, independent of the sovereign. If he attempted to deprive them of their rights he would find that he must wage war against a dozen small states, and would not find soldiers enough to reduce them all to obedience. Even should he succeed in doing so, the villages would be almost entirely deserted, and the population would seek refuge in impenetrable jungles and wildernesses. On the other hand, our villagers leave the prince free to act as he will. He can carry on war against other kingdoms as much as he pleases, and as long as the state of his treasury admits; and they never concern themselves with court intrigues and disputes."

"What a happy condition of things," said Siddha, "for both parties."

"But the union of state and people is not much advanced by it," remarked Parviz, joining in the conversation.

"No, that is true," answered the magistrate. "But do you believe it possible that there can be real unity in a State such as our present Hindustan, where so many and such different races and people are brought together under one rule?"

"I acknowledge that it may be difficult; still, it is worth trying for."

The conversation, which was very interesting to Siddha, continued for some time, and then the two friends, taking leave, mounted their horses and continued their journey. A brisk but rather long ride, which obliged them more than once to halt and rest, brought them in sight of the heights on which the palace of Fathpúr was built. However striking had been the first view of the palaces of Agra, this was not less so. The buildings rising one above another, as though built on terraces, stood out proud and stately against the sky, with their tall towers, and sharply cut battlements. Broad marble steps glittered in the sunshine, here and there overshadowed by the thick green of tamarinds and other trees.

As Siddha and his companion, leaving their horses to the charge of their servants, entered the precincts of the palace itself, the former, though less astonished, was far more delighted than he had been with his first view of Agra. The gardens pleased him more, and were more satisfying to the eye, for here no wrong was done to nature; the paths, instead of being laid out with uniform regularity, followed the unevenness of the ground, and were thickly overshadowed by luxuriant vegetation. And what a magnificent and refreshing view over the neighbouring hills and fields, rich and golden with corn, and over the silver shining river! For some time the two wandered about, sometimes through solitary groves, and then through galleries filled with guards and servants. At last Parviz proposed they should go to the lower town to seek their lodgings, and to obtain better refreshment than had been possible on the road. This proposal was willingly agreed to; and after the two friends had enjoyed the needful repose, they again sallied out to visit what was to be seen in the town.

"Excuse me," said Parviz, "if I leave you for a few minutes. I have to give some papers from my uncle to one of his officers here, and to speak to him about some affairs which will not interest you. He lives close by, and I shall be back immediately. In the meantime you can visit that old temple yonder, surrounded with acacias; or, if you like it better, pay your devotions there."

"Very much obliged," he answered, laughing; "I scarcely care to do that, but I will willingly visit the temple, and will await you close by."

Siddha had hardly entered the vaulted, dimly-lit building before he recognised it as a temple of Siva by the numerous emblematic ornaments on the pillars, and, advancing a few steps, he saw at the furthest end a kind of hall lighted from above, where was placed a colossal image of the god, seated cross-legged on a lotus, his arms and ancles ornamented with numberless rings, the symbol of the trinity on his forehead, and a necklace of skulls around his neck. Siva was the immortal ruler of the world, creating to destroy, and destroying to create afresh, endless in his manifestation and transformation of being, from whence all takes origin, and to which everything must return. Well as our young Indian understood the idea represented by these images and their symbols, the mis-shapen, monstrous figures struck him with the same feeling of repulsion as they had done when he first beheld them. The temple itself was not wanting in beauty, though disfigured by the grotesque representations on the walls.

He had not been long alone before he heard a voice behind him, although the silence was unbroken by any sound of footsteps.

"Om," sounded through the stillness; "Om, the unworthy servant of Siva's holy consort greets thee, O Moral Force."

Turning to the spot from whence came the voice, Siddha recognised the Durga priest Gorakh, whom he had seen in company with his uncle at Allahabad. "I greet you, holy man," he said, and awaited what the other should say.

"So, then, we have not forgotten each other since our last meeting," replied the priest. "In truth I have not lost sight of you since I saw you in the neighbourhood of Badrinath."

"Let that be as it will," answered Siddha, half impatiently; "but I scarcely comprehend, honoured lord, why you should concern yourself about me."

"Should not," asked the other, "the nephew of my old friend and pupil have claim to the interest I feel in him? and for that reason I feel obliged to give you a warning, if you will take it from me. You know who Gurupada the hermit is, do you not?"

"Gurupada?" asked Siddha. "Certainly; he is a hermit living in the mountains."

"Yes; but I mean who he was before he assumed his present name."

"Of that I know nothing—he never alluded to it."

"But your guru, Kulluka, must have told you."

"I never asked him; it was nothing to me."

Gorakh turned a penetrating look towards the speaker; but he would have been no true Indian had his countenance displayed ought but utter indifference. However, irritated by the persistence of his questioner, he proceeded, with less caution, to say, "Even if I knew who and what Gurupada had been, can you not understand that I would not tell you?"

"Ha!" cried the Yogi, "you mean you do not trust me. You mean to defy me. Do you remember that I am a friend of the Governor of Allahabad?"

"Yes, I know that," said Siddha, expressing vexation.

"What do you know?"

"I know what I know, and that is enough."

The priest regarded Siddha with anger, not unmingled with disquietude. What was the meaning of this tone, and what could he really know? Still for the moment the wisest course seemed to be to break off the conversation.

"Enough, then," said Gorakh, "both for you and for me; but bethink yourself, my young friend—though you are so little desirous of my friendship, and I will not force it on you,—think that the mighty goddess, to whose service all my feeble strength is devoted, not only protects but destroys also, and that there is no hope of mercy or chance of salvation for him whom, through her priests, she has chosen out for her service and who has turned from it." So saying, he disappeared down a side aisle, without waiting for any answer to his mysterious menace. Siddha looked after him with an involuntary feeling of anxiety; and though in reality the Durga priest was alone, yet he almost fancied he could see him followed by a long train of naked bronze figures, with white cords round their necks, just as he had seen him in the dimness of night passing along the wall of Allahabad fortress and vanishing in the jungle. And that night, as he went to rest, he thought it would be as well to question his faithful servant who awaited his orders.

"Vatsa," he said, "at Allahabad you assured me that neither you nor Kulluka's servant had spoken to any priest or penitent; but can you not remember some other unknown person to whom you might have talked of our journey through the mountains, and recounted to him some of its incidents?"

"I should never have thought of it again, Sir, if you had not brought it to my mind," replied Vatsa; "but now I remember that near the stable a half-naked, bronze-coloured man once talked with us, and told us much about the town and fortress, and then asked us about our journey."

"And you told him of my adventure with Gurupada's tiger?"

"I believe we did."

"And did you say anything of the hermit and his appearance?"

"Certainly," answered Vatsa. "His venerable and princely bearing had so struck us that we were full of it, and not thinking there was any harm in speaking of it we made no secret of our meeting with him to the stranger."

"Did you describe Gurupada's appearance exactly?"

"I cannot distinctly remember all we said; but I believe we did speak of it."

"There is danger," murmured Siddha to himself, "and more than danger. The priest naturally learnt enough from his spy about our journey to put me out of countenance. His suspicions seem to be aroused as regards Gurupada; and it is clear he tried to find out more from me. But what can he have to do with Gurupada or Nandigupta? And my uncle Salhana—is he also mixed up in this?"

"I hope we have done no harm by our talk with the stranger," said Vatsa, disquieted by seeing his young master sunk in thought.

"No, no," he replied; "and even had you done so, it was done unintentionally, and you are not to blame. We ought to have been more cautious, and to have warned you beforehand. But in future, Vatsa, do not speak to any one of the hermit, whoever it may be that asks you; do you understand?"

"Perfectly, my lord," was the answer; "and in future I have never seen the hermit, or even if I have done so, I have entirely forgotten what he was like."

"Nevertheless," thought Siddha, "it might be as well to warn Kulluka, and even Nandigupta himself. I will try and find a safe opportunity, whether Salhana has anything to do with it, or not."

---

1 Fathpúr Sikri was the favourite residence of Akbar from 1570 to the end of his reign. The chief glory of the place is its mosque. Fathpúr Sikri is 12 miles from Agra.

2 Akbar's system is fully described by Abú-l Fazl in the "A'ín-i-Akbari." The lands were divided into four classes with different revenue to be paid by each, namely:—

1. *Pulaj*, cultivated every harvest and never fallow.

2. *Paranti*, lying fallow at intervals.

3. *Checher*, fallow for four years together.

4. *Bunjar*, not cultivated for five years and upwards.

The lands of the two first of these classes were divided into best, middling, and bad. The produce of a *bígah* of each sort was added together, and a third of that was considered to be the average produce. One third of this average was the share of the State, as settled by Akbar's assessment. Remissions were made on the two last classes of land. The Government demand might be paid either in money or kind. The settlement was made for ten years.

In Akbar's reign the land revenue yielded £16,582,440, and the revenue from all sources was £32,000,000. Akbar also remitted many vexatious imposts, including the poll tax on unbelievers, the tax on pilgrims, ferry dues, and taxes on cattle, trees, trade licenses, and market dues on many articles.

3 See note further on.

Chapter VI.
Salim.

"Form quickly," said the commandant of the Rajpúts, as he stood in the court of the fortress, while the cavalry fell into rank; "and then march for the field where the Emperor reviews the troops to-day."

This order was obeyed without delay, and, when outside the fortification, they broke into a trot, until they reached a plain, at some little distance from the town, where the review was to be held. A splendid sight lay stretched out before Siddha, as, at the head of his detachment, he ascended a small hill. On the right was a whole town, as it were, of tents; long, broad streets, laid out with the utmost regularity. In the middle stood the imperial tent, made of red cloth, with a gilded dome-shaped roof,—if one might call a palace of cloth and wood a tent; and on the left, brilliant with many colours, were drawn up the different army corps—some horsemen in armour and some without, some armed with lances and some with guns; and there stood the artillery and war elephants; and further off, other elephants with luxurious *hauda*, on whose cushions were seated ladies, most of them veiled, who had come to see the spectacle.

Soon after the arrival of the Rajpúts the troops moved forward, and, preceded by their bands, defiled before the Emperor and his staff. Siddha did not hesitate long before deciding which was the Emperor among that brilliant group of officers, their arms and horse-trappings glittering with gold and jewels. Unmistakable was his whole bearing—a robust man on a splendid white horse, with the commander's staff in his hand, standing a few steps in advance of the others, his standard and umbrella bearer behind him. Instantly Siddha recognised in the mighty ruler the man with whom he had spoken in the gardens of the palace, a suspicion of whose real rank had for a moment crossed his mind.

When his turn came to pass before the Emperor with his men, he bent his head and pointed his lance to the ground, as he had seen others do; and stealing a glance at the Emperor, saw a smile pass over his stern features, from which he gathered that Akbar had not taken ill his bold words, and he remembered that excepting a passing outburst of anger, his interlocutor had maintained during the whole interview a frank and friendly tone. He came to the conclusion that he had no cause to dread his presentation to the Emperor, which Faizi had warned him would most likely take place after the review. This expectation was soon fulfilled. No sooner had the halt been sounded, a sign that the troops might for a time repose, than Siddha saw Faizi beckon, and on joining him he was guided through tents, the magnificence of which rivalled that of the palace itself; and a few minutes later he found himself in presence of the Emperor. Faizi was not a little surprised at seeing Akbar, without waiting for the official presentation, step forward to meet Siddha, replying to his reverential greeting with a gracious movement of his hand, and say, "Well, I saw you at the head of your troop, and it seems to me that you will turn out a good officer. Take care that my expectations are fulfilled. I have already made acquaintance with your friend," he continued, turning to Faizi; "we met a few days ago, although at the time he had no idea who I was."

"Even had I known it, Sire," said Siddha, respectfully, "I could not have regarded your Majesty with more reverence than I did the unknown stranger."

"But perhaps spoken a little less freely," said Akbar, smiling. "However, there is no harm done, and I had far rather hear what men think of me than guess what they say behind my back. Our former meeting induces me to command, or rather to request, for what I wish cannot be forced, that now you know me, you will trust me as you did when I was a stranger. You see to-day that your confidence was not misplaced. Turn to me, and not to others, when you think that you have cause of complaint against me or mine. I never refuse to hear grievances: if they are groundless I try to refute them; if real, to redress them. Boldness and free speaking, my friend Faizi here can bear witness, never arouse my anger, however much dissimulation and falsehood may do so."

After some questions and replies regarding the particulars of Siddha's service, the Emperor signified that the audience was at an end, and they took their leave, Faizi not a little bewildered about this first meeting, a full account of which his young companion soon gave him.

"You are indeed a child of fortune," said Faizi; "such things do not happen to every one, however easy of access Akbar is, and however willingly he enters into conversation. You seem to have made a favourable impression on him, and that rejoices me from my heart. But do I not see Parviz approaching? Yes, indeed; but what can he be doing here? Well," continued he to his nephew, "what is my lord the future councillor doing here among warriors in their tents?"

"As much as my worthy uncle the philosopher," answered Parviz; "but I willingly confess that I can rival him as little in statecraft and learning as in deeds of arms."

"No compliments, my nephew," answered the other, laughing; "they are not fitting between us. But shall I tell you my suspicions? That you have come to have a glance at those beautifully decorated elephants yonder: the lovely daughter of Todar Mal is perhaps not unaccustomed to your appearance, although you are supposed never to have seen her."

"Uncle, now in my turn I say, no betrayal of my secrets! However," added Parviz, good-naturedly, "I have none from my friend Siddha, and all the more, that I am sure of his sympathy whenever he thinks of his no less dearly loved betrothed, though I am less fortunate than he; and even if I hope to find favour in the eyes of the daughter, I am not so sure of doing so in those of the father."

"That will all come right in time," remarked Faizi, good-naturedly; "but enough at present of our confidences. See, here come others, for whose ears they are not intended."

"Who is that?" asked Siddha, as he saw a group of horsemen approach, in the centre of which rode a young man but a few years older than himself, and whose appearance for more than one reason attracted his attention. He was dressed with the most luxurious splendour: over his coat of gold cloth he wore no less than four necklaces of pearls of unwonted size; his turban was ornamented by a heron's feather and three jewels of priceless worth. On his arms, up to the elbows, were clasped numerous bracelets, all set with precious stones; and on each finger was a ring; while his weapons and horse-trappings were a mass of pearls and diamonds. But in strange contrast to all this splendour was the wearied white face, its sallowness still more marked by the jet-black eyes and finely pencilled moustache and eyebrows. Originally the features must have been noble and beautiful, but they were ruined and aged before their time, and bore signs of many a night spent in dissipation and riot.

"What, do you not know him?" answered Faizi; "that is Salim, the Emperor's son and heir."

With a silent greeting the Prince was about to ride by, but a sudden thought striking him, he drew in his horse by Faizi, and said, "Sirs, I am glad to meet you here; I expect some friends this evening in my palace to a feast, will you also give me the pleasure of your presence?"

"The invitation," answered Faizi, "would be to me a command, if a still higher one did not prevent me from obeying: the Emperor has invited me for this evening."

"And so you will give my father another lesson from your unbelieving philosophers; is it not so?" said Salim, with a half-contemptuous smile, not quite pleased with the refusal.

"What I myself may do," was the answer, "can depend on the will of your Highness; but what the Emperor may think good to do is, it appears to me, above your opinion and above mine. Also there may be a question as to which evening will be most profitably spent."

"Now do not be angry, noble Faizi," said Salim, good-naturedly. "I mean no harm; and if I leave your evening alone, let me have mine. And you, Parviz," said he, turning to him, "have you also some important business to prevent your enjoying some innocent amusement?"

"Certainly not," answered Parviz, "and even if I had, I would desire nothing better than to thrust it on one side before the pleasure of a feast in Salim's palace. But allow me, if it is not indiscreet, to present to your Highness a new friend of mine." And signing to Siddha to approach, he announced his name and rank.

"Oh yes," said Salim, "I remember hearing of his arrival; and if you," he continued, turning to Siddha, "will accompany your friend this evening, it will give me pleasure."

"It will be both honour and pleasure to me," said Siddha, bowing respectfully.

"There is not much honour in it," said Salim, "I am of no consequence at this court; still I hope that our meeting may give you pleasure. Till this evening, then." And turning his horse the Prince rode off, followed by his retinue.

"And allow me also, honoured friend," said Siddha, "to take my leave; it is time that I should return to my troop."

"If you will," said Parviz, "come and fetch me this evening; my dwelling is on the way, and we can go together."

"With pleasure," answered the other, as he turned away to return to his post.

Though Siddha had anticipated that Salim's palace would be one of great splendour, yet his expectations were far outstripped by the unheard-of luxury which surrounded him on all sides, as he passed through different ante-rooms and rows of servants, before reaching the brilliantly lighted hall where the Prince welcomed his friends. In spite of the richness of the imperial palace, there was something grave and sober about it; but here, on the contrary, in the midst of Moorish architecture and sparkling decoration, all breathed of luxury and the search after boundless enjoyment. Many coloured hangings of silk and gold hung from the finely cut arches, and the marble walls were partly covered with variegated mosaic work and gilding; thick masses of flowers spread fragrance around; broad mirrors reflected back the light, while the foot sank deep in soft carpets of fantastic designs; luxurious divans wooed the passer-by to repose; and there at his hand were drinking-cups of open-worked gold and crystal, and porphyry and marble coolers of every form. On one side of the hall was a kind of stage, lighted with coloured lamps, where dancers and players were to perform. All this formed a picture that at first sight would strike the beholder with surprise, however accustomed he might be to the palaces of India.

Salim quickly caught sight of the new comers among the other guests, who stood talking in groups, while others reclined on divans, and advancing towards them, he said, "You are right welcome to my humble dwelling, and I hope that this evening will afford you enjoyment; but let me tell you that etiquette has nothing to do with pleasure, and here we are all friends."

The Prince turned away, and at the same moment Siddha saw approach a well-known but unexpected figure—that of Salhana, Governor of Allahabad.

"Well, nephew," he said, giving him his hand, "I am very glad to meet you here; I have just arrived, and found an invitation from the Prince awaiting me."

"And how goes all yonder?" asked Siddha; "and how is——"

"Iravati," interrupted Salhana. "Very well; she sends her greetings. But see, there comes a man whose acquaintance you must make; he is not much seen at court, but, for all that, is a man well worth knowing."

No introduction was necessary, for the man was no other than Abdul Kadir, Badaoni, the Islam fanatic, whom Siddha had already met in the imperial park with Akbar. To his astonishment this man greeted his uncle with courtesy, although he was an unbeliever like himself; and even to his share fell a recognition which could not be considered uncourteous.

"I have already met your nephew accidentally," said Abdul Kadir, as Salhana was about to introduce him; "and I hope," he continued to Siddha, "that you regard the words I then spoke in the sense I gave them, for you see now that persons are not hated by me, however much I combat the false doctrines they hold."

"I honour your feelings, noble Sir," said Siddha, "although I regret that you are not one with us; perhaps——"

"Perhaps what?" began Abdul Kadir, angrily.

"No, no, my friends," interposed Salhana; "no disputes, I pray, over your different beliefs. Think rather of the grave dangers which threaten us all, we Hindus as well as you true sons of the Prophet, should the plans be carried out in true earnest that the higher powers now think of."

Some others, apparently trusted acquaintances of Salhana and the Muhammadan, had joined the speakers, forming a thick ring around them, while Parviz and some young friends had gone to the other end of the hall.

"Let us consider," continued Salhana, in a low but audible voice, "how we should bear ourselves should our otherwise honoured Emperor attempt, as is probable, to force upon us a religion alike abhorrent to our feelings, customs, and morals. Will you Muhammadans, the present rulers of the land, deny Allah, and kneel in adoration before the sun and stars, and perhaps——"

"By the beard of the Prophet," began Abdul Kadir, laying his hand on the hilt of his sword, "we should——"

"Let that be as it may," interrupted the other; "there are still worse things. Consider the words 'Alláhu Akbar'1 we now find on our coins and firmans; they are innocent enough if you understand them as 'God is great,' but far different if you read them in the sense of 'Akbar is God.'"

"That goes indeed too far," broke out Abdul Kadir, in bitter anger.

But Salhana again interposed.

"Let us be calm," he said; "we have at present only to do with suppositions, which may, as I hope, turn out to be groundless. But should it be so, could you, and would you, submit?"

This question was addressed as much to those standing around as to Abdul Kadir, and made a deep impression on Siddha. That Akbar had thought of founding a new religion had already come to his ears; but could it be that he thought of using force as an aid to conversion; was this possible?

"Therefore," concluded Salhana, "let there be no division between us; let us consider together, and by unanimity and the use of legitimate measures we may ward off the dangers that threaten us, through the excited imagination of an otherwise excellent sovereign being worked on by fanatics and intriguers. But I believe that the Prince already signs to us that the feast is about to begin. Let us for the moment break off our conversation; I shall remain at your command, my lords. Perhaps I am in error; from my heart I wish that it may turn out so."

As the guests were taking their places on the divans, Siddha heard, in passing one of the groups of talkers, a few words that attracted his attention—"And Kashmir," asked one of the speakers; "is she informed?"

"Thoroughly," was the reply; "the mine is almost ready to be sprung."

"And the letter?"

"Is in the best of hands."

Other guests divided Siddha from the two whose conversation he had accidentally heard, and he was soon seated, not far from Salhana, but divided from him by several young people, with whom he was soon in conversation; while servants carried round various refreshments, and rich wines flowed in the golden drinking-cups. Now and then the words he had heard crossed his mind, but their meaning was dark. Could they refer to secret divisions in his native land, which, according to Salhana were stirred up by Akbar. And the letter! Involuntarily his thoughts turned to Rezia's letter that he had entrusted to Kulluka; but what could that have to do with state affairs? His attention was soon engrossed by the dancers who, accompanied by musicians, appeared on the stage at the end of the hall. Their bronze-coloured arms and necks were bare, while a long robe fell to their feet. To the music of stringed instruments and cymbals, they commenced one of those dances so dear to both Indians and Muhammadans, and which they can watch unwearied for hours. Now and then, for a change, their places were taken by singers, who treated their audience with extracts from the Persian poets, which Salim and his friends listened to with great pleasure, but which to Siddha appeared a little monotonous.

"Where is Rembha," at last asked the Prince, "that she does not come and sing a few translated passages from an old Indian poem, that you, Siddha, doubtless know well—I mean the Gita Govinda?"

"Oh yes," answered Siddha; "the pastoral of Jayadeva, which describes the adventures of the god Krishna with the shepherdesses, and his reconciliation with the beautiful Radha. I have myself attempted a translation."[2]

"Let us listen," said Salim; "here comes Rembha." And on the stage appeared a dark but beautiful young woman, in rich and luxurious costume; and, accompanied by soft music, she began half to sing, half to recite, the following:

"In this love-tide of spring, when the amorous breeze

Has kiss'd itself sweet on the beautiful trees,

And the humming of numberless bees, as they throng

To the blossoming shrubs, swells the Kokila's song,—

In the love-tide of spring, when the spirit is glad,

And the parted—yes, only the parted—are sad,

Thy lover, thy Krishna, is dancing in glee,

With troops of young maidens, forgetful of thee.

"The season is come when the desolate bride

Would woo with laments her dear lord to her side;

When the rich-laden stems of the Vakul bend low,

'Neath the clustering flowers in the pride of their glow;

In this love-tide of spring, when the spirit is glad,

And the parted—yes, only the parted—are sad,

Thy lover, thy Krishna, is dancing in glee

With troops of young maidens, forgetful of thee.

"Dispensing rich odours, the sweet Madhavi,

With its lover-like wreathings encircle the tree;

And oh! e'en a hermit must yield to the power,

The ravishing scent of the Mallika3 flower.

In this love-tide of spring, when the spirit is glad,

And the parted—and none but the parted—are sad,

Thine own, thy dear Krishna, is dancing in glee;

He loves his fair partners, and thinks not of thee."4

"The poetry and the meaning," said Salim, as the singer paused, "leave nothing to be desired; but what, noble Siddha, do you think of the translation?"

"Not bad," he answered; "the imagery and spirit are well and freely given, even if here and there the word are not exactly followed; but that, I believe, in the poetry of the present day, would be difficult if not impossible. Is not the name of the translator known?"

"It is Faizi, with whom I saw you talking this morning," said the Prince, smiling at the confusion painted on Siddha's cheeks at hearing these words and thinking of the rather magisterial opinion he had just expressed. "Do not be disturbed," continued he; "Faizi will not take it ill that you do not consider his work faultless; but, on the contrary, will be grateful for any corrections. Now, Rembha, let us hear one piece more, and then for this evening we will not trouble you again."

"This," said the singer, "is the complaint of the forsaken Radha to her friend:

"Ah, my beloved! taken with those glances;

Ah, my beloved! dancing those rash dances;

Ah, minstrel! playing wrongful strains so well;

Ah, Krishna, Krishna, with the honeyed lip!

Ah, wanderer into foolish fellowship!

My dancer, my delight! I love thee still.

"O dancer! strip thy peacock crown away;

Rise! thou whose forehead is the star of day,

With beauty for its silver halo set;

Come! thou whose greatness gleams beneath its shroud,

Like Indra's rainbow shining through the cloud—

Come, for I love thee, my beloved! yet."5

For a short moment Rembha paused, and then continued in a slightly altered measure, and with a softer and sadder tone in her sweet voice, as though she from her heart threw herself into the rôle of the loving Radha.

"Go to him—win him hither—whisper low

How he may find me if he searches well;

Say, if he will, joys past his hope to know

Await him here; go now to him and tell

Where Radha is, and that henceforth she charms

His spirit to her arms.

"Yes, go! say if he will that he may come—

May come, my love, my longing, my desire;

May come, forgiven, shriven, to me, his home,

And make his happy peace; nay, and aspire

To uplift Radha's veil, and learn at length

What love is in its strength."6

Universal applause greeted the singer as she concluded: the beauty of the words, so fully expressed by her voice and bearing, came home to them all.

"Then follows the reconciliation of Krishna and Radha, does it not?" said Salim, "but that we will have another time. Tell me, worthy Abdul Kadir," he continued, perhaps not without intention, "does the Hindu poetry give you as much pleasure as our own, or, like others of the Faithful, have you a horror of the false ideas proclaimed by these Hindus?"

"With poets," answered Abdul Kadir, with difficulty suppressing his anger, "I have not much to do; and our Holy Prophet, blessed be his name, cursed with good reason the impious Amru-l Kais,7 however highly his *Mullakat* was famed by others. But that the Hindus, not content with writing the wanton poetry we have just heard, should dare to hold up such beings as Krishna and Radha as objects of worship, appears to me too gross."

Just as Siddha was about to attempt to show the fanatic that there was a difference between mythology and true worship, between poetry and faith, Salim hindered further discussion by saying—"No theology, gentlemen, I beg; let us leave that to my honoured father, who is, at this moment, I believe, occupied with the learned Faizi, and, it may be, with other philosophers also; but we younger ones have met together to pass a merry evening. Ho! you singers and players! A drinking song, and a gay one too, that may bring back the right tone amongst us; and let wine flow to rejoice our hearts. That no anger may linger in your mind, noble Abdul Kadir, think that even a poet, whom our great Prophet did not curse, and who is honoured amongst us,— think that Tarafa8 sang:

"Wouldst thou spend the livelong day

In the tavern bright and gay,

I with song would mirthfully

Bear thee joyous company.

"Ready on the board we'll find,

When the morrow breaks again,

Foaming goblet—rosy wine—

Which with joy once more we'll drain.

And why should we not follow the good advice?"

The sullen Muhammadan muttered behind his beard, but dared say nothing, for he had need of Salim, as the latter well knew, as an ally in the troubles that might arise from Akbar's forsaking the faith. He was silent, therefore, and ended with consoling himself for his wrongs by drinking as deeply as any, in spite of what the Prophet might have said.

The other guests made good use of their time, and the drinking-cups were no sooner emptied than they were refilled. Then the singers and bayadires, at a sign from Salim, mingled in the gay company, and took their places on the divans amongst them.

The beautiful Rembha seated herself by Siddha, and before long they were in conversation. He discovered her not only to be accomplished but good-hearted, from the compassionate manner in which she spoke of the unfortunate dancers, who, though not slaves in reality, were sold in their earliest years by their parents to the highest bidders, and then passed from one to another like so much merchandise, leading a life but little better than real slavery.

"And though," she said, frankly, "in the beginning mine was the same fate, fortunately I had a talent for music. My patron gave me a thorough education in it; and now I can support myself by means of my art. And when," she continued, smiling, "I become old and ugly, then——"

"Then what?" cried Siddha, who had listened with sympathy to all she said.

"Oh no," answered Rembha, "I know what you mean, and you forget yourself. When I become old and ugly, I need not descend to a life of adventure; being a Hindu of high caste, there will be no difficulty in finding employment in one of the temples to superintend the dancers and singers kept by the priests for their ceremonials."

Here the words were interrupted by a wilder and louder burst of music, and when it ceased other guests and women joined in the talk. But now the conversation became less guarded, and many an expression met Siddha's ear that until now was unknown to him, but the meaning of which he soon caught. By degrees he also began to lose his sense of decorum. Here and there lay a reveller, still clasping his empty goblet, and quite unconscious of all around. And there on the divan were groups whose bearing showed no recollection of the high presence in which they found themselves.

But the Prince had long ceased to take much notice of what went on around him; he had thrown himself carelessly back between two dancers, one of whom played with the hilt of his dagger, while the other examined the many bracelets on his arms. One of these he unclasped and flung at her, tossing at the same time two costly pearls, he had torn from his coat, to her companion; then filling high his goblet, he drained it to the last drop, and sank back senseless on his cushion. And now, as the conversation became more confused, so also it became louder and louder, while the music played, and the wine flowed in streams; and our Siddha, overcome by the noise, and heavy perfume of flowers, and still more perhaps by the wine, by degrees remarked less and less all that went on around him. But a heavy hand laid suddenly on his shoulder aroused him from his stupefaction. It was Salhana, who had approached him unnoticed.

"Come," he said, "it is time we departed; on occasions like these who can tell what quarrels or disputes may break out?"

"Yes," answered Siddha, with hesitating speech; "but can we go before the Prince gives the sign for leave-taking?"

"The Prince!" answered Salhana, contemptuously: "look! and judge whether he is likely to know or care whether we go or remain."

He glanced towards Salim, who reclined on a divan with closed eyes, his arm hanging over the cushion, while a few paces from him lay his newly-filled goblet that had fallen from his hand and rolled on the carpet. Though Siddha did his best, he could not see Salim; or, if he did, it appeared to him there were two Salims; and without resisting he let his uncle lead him from the hall, and assist him into a palanquin which awaited them at the door; and after giving directions to the bearers, Salhana, who had certainly not drunk less than his nephew, turned, with a firm and steady tread, towards his dwelling. As he passed through one of the narrow streets he saw under the shadow of a house a tall thin figure, which, after looking cautiously around, left its hiding-place and approached him—it was Gorakh the Yogi.

"Does all go well?" he asked.

"Nothing could be better," was the reply. "Our cause prospers; I cannot yet give particulars, but when I know more, and certainly in case we have need of you and your followers, you shall be warned at once."

"And our young simpleton? keep your eye upon him, for I believe he has suspicions of our understanding. When he is once with us that will not signify. But tell me, is the bird in the trap?"

"Not yet," answered Salhana; "but it will not be long before he is."

Gorakh laughed, and the men parted, each going his own way.

---

1 *Alláhu Akbar, jalla jaláluhu*: was the inscription on one side of Akbar's rupee, and on the other the date.

2 Jayadeva wrote the "Gita-Govinda," a pastoral drama, in about the twelfth century of our era. It relates to the early life of Krishna, as Govinda the cowherd, and sings the loves of Krishna with Radha and other of the cowherd damsels. But a mystical interpretation has been put upon it. There are some translations in the "Asiatic Researches," by Sir W. Jones. Mr. Griffith has translated a few stanzas into English. He says, "the exquisite melody of the verse can only be appreciated by those who can enjoy the original." A translation of the "Gita-Govinda" of Jayadeva was also published by Mr. Edwin Arnold in 1875.

3 *Jasminum undulatum*.

4 From Griffith's "Specimens of old Indian Poetry," p. 98.

5 From Edwin Arnold's translation of the "Gita-Govinda," p. 24.

6 Edwin Arnold's translation of the "Gita-Govinda," p. 28.

7 Amru-l Kais, was an Arabian poet and King of Kindah, living shortly before the era of Muhammad. He was the author of one of the seven *Mullakats*, or poems, which were inscribed in letters of gold, and suspended in the temple of Mecca. Pocock and Casiri give an account of the Arabian poets before Muhammad, and the seven poems of the Caaba were published in English by Sir William Jones.

8 An Arabian poet who lived after Amru-l Kais.—See "Casiri," i. pp. 71, 72. Casiri calls him Tarpha.

Chapter VII.
Secret Meetings.

Faizi's excuse for refusing the Prince's invitation was no feigned one, for at the moment when Salim's guests were assembling he was awaiting very different company in the private apartments of the Emperor. Preceded by a servant a man entered, by whose garb any one from the West would at once have recognised a Catholic Priest. It was the Padre Rudolf Aquaviva, head of the Jesuit Mission, and deputed to the court of Agra by the Father Provincial.1

"You are welcome, worthy Father," said Akbar, returning his greeting; "welcome in the name of the Great Being whom we both worship, although in different ways. I hope," he continued, "that the journey has not wearied you."

"I am grateful to your Majesty for the interest you take in me," answered Aquaviva. "Our journey, fortunately, has been accomplished without accident, although my health is feeble; but it is fitting that insignificant man should bear, without murmuring, what the Lord appoints."

"In that I agree with you," said Akbar; "but I have to thank you for the books that in your absence you were so good as to send me—your evangelists' and other writings. My friend Faizi here, who doubtless you remember, has translated the greater part of them for me, and I assure you that we have carefully read them, together with Abú-l Fazl."

"And," asked the Padre, gazing earnestly into the Emperor's face, "may we hope that the seed is fallen in good soil?"

"I believe that I can answer yes," said Akbar. "Some of your holy books I prize very highly, now that I have made closer acquaintance with them. What beautiful, elevated truth they contain, and noble ideas, almost beyond our grasp (which, however, are not entirely wanting in the teaching of Islam). What a noble, pure conception of self-denial and self-sacrifice, and, above all, what a pure idea of love and charity! and this is entirely wanting in the Koran. After this I can hardly tell you how far above Muhammadanism I place Christianity."

"The Lord be praised!" said the Jesuit, clasping his hands, and casting his eyes up to heaven. "That is the right way; first error recognised by comparison with truth, then is the soul steadfast. And how should it be possible that a man like Akbar, who is not only a powerful prince but a wise and learned scholar, should not be able to distinguish truth from lies?"

"I am flattered by your good opinion," said Akbar; "but am afraid I shall fall in it when you hear what I have to add to the words I have already spoken. Still I must say it, for I wish to act openly and fairly with you. Though I expressed my warm admiration of much that is to be found in your holy books, yet that does not prevent me from being ready to welcome all that is good and beautiful in other creeds: for example, some of the original Vedic ideas that are still extant."

"What!" cried Aquaviva, with irrepressible agitation,—"the terrible idolaters?"

"I acknowledge," replied Akbar, calmly, "that there are many amongst them to whom the name is appropriate; but that is not the case with all. Am I not right, Faizi?"

"Most certainly," was the answer; "and no one knows that better than my Emperor himself. He, as well as I, worthy Father, can testify to you that in these religions there is more than one passage, touching the points already mentioned, which are not inferior to your Christianity."

"It is impossible," said Aquaviva, firmly.

"And why impossible?" asked Faizi, smiling. "Are you intimately acquainted with all the religious systems?"

"All I know of them," said the Padre, "is what I have seen here and there; but I neither wish nor need a closer acquaintance with them; what purpose could it serve? And can there be more than one truth?"

"That speaks for itself," said Akbar; "but the question is, what is truth, and where is it to be found? Is it only to be found in one religious system, or scattered through many? You naturally will answer that you alone are in possession of truth; but then, I ask, what are your grounds for saying so?"

"The truth," replied Aquaviva, "has been declared to us by Jesus Christ, the Son of God."

"So you say," was the answer; "but my friend Abdul Kadir says that the truth was revealed to him through Muhammad the great Prophet; and if your Christ is really the Son of God, it would be well you should prove it, before calling upon him as such."

"And," added Faizi, "our Vishnuvites here say that truth was declared to them, not only by wise and holy men, but also through different incarnations of the Deity."

"The authority of the one true Church rests on the Bible, the Word of God," said Aquaviva.

"That again," answered Akbar, "resembles the authority of the Koran, the Khalifas and Ulamahs, and the authority of the canonical books, and the teachings of the Vishnuvites, of whom Faizi spoke just now."

"But surely the faith that stands firmly is of importance?"

"So are also all of like strength."

"There is no doubt but that Christianity is far older than the teaching of Islam."

"Yes, but not quite so ancient as the Vedas, on whose authority is founded the religious teaching of which we have just spoken. Buddhism is also far more ancient than Christianity; and while that, and I believe other religions, agree with yours in the teaching of true humanity, and also, to a wonderful degree, with the ceremonials of your church service, they go far beyond it in tolerance."

"In this manner we shall make no progress," remarked the Padre, angrily, in spite of his respect for the Emperor, in whose presence he was.

"No; I agree with you there, worthy Father," said Akbar, with a slight smile; "but perhaps all would be better if you would study our different faiths, and give yourself the same trouble that we have not spared ourselves in making acquaintance with the religion of our country. We could then at least compare the different teachings, and so in the end decide on their comparative worth."

"It was not for that purpose I came here," answered the apostle of the heathen; "I was sent to preach the gospel, and save souls from destruction."

"And in that," said Akbar, in his usual calm tone, "I wish you all success; but I doubt whether you will achieve much if you simply seek to force on others what you yourself hold for truth, without inquiring what they on their side may consider true."

"I believe," said Aquaviva, not alarmed at the difficulties in his way, "in the irresistible power of conviction possessed by our faith alone, which in the end can soften the most obdurate hearts, be they those of atheists or idolators."

"You mean by the teachings of your belief, do you not?"

"Certainly."

"Well, however much this teaching differs from that of the other religions we have mentioned, I am but little inclined to share the implicit faith you place in it. I respect all; and on those points where you find other creeds to agree with your own there can be no strife, and your work of conversion will be unnecessary. What do you think, friend Faizi, is it not so? You are a man of calm judgment, not an idealist as I or even our worthy Aquaviva, therefore your opinion is for us of great weight."

Whether the worthy Aquaviva agreed in this is very doubtful; however, he could not refuse to listen to Faizi, who thus began:—

"I do not think, Sire, that your Majesty requires any confirmation of your words from me. Still, I must assure the Padre, although in doing so I take from him his dearest illusions, that even though he may here and there make a convert, yet his teaching will never take root, neither among the Muhammadans nor among those it pleases him to call heathen. Those who cling alone to the dogma of the unity of God can never agree with what he inculcates about the Trinity, three persons in one God. There are others to whom this dogma will be less unacceptable, as they already worship the Great Being under more forms than one; but they will find other points which they also will never receive. For example, worthy Father, they will never allow it to be possible that God created man to let him fall, and that He offers Himself or His Son as a sacrifice, to save man; or that He created man as if He did not know that man would fall; and that by such extraordinary means of redemption alone could Divine justice and Divine love be again brought into harmony. They would, excuse me for saying so, consider such representations as utterly senseless, and feel no inclination for their sake to say farewell to the faith handed down to them by their fathers, which they find simpler and more rational. On the other hand, if you were content only to inculcate your doctrine of sin and reconciliation, and much of the same kind of teaching that I will not now allude to, and to declare nothing but your Christian morality, your ideas of humanity, of self-denial, and of love of man, to which all should gladly be sacrificed—when you have taught all this, it is nothing new here; and to say the least, your preaching is superfluous."

"But," said Aquaviva, "we hold fast by the truth we declare—the one truth that can save lost man and doomed souls from the eternal punishment of hell; and for this we are ready, here and everywhere, to take up our cross and suffer reproach for the sake of Jesus Christ, even should it be to the same martyr's death that He and so many of His saints after Him have suffered."

"But of that," said Akbar, laying his hand on the arm of the angry and enthusiastic fanatic, "there can be no question as long as I reign over Hindustan; nor, do I think, have you met with scorn anywhere under my government. On the contrary, honour has been shown you, an honour so high that many are jealous of it; and you enjoy the fullest liberty to declare your faith when and where you will. But we spoke, if I do not deceive myself, of the chances of your doctrines prevailing over those already professed in this country, and these, I must confess with Faizi, appear to me but slight."

"Still," Aquaviva ventured to remark, "if your Majesty would set the example."

"But I must first be convinced," said Akbar; "or do you wish that I should declare with my mouth what my heart denies?"

"Certainly I do," the other answered, "wild and absurd as the wish may appear; however, I do not urge it. But I had so hoped, so believed that the reading of the holy writings would have rendered the noble soul of Hindustan's wise ruler steadfast in the one true faith that alone can save his soul and ours from eternal perdition. And now I see my most cherished hopes lie shattered. Is it not, then, to be excused if I have expressed myself too strongly?"

"There is no need of excuse, my worthy friend," said Akbar; "I can quite understand your feelings. But I never said that I would not listen to you; on the contrary, I will willingly give you the opportunity of convincing me, if you can. For the present our conversation must cease; but let us regard this evening as the forerunner of others to come. This time we have touched on too many topics; on our next meeting we will keep to one distinct point, and who knows to what your learning and eloquence may bring me?"

If irony was mixed with the Emperor's grave words, neither his voice nor bearing betrayed it. All that the Jesuit remarked was that the audience was over, and thanking the Emperor for the honour he had done him in listening to his words, he respectfully took his leave.

"All are the same," said Akbar to Faizi, when they were alone; "if we listen to Abdul Kadir or Aquaviva, it is always authority, faith, revelation, never one word of reason or judgment, or of reasons founded on knowledge or experience. Still I always converse gladly with these zealots. From books we can learn the various theories of man's connection with the infinite; but the living words of the professors of the various persuasions teach us far more."

"Certainly," replied Faizi; "but as to this constant reference to authority and revelation, is it not natural and unavoidable in those who, not content with the lessons of experience and reason, seek the solution of the enigma of life in their own imaginations? If they are shown the groundlessness or senselessness of their propositions, what remains to them but to take refuge in the authority of a revelation declared and handed down to them by their forefathers? But it is singular that contradiction so seldom leads to the study and criticism of their own doctrines; were it to do so, they would soon become aware of the vanity of their theories. Proudly and defiantly the towers and pinnacles of their temple rise into the clouds, but examination would show them that the foundations are laid in the shifting sands of phantasy."

For some moments after Faizi ceased to speak Akbar was silent; on resuming the conversation, he said—

"I believe you are right, Faizi; still I have a sympathy with the people you reproach. And it may be that in some moment of enthusiasm and poetical imagination we may be carried away to the discovery of truth that we shall afterwards find to be supported by reason and knowledge. But for the present no more of this; we have other things to attend to, and presently I expect Abú-l Fazl, who has some important communication to make."

On a subsequent evening another interview took place at Agra, which had nothing in common with that just described, except that it also was hidden from indiscreet eyes and ears.

After his first interview with Rezia, Siddha had more than once sought for the servant who had guided him to her dwelling. At last he met her in the neighbourhood of the imperial gardens, and received anew from her an invitation to visit her mistress, which he hastened to accept. Since then the visits had been repeated, following one upon another, until at last the day that passed without Siddha sitting beside Rezia in the verandah appeared to him empty and void. All that Agra had to offer him of beauty and pleasure; however great the delight he took in the favour of Abú-l Fazl, and, later, in that of the Emperor himself; or the pleasure of conversation with Faizi, whose house was always open to him, and who treated him as a trusted friend; or the amusement he found in the society of Parviz and that of his joyous comrades; all sank to nothing in comparison with the quiet dwelling of the lonely Armenian. That the image of Iravati retired more and more into the background was not strange, nor that Rezia speedily became to him more than a pleasant, entertaining acquaintance; nor was she herself entirely insensible to the unconcealed homage of the young chief. A feeling of terror had overcome him when he first made the discovery that, instead of loving her as a dear friend, his feelings for her had in them a depth and passion that until that moment he had never known; but he had soon become accustomed to this thought, and from that moment only one desire was master of his soul, that of calling her his, and knowing that his love was returned.

On a certain evening Siddha was again seated on a divan beside his fascinating hostess; before them was a low table decked with fresh fruits and sparkling wine in golden drinking-cups. She seemed lovelier than ever to him, deeper than ever the expression of her soft blue eyes, that now full of tenderness, and now with an indescribable fire, gazed up at him, and then again were hidden under the shadow of long, silken eyelashes. The scent of roses and jasmine filled the air, and moonlight, almost as bright as day, fell on the verandah, and silvered the groups of trees and fountains in the garden.

"Siddha," said Rezia, with sudden gravity, interrupting their gay, laughing conversation, "you once did me a great service in undertaking that my letter should safely reach Kashmir; can I now ask of you a second, which, I tell you beforehand, may be of more consequence to yourself?"

"Command, and I obey," said Siddha, without hesitation; "whatever you may desire, do not doubt but that I will endeavour to fulfil it."

"Prudence, my friend," said Rezia, playfully lifting up her finger; "you are committing yourself before you know what I require; and you do this because, from your high rank and assured position at court, you think you can look down on what a simple woman like me can wish, and assume that the question is only how some one of my whims may be gratified; but in this you may be mistaken."

"I swear to you," was the impetuous answer, "no such thought crossed my mind. Now, then, demand what you will, and I obey your commands."

"Well," said Rezia, approaching her worshipper a little nearer, "you are perhaps more concerned in what I wish than I am myself. You imagine, perhaps, that I, leading this solitary life, know nothing of what goes on in the palaces of Agra and the Emperor's council. Accidental relations with people of high station give me the opportunity of knowing more than you perhaps suspect—more than you know of your own concerns, and of what should be known to your country and your people."

"I believe," said Siddha, "that I know what you mean; you allude to plans that may be formed to destroy the independence of Kashmir, as the many party divisions there give hopes that such plans may succeed."

"You are right," was the answer; "but what you do not seem to know is, that these plans are already ripe, that the imperial army is ready for the invasion, and that you yourself are destined to serve against your country and people; for your influence among the faithful Rajpúts, and your well-known name, will be important, should you remain blindly obedient to the commands of Akbar."

"But, dear Rezia," said Siddha, making a faint attempt to conceal under a cheerful voice the uneasiness that was mastering him, "even if this should be so, what is it to you? and what moves you to speak to me of it?"

"My own interests; but also the interest I take in you, my friend. I told you, as you will remember, of a friend who was exposed here to certain persecution. But now I will confess; I deceived you—it was not a friend, it was myself. The husband to whom my father's cruel command gave me, and whose tyranny I detest, will soon return, and my own desire is to fly from him, to be free, and some day perhaps in safety to be able to give myself to the one I choose; and to attain this I sought Kashmir as my place of refuge, and opened a communication with some of my friends there. But should this country also become subject to Akbar, my hope vanishes and I know not where to turn. Quickly you will again see me in the power of this man, who has my fate in his hands; our happy meetings will be at an end; and Rezia will cease to exist for you, as you," she added, with a slight sigh, "will for her."

"Never!" cried Siddha, passionately; "that shall never happen. But what would you have? what means do you know of? what do you ask of me?"

"Only this," replied Rezia, calmly, "that you should not allow yourself to be used as a tool against your own country, against yourself, against me. Remain by your own brave followers; but when the decisive day comes, do not lead them against us; but know how to go over to those of us, who, in spite of outward show of subjection to the Emperor, have a secret understanding. Then a powerful party in Kashmir will side with you, support you by their influence, and raise you to the greatest honour; and in the end, though that is of less importance, you will find a resting-place in my arms, who will ever be grateful to you for your protection."

"But," said Siddha, following, among all other plans and proposals, the thread of his own thought, "that would be treachery of the worst kind against the Emperor who has trusted me."

"Certainly, treachery," answered Rezia, with a contemptuous laugh. "As the Emperor has shown you some favour, he naturally has a full right to use you as a tool against your country and people, but you have not the right to repay him in the same coin. Now be subject—or slave! However, act as you please. Your assurances that you would do all I asked were nothing but the vain promises men are wont to make to simple women. But enough! Let our interview come to an end; not that I wish it, but it is better with firm resolution to part from one another, than to continue our intercourse only to see it inevitably broken off a few days later against our will."

"Never!" said Siddha, as Rezia turned from him, as though to hide her grief. "Nothing shall part us, and if for a moment I hesitated, I did not deceive you when I promised to do whatever you might ask. I repeat it, command and I obey."

"Your word."

"My word as a Rajpút. But why do you ask it? you know well that I can do nothing but what you wish. Why should I keep silence respecting that which you must long have known? At last let me say freely, that you are dear to me, above everything, dearer than life or even honour. I love you with a passion and devotion that until now I should never have thought possible; I believed I knew what love was, but what I took for it was only a childish liking. You have taught me differently; teach me more; teach me what it is when love like mine is returned. No slave can be more submissive to the will of his master than I to you; no slave of Akbar's or of any one but yourself. Whatever I may gain in the future, rank, esteem, riches, belong to you alone. And the power you have over me you may use or misuse as you will. But be mine, Rezia, mine as long as life lasts!"

"No, Siddha," said she, softly withdrawing her hand from him, "it is not fitting that I should hear such language, nor that you should use it. Remember that I am not yet free, and you yourself have other ties."

"Other ties!" cried Siddha, passionately; "I break them, or rather I broke them long ago; and could I not do so, I should curse the day when they were laid on me. And you, if you are not free, I will soon make you so. We will fly to Kashmir, to that far-away, beautiful country in the north, where, as you say, Siddha Rama's name and influence is well known, and where none will dare to injure you whom I protect, your hated husband least of all."

"And will that protection avail against Akbar and his favourites?" asked Rezia.

"Against him and his, as against all others," was the proud reply; "and against him we shall know well how to defend the liberty of Kashmir, if it were only for a place of refuge for you and for me."

"But I cannot be yours," interrupted Rezia; "and it grieves me, in truth, that you have so spoken this evening. You might have spared us all this, and then our friendly intercourse might have continued, and led perhaps later to another and a closer tie. Now all must cease, however deeply it grieves me. Go now, say farewell, and forget me, it is better for you and—for me, whom you say you love."

"In truth," said Siddha, as he rose, and, with his head sank on his breast, drew back a few steps, "to part at once is perhaps the wisest course. I see but too plainly that my love is despised. It is true that for me, without you, there is no life, no happiness possible. Still the continued martyrdom of meeting you, day by day, loving you more dearly, and yet knowing that you belong to that hated, cursed stranger, is more than I can bear. Fresh disturbances have broken out in the south, in the Dakhin, and the Emperor has ordered part of the army on service there. I will implore him to let me join them; and there in battle with the wild mountain races I may soon find, not forgetfulness, that is impossible, but an early and longed-for death."

"Ah, Siddha," said sadly the sweet, loved voice, "why such violence because a weak woman (who finds the strife against herself and her own heart too much for her) seeks for a moment's strength to withstand you? It is, as you said, better that we should part, and yet—I cannot let you go; remain, it is but a short pause; seat yourself again by my side, and let me enjoy, even though it may be for the last time, that quiet conversation, undisturbed by passion, that until now we have found so much pleasure in."

And before Siddha was quite aware of what he did, he was again seated by the side of her who had so mastered his whole mind and understanding. At her desire he seized the lute that lay beside them, and tried to bring back to his recollection one of the songs of his native land, for which, in the winning way peculiar to her, she had begged; but vainly he tried, sometimes beginning and then breaking off, his memory failed him, and dejectedly he laid down the useless lute.

"I know no more," he said. "I can neither think nor remember."

"How now, my singer," said Rezia, laughing; "must I set you the example? But let us first drink to one another." And lifting a golden goblet to her lips, she made Siddha empty his, and then began, in soft, melting tones, a Persian love song that soon brought Siddha back to himself.

"Now, then," cried he, as Rezia finished, and he began the description of a lover's reception from Kalidasa's "Seasons,"[2] "The Bride represented by the Return of Summer."

The singer ceased, and she who listened to him had drawn nearer, gazing at him with her fascinating eyes, that now shone with an unwonted glow. Suddenly he seized both her hands, and drew her to him with irresistible force.

"Rezia," he said, "Rezia, be to me as Kalidasa's bride—now and always mine!"

She softly murmured Siddha's name and flung her arms around his neck.

More than once since that evening a manly figure might have been seen in the darkness of night carefully looking around him, and then following the cactus road that led to the dwelling of the Armenian. Iravati's lotus flower had struck against the frail vessel on which he had embarked, and had been wrecked by a sultry wind.

---

[1] Akbar received a Portuguese embassy in 1578 from Goa, at the head of which was Antonio Cabral. He afterwards wrote to Goa, requesting that Jesuits might be sent to him with Christian books. Rudolf Aquaviva, a man of good family, who was afterwards murdered at Salsette, Antonio Monserrat, and Enriques (as interpreter) were selected for this mission, and despatched to Agra. They were most honourably received by Akbar, and great hopes of his conversion were conceived. But there was no practical

result. Some years afterwards, in 1590, Akbar again applied for instructors, and in 1591 three brethren came to Lahore. But after a while, seeing no hope of good, they returned to Goa.

2 Kalidasa is the most popular poet of India. His "Sakuntala" has been translated into English by Professor Monier Williams. His best known lyrical poems are the "Cloud Messenger" and the "Seasons." Portions of the latter have been translated into English by Mr. Griffith.

Chapter VIII.
A Tempter.

Once more the lovely lady of Allahabad sat on the balcony looking out towards the far-away mountains, from whence, now long ago, had approached the eagerly awaited one. Nothing had changed since that time: the same calm, silver waters and thick shade of trees, and far beyond the mountain tops, while the same cloudless sunshine lighted up the whole landscape. Ah! if only he were as unchanged—he that now took part in all the dissipation of the court and the many pleasures of the great city. Did he still think of her, and daily regard her likeness as she did his? These doubts, that had involuntarily arisen in her mind, appeared to Iravati an injury to the man whom she esteemed as highly as she loved him, and who at their last interview had so fervently pledged his word to her, and had repeated the same promises in his letters. But these had now for some time ceased. And why did he not return to her? Could he remain so long parted without making any effort to see her again, even if it were but for a day? Without doubt his duty prevented him, and he was not yet able to obtain leave of absence. But oh! how long was the time, and how the days and hours appeared to creep, as she waited and watched alone!

As on that morning long ago, her musings were interrupted by the appearance of her father the Governor.

"Iravati," he said, in his usual measured tones, "a guest has arrived."

He had come, then; he already awaited her; and her whole heart was filled with impatient joy, but of which she showed no trace.

"A guest," continued Salhana, "that for you to receive will be as great an honour as a pleasure. It is Salim the Prince, who, in obedience to his father's wishes, comes to pass some time at Allahabad."

With a great effort Iravati concealed her bitter disappointment; but to speak was to her impossible.

"Well," asked Salhana, "is not the news welcome to you? There are many who would give all they possess to enjoy the honour that awaits you. Naturally I do not wish that any of the Prince's followers should see you, but the future emperor is different; and it may be of importance both to me and to Siddha that you should gain his favour. Follow me."

As Iravati and her father entered the gallery where Salim was, he advanced to meet and greet her with his usual light-hearted courtesy. But suddenly all his boldness deserted him, and he stood still and silent. Such a noble bearing, mingled with so much modesty, beauty so grave, with an expression so winning and lovely, he never remembered to have seen in any other woman; and, contrary to his custom, he waited until Salhana had presented his daughter before greeting her.

"Noble lady," he said, "I am indeed grateful to you for the trouble you have given yourself in coming to welcome your guest. I have heard of you more than once, and—" but the courteous phrase that trembled on his lips appeared too insipid and meaningless, and he continued—at the moment not being able to find any better speech—"It is indeed a pleasure to make your personal acquaintance."

"The honour shown by your Highness to my father and to me, I prize highly," answered Iravati; "and I trust you will not find our quiet town at Allahabad too dull in comparison with the capital, with its many pleasures and diversions."

"If," returned Salim, "the noble daughter of the Governor will sometimes give me the pleasure of her company, I need not fear that my sojourn in Allahabad will be tedious. But you speak of the capital; you know it, I hope?"

"I have never been in Agra," was the answer.

"Never?" said Salim; "it is indeed time, my worthy Salhana, that your talented daughter should see more of the world than is possible in this remote fortress."

"The time will come," answered the Governor, "when my daughter is under the protection of her intended husband, my future son-in-law, whom your Highness has received with so much kindness."

Whether this recollection did not please the Prince it was difficult to discover, but he at once became silent and knitted his dark eyebrows; and when he spoke again it was on quite another subject. The conversation continued for some time longer, and then Salhana gave his daughter leave to return to her own apartment, and with a deep reverence, Iravati took her leave, rejoicing that the interview was over. The only impression left on her mind by the Emperor's son was the magnificence of his attire, although Salim himself only regarded it as a simple travelling costume.

A few minutes later, Salim, the Governor, and a third person were seated in one of the inner apartments of the fortress, well secured from all intruders or listeners, engaged, apparently, in consulting over more important questions than how time should best be spent at Allahabad. The third person was Gorakh, the priest of Durga.

"The good for which we strive, my friends," began the Prince, "seems nearer; and it appears to me that it would be wise to consider the present state of affairs, and then to think what further preparations had better be made. You,

Salhana, are, I believe, the best informed of us three; as for me, at the court much is suspected, and I come here in obedience to the wish, or rather the command, of my father. Abú-l Fazl—may Alla curse him!—is, I know, at the bottom of this; but I hope one day to have the opportunity of repaying him. And now for you, Salhana."

"I must say," he began, "that all now goes according to our wishes. In Agra, Delhi, Lahore, and other places, are the true Muhammadan Umaras and other nobles embittered to the utmost against the Emperor, through the contempt he shows for their religion and by reason of the loss of many privileges of which he has deprived them. Nothing will be more welcome than a revolution, and many will join it; including more than one of the principal mansabdars. Abdul Kadir has been of great use in all this, but we must not count much on him; he wishes to act openly, and every now and then misgivings come over him of what he calls treachery."

"And your nephew?" asked Salim.

"Is entirely one of us. How he has been won over matters not; it is enough that so it is. I had at first destined him as a spy on Akbar, but soon saw that he would be worthless as such; he is too simple, and too strictly brought up according to Kulluka's ideas, to be of any avail for such a rôle; and then, too, Akbar entirely won him over, in his usual manner, at their first meeting. But in another way he will do us better service: he has obtained the rank of mansabdar, and will soon have the chance of further advancement; so when the time fixed on comes, he will be in command of an important body of Rajpúts; and in Kashmir his name has great influence. Then, when our plan is carried out, his co-operation will be of no slight importance. At the chosen moment he will turn his troops against the Imperialists, and doubtless his example will be followed by the greater part of the Rajpúts and Patans."

"But now the plan itself, as it concerns Kashmir?" asked Salim again.

"It appears to me that nothing could be better," was the answer. "The interior strifes, for the most part fomented by us, have come to a crisis; both parties have had recourse to arms, robbers desolate the land; and, what is of greater importance, the adjacent countries which form part of Akbar's kingdom are also convulsed. This gives him a pretext of marching his army to the north, and attempting to re-establish a lasting peace by the conquest of Kashmir. His army is ready, and, if I do not deceive myself, his intention is to place himself at the head of it, after the annual celebration of his birthday has taken place. When the war begins, then suddenly our Siddha and other followers will fall from him, and join the army of Kashmir; and Akbar will have enough to do in making good his retreat. In the meantime our party in Agra will have proclaimed Salim emperor, and taken possession of the fortress and treasure. So if Akbar succeeds in his retreat, he will find more fighting awaiting him, and the end must, I suppose, be his abdication in favour of the Prince Royal."

"All," said Salim, "is well calculated, and quite in accordance with our original plan, which I see, with pleasure, is now almost ripe. One question, however; is there no danger of any part of our plan becoming known? is all arranged with caution? That letter, for example, that was sent to Kashmir,—supposing it should have got into wrong hands?"

"That letter," answered Salhana, "has safely reached its destination; and who do you think carried it? No one less than Kulluka himself."

"What unpardonable rashness!" cried Salim.

"Not in the least so," was the calm reply. "The good man had no idea of what he was undertaking, and the letter was given to him by Siddha himself, who equally had no idea of its contents. He was trapped into charging himself with its safe delivery; and had he, at the worst, glanced at it he could have given no information, and no suspicion could have fallen on us, who were naturally not named."

"Well done," said Salim, approvingly, and laughing heartily. "We thank you, Salhana, for your information. But has not our worthy Gorakh his share for us?"

"Indeed, yes," answered the Yogi, who had hitherto listened in silence; "I have not been idle; as I told you, but you thought it improbable, I have made my way not to the palace alone, but to the private apartment of the Emperor. You know how anxious he is to study the various religious systems and philosophies that are found within his realm; and so he desired to become acquainted with the ancient Yogi teaching, of which, although he had heard much, he knew little or nothing, and on which neither the learning of Faizi nor of Kulluka could throw much light. Then I found means, through some confidential friends, of letting come to his ears my great knowledge of the Yogi mysteries. Not long afterwards I was invited to court, and Akbar received privately from me the first indications of the teaching of *Concentration*,[1] whereby mortal man comes more and more into relations with the immortal Being, resolving all his thoughts in the absolute, and participating in the infinite existence, so that he attains to the power of being able at will to transport himself to the greatest distance, while apparently he remains in the same spot, and of assuming any form he pleases, or of making himself invisible or lighter than air. To support this, and not to rest on assurances alone, I brought one of my people before him, who is a great adept in magic or trickery, and made him perform a feat, at which, not without reason, the Emperor was much astonished. The man seated himself on a low wooden stool, to which was attached a bamboo, with a crooked handle like a walking-stick. Then a white cloth was spread before him, so that he was entirely concealed; and when it was again removed, he was found seated in the air, about two feet above the stool, supporting himself by resting his out-stretched hand on the crook of the bamboo. A most wonderful feat, and one that you must some day see when we have time.2 But enough: Akbar was not only astonished, but still more desirous of being admitted to our mysteries. As you understand, I took good care to tell him no more than was necessary, still more to excite his curiosity; and now I have always the opportunity of being admitted to his presence, a privilege of which I make but a sparing use, but, as you may be assured, a good one. Through my people I hear all that is of importance for our affairs. Akbar's palace and private apartments are filled with people who seek out all that happens, although in them he suspects nothing more than the followers of a religious fanatic or ascetic. By these means I can give you, Salim, and our friend Salhana information on many matters, that would not otherwise have been easily obtained."

"In truth," said Salim, "we must confess that you are almost a magician. But what do you demand as recompense for the services that you render us? Salhana, we know, wishes, when our power is established, to be named Viceroy of Kashmir; and if all goes well his wish shall be fulfilled. Nothing for nothing I say with him; but you, what are your wishes? It is best that all conditions should be settled beforehand."

"Mighty Prince, allow me to call you so by anticipation," answered Gorakh; "if I ask you nothing, simply nothing, that astonishes you, does it not? But I will try to make it simple. In my turn I ask, what do you want for yourself? You have already, one would think, everything the heart of man can desire; you have treasures, palaces, lovely women to serve you, joyous friends and companions, the most splendid wines, and only stand next to the Emperor in this powerful and flourishing kingdom, and are certain of succeeding him. And yet you have recourse to our help and that of others, your inferiors, to carry out your dark, difficult, and even dangerous plans. Why? Because you wish to govern at once, and cannot wait until the death of your father leaves the throne vacant for you. See, then, what you ask for yourself is what I ask for myself—to govern. And while you, to-day, may be said to be ruler over nothing, I reign already, though I ever strive for a more extensive power. Hundreds who, if need were, would become an army against the great of the earth, obey unconditionally my slightest sign without question or hesitation. I, the poor, unknown priest, despised by many, possess a power that you, in all your greatness, cannot rival. And by what might are they thus subject to me? Through that which nothing can resist, by which reason is silenced and the will destroyed, so that man is nothing more than a living, moving corpse—the power of religious fanaticism. Just a sign of my finger towards whom I will, towards you or some other, is enough to show more than one of my followers what new offering will be the most welcome to the never-satiated Durga; and the higher the rank, the more welcome is the victim. Even should the doomed one be warned beforehand, let him take what precaution he will, let him surround himself with servants and guards, yet nothing less than a miracle can save him. Close to him, amidst his followers, are my trusted ones; and when the right moment has struck, in the stillness of night, with no sound to awake suspicion, suddenly the cord is round his neck, and with no time for cry or groan, the long list of victims is swelled by another name. It is true that occasionally, but seldom, the intruder is seized; but he who tries to hold him grasps a body slippery as a snake, that glides from his hands, and disappears as suddenly and silently as it came. But suppose it came to the worst, and one of my Thugs was really taken, what matters it? he dies with the certainty of participating in endless bliss; and hundreds are ready to attempt to carry out what he failed in, and sooner or later success will be theirs."

The Yogi was silent for a moment, but neither of his listeners spoke. Salhana, who was well acquainted with these strange confidences, had listened with calm indifference, but saw no room for speaking; while Salim, although not wanting in personal courage, turned pale at the priest's words, and remained lost in thought, gazing before him.

"So," continued Gorakh, "I also govern in my fashion. Those who withstand me, I sweep unsuspected from my path, and those who know my power fear me; and be they of high or low rank, they do my bidding. And do you not think that power so exercised has not equal pleasures with yours? Can you imagine no feeling of pride at seeing yourself looked down upon and treated by men with slight respect, and then to know that their actions, their life and death, are to be disposed of according to your will? And I am not the only one who so thinks. I know there are others, and in far and distant lands, who, in silence and darkness, strive to govern those who are looked on as the greatest rulers in the eyes of the world. More than once in Agra, and in other places, I have spoken with men from the far West, who have come hither to try and win converts to their teaching, and, under the pretence of lending a willing ear to their preaching, I have gradually become acquainted with their aims; and from what I have learnt from them respecting the institution and working of their order, I discover that they, or at least their chiefs, seek the same God as I, though by another path. Their means, I say, are different, though scarcely more humane: we strangle men, they burn them alive. But though often they are resisted and persecuted, yet they know how, in the name of the so-called faith, to rule over not worldly sovereigns alone, but also over the spiritual head of their own Church, while they flatter him by unconditional submission and obedience to his will. And so you see, however strange it may at first appear, that the existence and enjoyment of power does not lie in its outward display, nor in its acknowledgment by others."

Still Salim remained silent as Gorakh finished; but the look which he cast towards him said more than words.

The priest laughed. "I understand," said he, slowly, "what thoughts at this moment occupy your Highness. An ally such as I may become dangerous, and the question is whether it might not be wise to get rid of him at once. But I am not simple enough to venture into the tiger's den without the certainty of returning from it in safety. My followers await me in yonder temple on the mountain; if by the morning I do not rejoin them, they know well who the goddess requires as an expiatory sacrifice for the death of her chosen priest."

"Arranged with your usual prudence," said Salim. "But, worthy Gorakh, your prudence was superfluous; we have need of your help in many cases, and should I, without reason, deprive myself of it? But we have, I think, rather wandered from the subject of our consultation. About one thing I am rather uneasy. What are we to expect, Salhana, from your brother the Minister of Kashmir? Will he choose our side? And if not, has he the power of injuring us?"

"I fear greatly that he has," answered the Governor. "He will not forsake the cause of the present king; and should he fall, would rather turn to Akbar than to us, from whom he expects nothing but mischief to his country and people."

"In that case, hand him over to me," said Gorakh.

"What do you mean?"

"No questions. I say, hand him over to me, and he shall not long stand in your way. There is another point of far greater importance: I have reason to believe that a certain important person of Kashmir, who has long been considered dead, but who, should he return to his native land, would overturn all our plans, is still alive."

"How! what!" asked Salim, much disquieted. "You don't mean——"

"I mean he whom you have already guessed—Nandigupta."

"Nandigupta! it is impossible."

"And why so? Was there ever any certainty about his death? All we know is that he suddenly disappeared and has never more been heard of, that is all. Some little time ago I discovered that among the Himálayas, near Badarinatha, a hermit now lives, whose description answers to that of the former king, and whom Kulluka, with Siddha Rama, visited on their journey here."

"That, indeed, seems dangerous," said Salim.

"In the meantime," continued Gorakh, "I have set some of mine on the track to discover the truth; and should my suspicions turn out to be just"—here he made a sign that both his hearers understood—"then he certainly will be amongst those that Durga will welcome. It is now time for me to return to my followers, and your Highness will excuse me if I take my leave."

Salim nodded his assent, wishing no doubt that it were possible that the priest should never more set his foot outside the fortress; and so for the present the three separated.

Evening after evening since that first day the sound of feasting and revelry from the lighted walls of the fortress had fallen on Iravati's ears, as she wandered alone through the park. There feasted the future emperor of Hindustan with his boon companions and dancers, seeking thus to repay himself for the weariness of the day, and to forget for a while the cares that his own ambition had brought on him. At times the faithful Nipunika, who mingled with the other servants, and often looked in at these feasts, told her mistress particulars of them, which made the blood rise to her innocent cheeks, while she enjoined silence on her servant. Could it be possible that Siddha took part in such festivals at Agra? And Salim, the future governor of so mighty a kingdom, and undisputed ruler over so many peoples, how had he sunk! in spite of the high position to which fortune had raised him.

And yet Iravati found no reason to despise the Prince when she met him, as often was the case, in company with her father. His manner, when he conversed with her, was that of a polished nobleman; and far from allowing himself the slightest freedom, the respect and reverence with which he treated her was such that the greatest princess could have found no fault with it. There was no trace of flattery or empty politeness in the words he addressed to her, but all was simple, unconstrained and natural; while his conversation was amusing, and bore witness to an unusual cultivation and extended knowledge. "Oh, if," she often thought to herself, "he would but make a better use of his many gifts, and would consider that to follow the great example set him by his noble father is his holiest duty and task!"

One evening, as, lost in thought, Iravati seated herself on one of the benches in the park, she became aware, to her astonishment, that the silence that reigned around her was unbroken by any joyous sound of revelry from the castle, and that no lights showed themselves from the windows and galleries. Only a warm wind murmured through the leaves, gently moving the branches of the trees, and every now and then a sound of flutes or bells from distant villages told of some peasant fête. Suddenly a sound of footsteps broke on the silence, and through the evening twilight a man's figure became visible, approaching the spot where the daughter of Salhana was seated. With a feeling of terror, she rose to her feet, but, to her great astonishment, recognised in the intruder the Prince himself, who, drawing nearer, greeted her with his usual respect.

"Forgive me, noble lady," he said, "if, unaware of your presence here, I unwillingly have disturbed you; receive my evening greeting, and I will not trouble you longer."

"The disturbance," said Iravati, courteously, "cannot be otherwise than agreeable to me; still I must confess that I was a little surprised. I believed your Highness was wont to pass your evenings in another and more mirthful manner than by quiet, solitary walks."

"It was so," answered Salim; "and you have a right to reproach me. I should have treated with more respect the roof that sheltered you. But let bygones be bygones. In future no unfitting noise of carousal shall disturb you in your palace, and break the silence of the night."

Iravati listened to him with astonishment. Why should he make this declaration? and what was the cause of so sudden a change?

"A change has come over me," continued Salim, "and I believe no slight one, although the time has been short. Until to-day I was—listen to me and do not draw back, I will confess all to you—I cared only for pleasure; I was dissipated and even a drunkard; I conceal nothing. But I have ceased to be all that; I have broken with my former life, and the Salim of to-day is a very different man from him of yesterday. From this hour I will live for duty and honour alone, and for the weal of the people that may some day be confided to my care. I will say farewell to all ambitious and unlawful projects, and above all to those debasing, worthless diversions, in which, until to-day, I sought distraction but never true enjoyment. I will do all this if one wish may be granted, a wish on which my happiness and my future depend, and also to a great extent that of my kingdom; and the granting of this wish depends on you."

"I do not understand you, my lord," said Iravati, who, alarmed as she was, would have been no woman had she not guessed to what the words of the Prince tended.

"You will soon understand me," he replied, "when I tell you what has caused this sudden change in my whole being. But should I not rather leave it to you to guess, if you have not already learned from my words that it can be no one but yourself? And so it is," he continued, with ever-increasing enthusiasm, though never out-stepping the bounds of reverence. "From the first moment I saw you, I knew, or rather felt, that you had an influence, a serious one, over my fate; I who never before had cast my eyes down before any one, did so at once before you, and in your presence felt myself small and nothing; and so whenever I saw you and spoke to you, and came to know you better, I felt still more clearly that my future lay in your hands. I began to feel a horror of myself, my manner of life, and so-called friends who aided me in passing evenings, and often nights, in so unworthy a manner; yet I would not at once resolve to break with it all; and I confess that when our feasts were in progress your image often faded away from my mind, as wine obscured my senses; but then when morning broke, with what shame and anger I regarded myself! To-day my resolve is taken, and, as you see, is carried out. All is quiet, there is no sound of revelry, my dancers are dismissed, and most of my guests have already taken their departure from Allahabad, or will do so to-morrow. All that is your work, and may it be carried out still further! For that one thing is indispensable, we must no longer remain acquaintants, meeting occasionally; a closer bond must unite us. Iravati, is it possible to say more clearly what I feel for you? Well, then, I——"

"Ah! no, no, my lord!" cried Iravati, clasping her hands supplicatingly; "do not say the words that are hardly on your lips, for I may not hear them."

"May not," repeated Salim, "or will not? When a request is made to you by me, it seems there should be no question whether you may hear it."

"Both then," replied Iravati, firmly, "both may not and will not; may not, because my word and faith bind me to another; and will not and cannot grant your wish because my whole heart and life are given to that other."

It was fortunate for her that the increasing darkness hid the fierce expression that these frank, imprudent words called forth on the Prince's face; had she seen it she would have shuddered at the thought of what might befall that other from such a rival.

"Consider well," said Salim, after a moment's silence; "think what you recklessly fling from you for the sake of a young man once dear to you, and who for the moment still appears to be so, but who, even should he remain true to you, can never offer what the future ruler of the empire of the Mughals can give. I do not speak of the treasures that should be yours, or of the luxury that would surround you, seated by my side, and ruling over the kingdoms and princes of Hindustan, for I know how little temptation there is in all that for a soul noble and elevated such as yours. Still it is not to be despised. You think you know what riches and luxury are, but what you have hitherto seen is but tinsel in comparison with the splendour of the palaces and gardens of Agra and Delhi. But let that be. Think what a glittering future you throw from you in choosing to become the wife of a simple unknown nobleman, instead of ruling over the deeds of the mightiest monarchs, while all the great and noble bow before you, and the prosperity of millions depends on you. Even as I place my lot in your hands, so I swear from to-day to place also that of my future subjects. Your decisions shall be my laws, for I know well that you will command nothing but what is noble, good and wise, and no one in the whole kingdom oppressed justly or unjustly but will find protection in you."

Vainly the future ruler awaited an answer. Iravati was silent, but it was a silence that gave no hope of consent. She had turned from him as if to hide her sorrow, and buried her face in her hands. Even this glorious future made no impression on her.

"Iravati," said Salim, in a deeply moved voice, "do not at once deprive me of the peace with which your appearance filled my whole soul. Through you I had become quite a different man from what I was; do not let me fall back again. Have pity on me, and on the thousands that with you by my side would find a benefactor in me, but without you, in all probability, a tyrant. I am weak, I know, but I would be strong as a hero, if from your words and presence I might draw my strength. Why should it be refused me? It will only cost you one word, and the crown of India lies at your feet; and you have nothing to do but to stretch out your hand and place it on your head. But I see," he continued, passionately, "that my respect, my admiration, and my love are nothing to you; you despise the prince for a miserable adventurer, to whom you are bound by chains forged without thought; but think well what you do, what you venture, and what fate may await you and him also, if ever the love of one powerful as I is turned to rage and hate. But I am speaking wild and foolish words," he added sadly, letting his head sink on his breast. "What right have I to your love? However high my station, I am not worthy of you. I am old before my time; that other is young, beautiful, with a heart unspoiled by the world. Why should I then complain? what I am is my own doing, and that of an unhappy fate, which has placed me in a station for which I am unfitted. But ah! how different, how different might all have been, if fate had thrown you in my way earlier! Now it is too late, too late!"

"My Prince," said Iravati, gently, "you do yourself wrong; you have reason for reproaching but not for despising yourself. And be assured, I do not despise or scorn you, even if I can never be yours; in truth, had I known you earlier, even as you are now, but before another had won my love and faith, I might have returned your affection. You cannot really wish me to break my pledged word; and if I did you would lose the respect for me on which your love is grounded. But even in that case, which now is impossible, your high rank would have been no temptation. The luxury and splendour in which you live could never have been my element; and the great responsibility you were ready to lay on my shoulders, I could never have borne. But why should we lose ourselves in thought of what might have been, but can never be? The unknown powers that rule our fates have willed otherwise, let us submit to their decision, which must be just and wise for you as well as I. And so leave me, my gracious prince and lord, in the lowly state which you found me; go and forget me, now and always; and if you do remember me, let your thoughts be of that moment when nobler and more elevated feelings made themselves master of your soul. As for me, my thoughts will follow you in your future, which will, I hope and trust, be rich in noble deeds, when you succeed to the throne of the great Emperor; and be certain that amongst your numberless subjects none will watch your path in life with deeper interest than she who now implores you to leave her, and to release her from the hard duty of disobedience to your wishes."

Seeking for an answer both fitting and convincing, stood the despot who perhaps never before in his life had met with contradiction. Silently he stood before the young girl; now about to speak, and then restraining himself, seeking vainly for words to give expression to the conflicting feelings that thronged his brain. At last he approached Iravati, seized her hand and lifted it to his lips, then turned and disappeared in the darkness, without a single word.

The next morning, greatly to Salhana's alarm, he heard that the Prince had left the Castle of Allahabad accompanied by a single servant, but whither he had gone no one knew.

---

1 *Yoga* (concentration) is the name of the second division of the Sánkhya system of Hindu philosophy. It was first taught by Patanjali. He asserted that the soul *was* Iswara (God), and that man's liberation is to be obtained by concentrating his attention on Iswara. *Yoga* is, therefore, the union of man's mind with the Supreme Soul. When a man is perfect in profound meditations or "steadyings of the mind," he gains a knowledge of the past and future, he has the power of shrinking into the form of the minutest atom, and gains mastery over Nature's laws.

2 Professor Wilson records instances of a Brahman sitting in the air wholly unsupported for twelve minutes, and another for forty minutes.—"Wilson's Works," i. p. 209.

Chapter IX.
The Weighing of the Emperor.

What a bustle was there in the thronged bazar as Siddha, in the morning, wandered through the busy rows of shops, on which were spread out in rich abundance everything that could tempt the eye and purse. And what a strange and wonderful mingling of various peoples and races, the different representatives of which jostled against and crossed each other's paths without betraying any surprise, so well accustomed were they to the sight. Here the natives of the land, Hindus of more or less pale complexions, their servants of various bronzed shades; there, too, the proud ruling races—Persians, Arabs, and Tatars, Armenians and Jews from the west, and also sons of the Celestial Kingdom, with their long tails and wide flowered robes; and there men who especially struck Siddha, as he had never before seen their like, men most strangely clad, with pointed, broad-brimmed hats decorated with feathers, short doublets, wide velvet trousers, and high boots, and with long, straight swords hanging from coloured shoulder-belts. They were in company of the spiritual Fathers, one of whom but a short time since, had been admitted to the presence of the Emperor.

Among all this throng many had come to make their own purchases, others only to wander and contemplatingly watch the bustling crowd. Numbers of women, of many nations and classes, were also to be seen, some in the costume of the people, simple, but graceful and pleasing; others in coloured and gaudy Persian attire, and some closely veiled, according to the strict Muhammadan law, and showing nothing human excepting a pair of red-slippered feet, and a pair of dark eyes that glittered through round holes in the upper veil that enveloped everything. Some were busied with household purchases, others with the acquisition of useful knick-knacks.

Just as Siddha was about to inquire from some of the passers-by who the strange men were, he saw his friend and benefactor Faizi approach, and addressed his question to him.

"They are Franks," was the answer, "called Portuguese; they come from far-away countries in the West, for the sake of commerce; and those with them have come to try and convert us to what they say is the only religion which can save souls."

"And those two," asked Siddha, "coming from the other side? do they belong to them? They wear nearly the same clothing, but their companions appear to me fairer, and how red their beards are!"

"They are also Franks," answered Faizi, "though not quite the same as the others. They are English,[1] who seek to drive out the Portuguese, but with little success; however, they are well received by our Emperor and our great people."

A few years later, Faizi would have been able to point out others among these visitors from the West, who, though also included under the name of Franks, yet were quite different. He could have pointed to the robust and somewhat plump figures and good-humoured faces of Hollander and Zeelander, who, under Pieter van der Broeche,2 came to seek their own fortunes and those of their masters the Directors of the East India Company. For long years they were considered both by English and Portuguese as their most formidable rivals in the markets of Hindustan, and as men who knew how to sustain the fame of the flag of the Netherlands in the Indian waters against the Gijs, or "Gijsooms" as they mockingly, though not very grammatically, named their arch enemies. But their time was not then come.

As the two Englishmen passed by, Siddha looked at them with a curiosity which, though perhaps natural, at first seeing such strangers, yet was far from courteous; but Siddha felt—although he had heard nothing of these people—very little respect for them, and even Faizi seemed to consider them hardly worthy of a glance.

"Cursed proud Moors!" muttered one of these sons of Albion in his own tongue as he passed. Had these men, the haughty Indians and half-despised English, been able to cast one single look into the future, and could the former have guessed that the descendants of the latter would one day rule over their people and country, they would certainly have observed them with more attention. With still closer interest would they have gazed, if anyone had told them that these strangers sprang from the same race, and stood nearer to Siddha than many of his friends whose origin was from the Semitic race.

"The visits of all these strangers," said Faizi, "do us no harm; on the contrary they give fresh impulse to our trade and various industries; and from them also we have many good painters and other artists. Then we have learnt much from them respecting their own countries. Still they must not attempt to play the master here, which appears to be rather according to their tastes."

"Then surely we should show them the door," said Siddha.

"That would soon happen, I can assure you. But now for another subject. Have you tried my bay that we spoke of the other day?"

"Indeed I have," answered Siddha, "and with the greatest pleasure; it is a magnificent animal." And he broke out with praises of Faizi's horse.

"You are pleased with him, then?" he answered. "I will send him to your stables; you can keep him if you will; and in the coming campaign he will be of use to you. Your grey is a beautiful horse and well broke, but scarcely strong enough; and the bay is uncommonly so. I ride him but seldom, for I must confess I have become rather lazy and prefer a quieter animal."

"But," said Siddha, overcome at such goodness, "this is indeed a costly present, which I have not deserved. Your bay is a splendid thoroughbred Arab, such as I have never before ridden."

"When I offer my friends anything it ought to be worth having," said Faizi. "Now I want to tell you of something else: about a meeting that took place yesterday evening at the palace, and at which I wish you had been present. In spite of state troubles that again overwhelm the Emperor, he found both time and inclination to hold one of his philosophical and theological gatherings, for which, just now, there is an opportunity, as the Christian missionaries from Goa are again here. Yesterday a number of Ulamas and Mullahs were assembled in one of the great halls of the palace. Among them naturally Abdul Kadir appeared; then there were the Jesuits, a Jew, and a Parsee, and your former tutor Kulluka, who has returned here, and whom doubtless you have already greeted; my brother Abú-l Fazl was also present, and I also had that honour, and took for my part in the course of the discussion your ancient atheistical philosophy of nature. Akbar himself inclined a little my way, while Kulluka defended the orthodox Brahmanical Vedanta,[3] and Abú-l Fazl the ordinary human ground. Kulluka detected him now and then in Buddhistic heresies, but let them pass, saying there was no Buddhist present to defend his creed. You know there are some here, but none fit to take part in these discussions. The Emperor scarcely took any part in what went on, but only listened; and perhaps the most remarkable part of these discourses was their conclusion. Nothing could be better ordered or more courteous than the beginning; our Mullahs, calm and grave, saying but little; nothing could be more gentle than the Padres, piping as sweetly as bird-catchers; the Jew, a follower of Maimonides,[4] was the same, but very silent, and not quite at his ease; the Parsee was poetical and not always very intelligible; and as for us, we every now and then threw in some problem or argument, gathered from the philosophers of old days, or that we had learnt from the Arabs or Persians, and which did not appear to be quite to the tastes of the disputants. By degrees they began to grow warm, and from arguments proceeded to assertions, and from assertions to hard words, especially between the Muhammadans and Jesuits, though on the whole we were not spared; and in the end there was shouting, cursing, and noise, in spite of the presence of the Emperor, enough to deafen us. In all this the Mullahs were foremost, who, as you understand, consider themselves as the most injured. Akbar sat watching this foolish scene, not without secret satisfaction, and glanced every now and then at me with a smile; but at last it became too much for him, and he saw that in his presence it was not fitting such a spectacle should continue. 'Faizi,' said he, signing to me, 'have the door opened to these people, as they no longer know how to conduct themselves. I gave them the fullest opportunity for defending their various religious theories against each other, in order that I might decide who had the best grounds for his opinions; and what have they done? Each has endeavoured to outdo his neighbour in shouting and cursing; nothing else. Let there be an end of it.' 'Sire,' I answered, 'we had better send them all away; if two only should remain, there will be no end to the strife.' Akbar laughed, but rising from the seat where he had calmly remained all through the storm, he said, in his powerful voice, which at once enforced silence on all around, 'We thank you, gentlemen, for the pleasant evening we have passed, due to your kindness and interesting discussions. We hope for another such interview before long, but the present one is closed,' and with a sign of his hand he dismissed them. The greater part withdrew, grumbling. Oh, Siddha, how foolish men are thus to curse and hate each other for the sake of abstract problems, of which they know nothing, and which, even if they did, would not advance them one single step in the practice of what honour and duty enjoin!"

"I quite agree with you; and to follow the two last are often hard enough," answered Siddha, with a sigh, knowing far more of the difficulties of which he spoke than the other suspected.

"But now tell me," said Faizi, "how it comes that you are here; I thought that you, with your men, were already on your way to join the camp."

"We had started," said Siddha, "but received counter-orders on the road. We are to remain some days longer at Agra, to my great pleasure, as it gives me the opportunity of being present at the great festival of to-day, which celebrates the Emperor's birthday, of which I have heard so much."

That there was another reason for rejoicing at a longer delay in Agra, Siddha did not think it necessary to add.

"That reminds me," said Faizi, "it is time to go to the palace before the durbar. The Emperor receives, as you know, the foreign ambassadors to-day. Come with me, and you can take your place among the officers of your rank."

Although Siddha had been more than once present at a durbar, yet as with Faizi he entered the great throne-hall, where the Emperor had already taken his place, the impression made upon him was almost as great as on the first occasion. He looked with admiration at the splendid white marble columns and walls inlaid with beautiful mosaics, delicate arches, with silk and velvet curtains falling in rich folds. He was much struck by the great assembly, which was larger and more splendid than any he had yet seen. At one end of the hall, lit by a softened light from above, was the Great Mughal, seated on a throne sparkling with precious stones; on both sides, standing in long ranks, were the Umara,5 the ministers, generals, and nobles of high rank, and then ambassadors from neighbouring countries in their various costumes, among them the two Jesuits; and at the end the lesser officials and officers, amongst whom Siddha, according to his rank, had taken his place.

The chief part of the ceremony was the exchange of presents. The ambassadors and others approached the Emperor in their turn. On reaching the throne they raised their right hands to their foreheads and bowed their heads before the Emperor, then placed their presents, consisting chiefly of costly objects of art, by the side of the step on which the throne was raised, and in their turn they received presents on behalf of the Emperor. Aquaviva also drew near the Mughal, bearing a splendidly bound Latin Bible, which, according to custom, he was about to lay down; but Akbar, rising from his throne, advanced a step or two, and took the book from the hands of the missionary. "We thank you, worthy Father," he said, "for this kindly thought, and trust that what we have to offer will not be less welcome to you," and taking from the hands of a Brahman standing by his side a voluminous and beautifully ornamented manuscript, he presented it to the Jesuit, saying, "This is a copy of the 'Atharva-Veda,'6 one of the most ancient of our holy books of India; it is accompanied by a Persian translation."

With deep respect Aquaviva received the imperial gift, though one might question whether in truth he was much pleased, and if he did not see in it some allusion to the meeting of the preceding evening; which was the more probable as the Emperor was always informed beforehand what presents were to be made him, that the return might be appropriate. But whatever the Padre thought, it was not difficult to guess what impression this affair made on the orthodox Brahmans. There was a frown on almost every forehead in their ranks, and Abdul Kadir could scarcely restrain his indignation. They could not read the meaning of the return present, and how by it Akbar wished to show that he took no part with the Christians. All they saw was the special honour shown to a Christian. Abú-l Fazl, who understood it better, nevertheless shook his head, vexed at the needless defiance and insult to the Muhammadans offered by the (in other respects) humane and wise Akbar; still he confessed that they almost deserved it for their unmanly conduct of the previous evening.

After the ceremonial of the reception of presents was over, the Mughal was for some time occupied with giving audiences and appointments; among others our Siddha was called to him.

"Siddha Rama," he said, "with good reason we are content with you, and, to prove it, we name you from to-day Mansabdar over a thousand; show yourself always worthy of our trust and favour."

A deep colour mounted to Siddha's face, as silently, according to the usage, he bent his head before the Emperor, in token of his gratitude for this fresh favour. He worthy of Akbar's confidence! Could there be one in the army that deserved it less? Yet the Emperor had need of his interest and assistance in Kashmir, so that it was not generosity and kindness alone which led to this promotion. Akbar only saw in the confusion of the young warrior an easily explained and praiseworthy modesty at finding himself so openly laden with favours, and nodded to him kindly as he signed to him that he might withdraw.

It was now almost time that the people's feast should begin, and for it was destined a field not far from the town. Towards it was now streaming from all the streets and along all the roads a brilliantly coloured throng, some on foot, some riding either on horses or richly caparisoned elephants; some, too, were on camels laden with eatables and refreshments of all kinds for the many that cared to take part in the rejoicings. Mingling in the merry crowd were Siddha and his friend Parviz, whom he had met on leaving the palace, and who had heartily congratulated him on his new command.

"And you," said Siddha, "how go your affairs?"

"You mean my own private ones, do you not?" answered the other, laughing. "On the whole they go on well. Lately I have several times seen her to whom my heart belongs; and, though of course it was in secret, yet I have reasons for suspecting her father, Todar Mal,[7] knew all about it, although he gave himself the airs of knowing nothing. I believe my uncle Faizi has something to do with this favourable change in affairs. 'May Allah bless him!' as the pious Abdul Kadir would say." And here the good Parviz wandered off into a stream of praises of the beauty and virtues of her he loved, which, deeply interesting to him, was not quite so much so for his hearer. However this might be, the one subject occupied the two friends until they reached the spot where the festival was to be held. Here the view was as full of life as that of the court had been, but far fuller of mirth and merriment. Endless numbers moved in lightly coloured groups over the great undulating plain where countless tents, great and small, were pitched. Above all, the elephants with their dark bodies, bright-coloured cloths, and richly ornamented *haudas*, contrasted picturesquely with the riders and those on foot. The imperial elephants were decorated with golden breast and head plates, set with large smaragds; and their gigantic bodies bore a treasure enough to make the fortune of any simple burgher. On one of these the Mughal himself was seated, and dismounting in a circle of his courtiers, and followed by them, repaired to the spot where the great ceremony of the day was to be celebrated. This ceremonial deserves attention, so strange and impressive was it. Many have endeavoured in different ways to explain what it betokened, but the true meaning has hitherto escaped all historians.[8]

On a little height was erected a large and strong pair of scales, large enough easily to hold a man. One scale was heaped with gold, silver, and precious stones, while the other stood empty, high in the air. On this the Emperor now took his place, in sight of hundreds and thousands of his subjects, who crowded round from all sides; and the other scale was added to or taken from until it exactly balanced the illustrious person of the Great Mughal, who well held his own against the precious metal. It was a pity that other things could not be laid in the scale, such as duty, honour, faith, and enthusiasm for all that is good and beautiful; then surely Akbar would not have been found wanting in the balance. When the weighing was over he stept calmly from the scales, and the gold and silver were distributed amongst the crowd. Towards the end the Emperor mixed among those around him, throwing among the bystanders small golden objects in the form of flowers and fruits, addressing here and there kind and friendly words—confirming many afresh in their conviction that in Akbar the people had not only a great and powerful, but also a benevolent ruler, to whose heart the well-being of his subjects was dearer than his own greatness.

After the grave ceremonies of the day were over, the real festivities began, and every kind of diversion occupied the numberless visitors. Here the jugglers and conjurors displayed their foolish art, and performed feats of strength; there dancers to the sound of monotonous music, and with slow movements, performed their dances; and further on, horsemen at full gallop lifted rings from the ground at the end of their long lances. On one spot was a wonderful and horrible exhibition of two of those beings peculiar to India, who think they combine a religious act with self-torture. They were suspended twenty feet above the ground by means of an iron hook driven into their backs and hung by a rope to a cross-beam.9 Here, where such a sight was rare, it excited great attention, and Parviz stood gazing at it with interest, very different from Siddha's indifference, who was well accustomed to such spectacles.

"What can possess the people?" said Parviz to his friend. "It is said they do this prompted by religious fervour; but if so, why do they choose a day of public rejoicing and festivity to exhibit themselves? It is not a pleasant sight, but I cannot understand how it is they appear so at their ease, and so free from pain."

"Perhaps I can explain it to you," said Siddha. "You know that such tortures as we are now looking at are considered by our fanatics as meritorious actions, by which heaven may be gained; and those that gaze upon these martyrs, and give them money, participate in the merit; and the more superstitious the people are, so much the greater are the gains. But the secret of their art is not known with certainty, although I believe there are grounds for suspecting how it is done. If I am not deceived, they are always accompanied by women, although they are never seen with them, and these for about half a day before an exhibition pinch them between the shoulder-blades until the spot is without feeling, and the hook can be inserted without causing them any pain."

"A wonderful kind of pleasantry," remarked Parviz.

"Yes, and a wretched one, too. Whatever support it receives from superstition, by respectable Brahmans it is only looked upon with contempt. But did you not say there were to be elephant and wild beast fights?"

"Certainly, and by yonder flag I see they are about to begin; let us make our way there and find a place."

This was not difficult, for their rank gave them instant admission to the space railed off, and provided with seats, where the combats were to take place. In the midst the Emperor was seated surrounded by his courtiers. They had not waited long when from the opposite sides the fighting elephants entered the arena, each covered with a splendid cloth, and mounted by a brightly dressed mahout. Very little preparation was necessary. No sooner did the gigantic animals approach each other, than, rising on their hind legs with a snort, they seized each other with their trunks, each endeavouring to stab his foe with his long tusks, while their riders, now clinging by their knees behind the creatures' ears, and now holding by their hands to the girth of the cloth, still kept their places. For some time the fight continued with uncertain fortune; now one elephant was driven backwards, and now the other. At last one was overthrown. His mahout leaping nimbly to the ground alighted on his feet, and the rider of the victor struck his hook into the constantly kept open wound behind the ears, and forced him to draw back without injuring his fallen foe. The Emperor applauded loudly, his example being followed by the courtiers and spectators, and then they slowly left the tribunes.

"Akbar seems to have a great liking for these combats," said Siddha to his friend, as they continued their walk.

"Yes," was the answer; "Akbar likes everything that displays courage and dexterity, whether in man or beast. As you know, he is of unusual strength himself, and unsurpassed by any in the use of arms; and his personal courage in war and hunting is of that description that one might call recklessness. He seems to seek danger instead of avoiding it, and his generals and hunting comrades have at times enough to do with him when his blood is up. You must have heard of his adventures; certainly some are exaggerated, but you can trust to Faizi, who has been present at many, and who will tell you about them some day."

Thus talking they wandered on, and at last having seen all they wished, turned towards the city. Suddenly Siddha stood still, struck with astonishment: his eye had accidentally fallen on the *hauda* of a magnificently caparisoned elephant, and the lady he there saw, with one or two others leaning back on the silken cushions, could be no other than Rezia! Her thin veil fastened with diamonds had been pushed on one side, there could be no mistake, and there by her side was the well-known servant. But what was she doing here, she who lived in solitude, carefully hidden from all eyes—just at this moment, too, when she believed that Siddha had marched with the army! Could she have deceived him? could she be other than she had told him?

As calmly and indifferently as was possible, he asked his companion, pointing to Rezia, who had not seen him among the foot passengers—"Do you know that lady?"

"She with the veil thrown back, and a servant holding a fan of peacock feathers?" asked Parviz. "Certainly I know her, and I wonder that you do not; however, of late she has shown herself but seldom. She is"—and here Parviz named a name which gave our friend such a shock as never before in his whole life he had experienced; and he felt as if, standing on the brink of a precipice amongst his northern mountains, he had been seized with a sudden dizziness and fallen into the abyss beneath. "She is," said Parviz, "a lady of whom, at any rate, you must have heard—Gulbadan,10 Faizi's wife."

---

1 These Englishmen were John Newbery and Ralph Fitch, merchants, William Leedes, a jeweller, and James Story, a painter. They came to India by way of Aleppo and Ormuz, and were sent prisoners to Goa by the Portuguese Governor of Ormuz. At Goa they fell in with a priest named Thomas Stevens, who was an Englishman, a native of Wiltshire, and who afterwards wrote an account of his voyage. They also met the Dutch traveller Linschoten. This was in January 1584. Stevens interceded for them, and "stood them in much stead." In September 1585 they reached Agra, and also visited Fathpúr Sikri. Thence Newbery set out on his return journey through Persia. Fitch went to Bengal, whence he visited Pegu and Malacca, and eventually took ship for Cochin and Ormuz, in 1589. Leedes took service under Akbar, who gave him a house and suitable allowances. Newbery had a letter from Queen Elizabeth to "Zelabdim Echebar."—See "Hakluyt," ii. pp. 375 to 399, 2nd ed.

2 Pieter van der Broeche was the President of the Dutch factory at Surat. He had an intimate knowledge of the commerce and exchanges of the East, and of Akbar's revenue system; and was also a man of great learning. He supplied much valuable information to De Laet, which appears in the work entitled, "De Imperio Magni Mongolis, sive India vera. Joannes de Laet. Lugduni Batavorum. 1631." Indian events are brought down to 1628 in this work.

3 The Vedanta is the second great division of the Mimansa school of Hindu philosophy. The name is from the Sanscrit *Veda* and *anta* (end), meaning that it gives the end or ultimate aim of the Vedas, which is a knowledge of Brahma or the Supreme Spirit; and of the relations in which man's soul stands towards the Universal Soul.

4 Moses ben Maimon, or Maimonides, one of the most celebrated of the Jewish Rabbis, was born at Cordova in 1133. He studied philosophy and medicine under Averroes. He retired to Egypt, where he died at the age of seventy. His chief work is the "Moreh Nevochim" ("Teacher of the Perplexed") in which he explains difficult passages, types, and allegories in the Old Testament. He wrote several other treatises on the Jewish law, and founded a college at Alexandria for his countrymen.

5 *Amír* (corruptly *Emir*) is a Muhammadan nobleman of high rank. *Umara* (corruptly *Omrah*) is the nobility of a Muhammadan court collectively.

6 The "Atharva Veda," in the opinion of Professor Wilson, is of later date than the "Rig," "Yajar," and "Sama" Vedas. It contains many forms of imprecation for destruction of enemies, prayers for averting calamities, and hymns to the gods.

7 Raja Todar Mal, the celebrated financier and administrator, was a Khatri and native of Lahore. His father died when he was a child, leaving him no provision, and he entered life as a writer. He was employed by the talented Afghan ruler Shir Shah, who drove out Humayun, Akbar's father, and afterwards under Akbar himself. His revenue settlement of Gujrat was highly approved by the Emperor; and he was similarly employed in other provinces of India. Abú-l Fazl says of him, in the "Akbar-nama,"—"For honesty, rectitude, manliness, knowledge of business, and administrative ability, he was without a rival in Hindustan." Todar Mal died at Lahore on November 10th, 1589.

8 See Blochmann's "Ain-i-Akbari," i., p. 266, for an account of the ceremony of weighing the Emperor.

9 The *Charak-puja*. It is the swinging festival held on the sun entering Aries. As a religious observance it is confined to Bengal; but the swinging is practised in other parts of India as a feat of dexterity, for obtaining money. The swinger is suspended by hooks passed through the skin above each blade-bone, and connected by ropes with one end of a lever traversing an upright post with a circular motion. *Charak* means a wheel.

10 "Gulbadan" means *rose-body*. The Emperor had an aunt of that name, own sister of his uncle Askari, who married Khizr Khan, Governor of the Punjab. She made a pilgrimage to Mecca.

Chapter X.
Surprises.

"How can the name of that woman affect you?" asked Parviz, astonished at Siddha's strange bearing. "You have not, I trust, fallen in love with Gulbadan at first sight? I would scarcely advise you to do so; although Faizi is goodness itself, he is not always quite gentle where his wife is concerned, with whom he is desperately in love."

"It was a passing remembrance," replied Siddha, recovering himself as well as possible, "awakened by that name, but which has nothing to do with Faizi's wife."

"So much the better," rejoined the other; and they silently proceeded on their way.

To be alone, to escape from Parviz as soon as possible,—no other thought occupied his companion, and seeing one of his men walking up and down, "Excuse me," he said, "but I have to speak with that man, and, thanking you for your pleasant company, I must for the moment say farewell." And hastily greeting his friend, and beckoning to the horseman to approach, he was soon in conversation with him on subjects connected with the service, but as suddenly broke it off directly Parviz was out of sight. He then hurried on, not minding where his steps carried him, only on and on, thinking and dreaming, as though bewildered with drink. "Gulbadan, Faizi's wife!" Treachery again, then, though this time involuntary, yet of the worst description, against the man by whom when a stranger he had been received with the utmost kindness, and in whom he had always found the truest of friends, and to whom he owed privileges and favours that no one in his place could have obtained without such protection. Treachery, too, against the Emperor, who had laden him with unexpected and undeserved favours; treachery and shameless faithlessness against her to whom once he had given his heart and pledged his word; and all for the sake of one who had deceived him,—and whom he must despise,—and yet love above everything and for ever. What should he do? Honour and duty spoke loudly,—flight, instant flight, alone could save him. He knew and felt that delay would only again place him on the brink of a bottomless abyss. But to leave her so suddenly, without any preparation, any explanation—she, who, though weak, still loved him; and if she had led him astray, she, too, had sacrificed honour and duty;—would that be acting rightly? would it be fair? was it possible that he could do it?

For a long time Siddha wandered on, not knowing where he went. At last he looked round, and found he was not far from the city, and near the habitation of Rezia—the Rezia of happy days now gone by—and which, as now he remembered, was situated close to Faizi's villa. Evening began to close in; it was the hour that he was wont to approach the garden wall, and, at a well known signal, to be admitted by the servant. A few moments later he again stood by the wall, gave the signal, and, as the door was opened, hurried in.

Rezia, or rather Gulbadan, was reposing comfortably on a divan by the verandah, little thinking of Siddha, who she imagined was on his way to join the army, when suddenly the man she thought miles away rushed into her apartments.

"How, Siddha!" she cried, starting in alarm to her feet. "I thought you were gone."

"Rezia, Gulbadan!" said Siddha, with assumed calm, "I know you now; you have deceived me, and the man to whom I owe so much, if not everything. I come to bid you farewell; honour commands me to go, but without flight I know that I could not. To-morrow or to-day I leave Agra, never to see it again, nor you."

In a second, and before Siddha had finished, Faizi's wife had comprehended all. She had, convinced that her lover had left in command of his detachment, seen no reason why she should not openly show herself at the great festival, nor for keeping herself veiled. Then he must have seen and recognised her, and have heard her real name; the affair was too plain to require any explanation, nor were questions and explanations among her tactics. She looked at him entreatingly with her soft blue eyes, raising her clasped hands towards him, then tottered, and without one word sank back on the divan, hiding her face in the cushions.

For some time Siddha gazed silently at her; so beautiful, so irresistibly lovely had she never appeared to him as just in that moment when he had determined never again to see her; and he felt that this last look would be imprinted on his mind for ever.

"Go, go at once," whispered a voice to him; "no words more, nor farewells, or it will be too late to escape the enchantment, that already begins to work."

Then she slowly raised her head, thrusting back the luxurious locks that fell in waves around her, and passed her hand over her face, as one that awakes from a deep sleep or swoon.

"Rezia," said Siddha, "let me call you so once more; I thought to leave you without one word of preparation would not have been honourable; but do not make this parting still harder to me. You, I trust, will agree that to part is unavoidable. Unknowingly, I have sinned against hospitality, and repaid the truest friendship with the grossest ingratitude. To continue doing so would be the worst of crimes."

"You are right, my friend," said Rezia, gently. "To part, I feel, must to you appear unavoidable. I have long feared it, and for that reason dissembled my name; but hear me for a few moments before you leave me for ever, for I would not that you should remember me with contempt. Listen to what I have to say, not in defence, but in excuse of my conduct. I deceived you, it is true, and more than once. I began by deceiving you the first time we met. I had seen you shortly after your arrival at Agra, though you did not see me, and that first sight of you awoke an interest that was not diminished by what I heard in answer to my inquiries, and then rashly I determined to make your acquaintance, making use of that letter to Kashmir as my pretence. To what that acquaintance led, aided by my weakness and love, alas! you know too well; but then, indeed, I did not know that there was any bond of friendship between Faizi and you. And when later on, to my horror, I discovered it, I should have had the courage to break off all that we were to each other by confessing who I was. But, ah! I was weak, Siddha; weak as only a woman who loves can be, who loves the man of her choice with passionate fondness. I feared the parting that your sense of honour would pronounce to be necessary, and I was silent. Can you forgive me, Siddha, before we bid each other good-bye for ever?" And timidly, as though afraid of his anger, she stretched out her hand to him, and sank back, slowly and wearily, on the cushions, her eyes filled with tears.

For a time he struggled with himself a bitter and terrible battle, but, alas! of too short duration.

"Rezia," he cried, clasping in his arms the woman who not only ruled him but forced him to forget all that honour bade him to hold dear,—"Rezia, without you there is neither life nor existence, and with you no crime and no shame."

He had indeed spoken the truth, and made use of no exaggeration when he told her that she was dearer to him than life, and dearer than honour. And so the evening passed on. Siddha was partly disturbed, partly overwhelmed with an indescribable happiness; sometimes despising himself, and then again rejoicing in his fatal passion. It was late before he passed down the well-known path, and was about to open the little door in the garden wall, when, to his astonishment, it opened, and the figure of a man passed through, who, without remarking him, attempted to close it after him. But a sudden exclamation from Siddha made him turn round. Who could it be? Faizi himself perhaps. Siddha could have bitten out his tongue for his foolish imprudence, but it was too late.

"What, in the name of Shaitan, are you doing here?" cried the new comer; and Siddha at once recognised the voice of Prince Salim, whose figure was scarcely visible in the dimness of night.

"With an equal or a better right, I might ask that of you," was the bold reply. The clatter of arms told Siddha that the Prince had laid his hand on his sword, and he on his side did the same. Salim approached a step or two, and recognising his opponent, let his sword fall back into its sheath.

"Ha! my friend Siddha Rama," he cried, in no little astonishment, "so we catch you in one of your nightly adventures! Still, there is not much harm in that for a young man like you. Do not fear that I shall betray you, nor need you be jealous. You must know that the chosen one of your heart is, to a certain degree, mixed up in our plans, and I come occasionally to talk them over with her in secrecy and under cover of night; but perhaps at this moment she will be hardly inclined to discuss such dry subjects, and it will be as well for me to put off my visit."

And Salim turned towards the doorway, and, having let Siddha through, carefully shut it.

"I suppose you are now returning to your lodging? My path lies in the opposite direction," said he; "but," he added, to Siddha, who, not knowing what to say, stood silently listening to him, "let this meeting remain a secret between us, it will be our wisest course." And so saying, Salim disappeared in the darkness.

"He has accidentally rendered me a great service," muttered the Prince to himself, as he hurried on; "he has put me in possession of a secret that can be of inestimable worth. In all this I recognise that snake."

The next day one of Salim's most trusted men was wandering round the country house, and before long found an opportunity of talking with Gulbadan's servant. The bargain he proposed was quickly concluded, the servant betraying her mistress's secrets willingly, for the Prince, naturally, could pay more than she and Siddha together. On the evening of the same day the servant presented herself at the palace, and was received by Salim's confidant, to whom she gave two papers folded in the form of letters, and hurried back to her mistress's abode with the price she had received for them. The following day Salim was on his road back to Allahabad with a small escort.

There sojourned one solitary and sad. For a long time Iravati had heard nothing of her betrothed. In the beginning, shortly after his arrival in Agra, he had, as she well remembered, written her two letters, as overflowing as his earlier ones had been with assurances of his love that could never be shaken; since then she had received no letter from him, though she heard from others that he was well and rising in favour with the Emperor. What, then, could be the reason of his continued silence? A terrible doubt began more and more to make itself master of her, but she strove against it, drawing fresh strength from her faith in the word and honour of her Siddha. Once as she sat lost in musings, idly turning over the leaves of a book that in earlier days she had read in Kashmir with her lover, she was disturbed by the appearance of the faithful Nipunika, who approached her with a troubled face, first hastily and then hesitatingly, as though she doubted whether to speak or keep silence.

"What have you to tell me?" said Iravati. "You seem to be the bearer of bad news."

"Alas!" answered the servant, "I would that my mouth were gagged; yet I cannot leave you in ignorance of what I have heard. It concerns you too nearly for me to dare to keep it from you."

"Speak at once, without further preface," said Iravati. "I am ready to hear what you have to tell."

Then she recounted her meeting with a soldier from Agra, and what he had told her of Siddha. At first she spoke guardedly, but ended in repeating all that Salim had discovered about Faizi's wife.

The consequence of this tale was as Nipunika had feared. As though lifeless, Iravati sat there, gazing before her; and some minutes of silence ensued before she spoke. Then she sprang to her feet, asking, with a passion unwonted to her, "Who told you all this? Was it a soldier? Speak the truth, with no shifts or excuses."

"Noble lady," answered Nipunika, "how should I dare to deceive you, and what reason could I have for doing so? The man from whom I heard what I have now repeated to you is a servant of the Prince."

"Then the whole story is a lie!" cried Iravati. "I understand it all now. What a contemptible plot!" she added to herself; and then turning to her servant,— "It is well, my good Nipunika, and I thank you for your report, which you brought, I doubt not, prompted by the real interest you take in me. But now that I know where it comes from I care not for it. Leave me now for the moment, and in future do not have to do with the man who told you these tales."

Still the arrow had been better aimed than Iravati would allow, either to herself or to her servant; and left alone, she sat for a long time, her head leaning on her hand, thinking over the possibilities and probabilities of what she had heard. But she felt her courage rise again when, some time after, leaving her apartment, she met Prince Salim in one of the galleries, whose return had not been announced to her. It was all plain to her. No one else had invented the whole slander in order to estrange her from Siddha; and she bent her head coolly and half contemptuously in acknowledgment of her visitor's respectful greeting.

"Iravati," he said, "you would have reason for surprise at my return here after our last, and for me discouraging interview, if the explanation had not been given you by what has come to your ears through your servant, and which I could not personally tell you."

"I understand well," said Iravati, without anger, but without circumlocution, "that you think scandal may aid you where persecution has failed; but this I had not expected, and, above all, from you."

"Scandal!" repeated Salim; "that would indeed be a contemptible manner of attaining the goal of my passionate, and for you not injurious, wishes, and a very vain one. Of what avail would such tales and empty gossip be? But it is different when truth is supported by proofs."

"How? Proofs! What do you mean?"

"I mean the kind of proofs that the strictest judge cannot condemn. You know Siddha's handwriting, do you not?"

"Certainly."

"Well, look at these letters." And Salim handed to her two papers folded as letters, which Guldbadan's trusted servant had stolen from her mistress and sold to him. They were hastily and passionately written, full of every expression of love, and contained one or two verses, written by Siddha, in which the name of the adored Rezia was repeated several times.

Iravati hastily read them through, and then read and re-read them, turning the letters round and round, looking at them from every side; then suddenly she let them fall from her hand, and would have sunk senseless to the ground if Salim had not supported her and placed her on a seat.

However deeply Iravati loved, she was no weak, nervous girl. In her veins ran the blood of an ancient and heroic race; and quickly recovering herself, she stood before the Prince, looking him firmly in the eyes.

"My fate," she said, "is decided; for I must confess that what I have heard is really true. Another has taken possession of the heart that until now was mine, and mine alone. But do not think, Prince, you who rule over everything except a woman's heart, that the way to it that was closed is now opened by your discovery; do not think that my promise is now vain because the word that was pledged to me in return is broken. As long as mine is not returned to me it is sacred."

"How?" cried Salim in astonishment. "The lover whose faithlessness is known to you, forsakes and abandons you for another, and yet you are not free, and may not listen—I do not say at once, but some time hence, when other memories fade at last and disappear—to him who loves you above everything, and can lay at your feet power and honour, such as no one else can offer?"

"Salim," answered Iravati, gently, as she strove to collect her thoughts; "you do not understand me, and perhaps you cannot do so. You do not understand us Hindu women, so different from those to whom you are accustomed. You think that the highest happiness for a woman is to be the favoured Sultana of some mighty ruler, and for many it does appear so; and you think it is enough to convince a Hindu woman of the faithlessness of her lover, to cause her to say farewell to all thoughts of the unworthy one."

"And is it not so?"

"Our women," was the answer, "know nothing of the temptations of greatness, where either duty or honour are concerned, and to their husband, or, which is the same thing, their betrothed, they remain faithful, even if their love is repaid by treachery. There are no bounds to the loyalty of a woman to her husband; and you know, though you may consider it only the consequence of superstition or exaggerated feeling, with what willing enthusiasm they will throw themselves on the burning pile that consumes the body of their dead husbands. You must have heard of our holy legends and heroic traditions, which describe the devotion of a wife to one unworthy of her. Doubtless the touching adventure of Damayanti must have come to your ears. Well, as far as in me lies, I will be another Damayanti.1 Siddha has deserted me, but that is because the wicked Kali2 has got possession of him, and tempted him to evil; not he himself that has brought this bitter sorrow to me. And when he awakes from this enchantment he will return, another Nala, and find me pure from any spot, and acknowledge that I knew better than he, how to watch over the honour of his name."

"I willingly leave you," said Salim, after a moment's silence, "the happy hope of his return, however much it grieves me. But do not flatter yourself with such expectations. Believe me, I know the woman into whose snares he has fallen. I loved her till I saw you, and know that she is irresistible until a purer love conquers the passion one feels for her. Believe me, I know no more fascinating woman, as I know none purer or nobler than you."

"Prince," said Iravati, in answer to this declaration, "I implore you to grant me a favour, although it may sound uncourteous. Leave me for the present. After all that has passed, I feel that it is necessary to be alone. A prince, a nobleman as you are, will not refuse me this."

"I should be," replied Salim, "unworthy of the name, if for a moment longer I misused your goodness; also I feel but too well that further persistence is now not only useless but prejudicial to my cause, therefore I obey your request." And turning, he left the gallery with slow footsteps.

No sooner was he gone than Iravati's courage and firmness forsook her, and, worn out, she sank on a seat near, and covering her face with her hands, wept bitterly.

Her repose was but of short duration, the sound of approaching footsteps made her look up in alarm, and she saw Salhana before her.

"My daughter," he said, in a gentler tone than she ever remembered to have heard from him, "I know what occupies your thoughts and bows your head with sorrow. I have long known what you to-day have heard. I discovered some time ago Siddha's faithlessness in Agra, but concealed it until the time should come when it would be necessary that you should know it. Now all is known to you, and I trust that you will recognise that the respect you owe, not to yourself alone, but to me and my house, should oblige you to banish all thought of the man who in so shameful a manner has flung from him the alliance with our race. No, listen to me," he continued, as Iravati was about to reply. "Believe that I feel the deepest sympathy with you in this fatal moment; still I must not neglect to remind you what a daughter of our noble race owes to her honour and good name. At the same time, I will tell you, though in confidence, what I have discovered, which, though it cannot heal the wound you have received at once, will in the end bring consolation. A splendid future awaits you, Iravati; that which every woman in the whole of Hindustan would look upon as the most enviable lot can be yours—Prince Salim. I suspected it some time ago, and when I gave him the opportunity, he acknowledged all to me. Prince Salim loves you, and asks you for his wife."

"I know that," said Iravati.

"You know it! and how?"

"From the Prince himself, this very day."

"And your answer?"

"I refused his flattering offer."

"What!" cried Salhana, in the greatest astonishment and anger. "Refused! Are you out of your mind?"

"I believe not; but I am engaged to Siddha."

"Well, what has that to do with it? you are still free to choose; you are not yet his wife."

"No; but, what is to me the same thing, I have sworn faith to him, and he has not released me from my promise."

"Let that be. Before, this might have had weight; but now he has himself broken faith, and so released you from your word."

"So, perhaps, might others think, who have been brought up with different ideas. Mine forbid me to do as you wish. And if these opinions now stand in your way, you must blame yourself, Father, who have had me brought up in them. Above all—I will make no secret of it—I still love Siddha, in spite of all; and after him I can never love another."

"There is no necessity for talking of love! It is enough that Salim loves you, and that you can make use of the influence you have over him. But this you do not choose to accept, simply from devotion to antiquated and exaggerated habits of thought, and from a silly passion for one unworthy of you. Think what you throw from you if you persevere in your foolish refusal. A kingdom is offered to you, to which the whole world can scarcely show a rival; and you throw it from you with contempt, for the sake of a dream—a whim!"

"It may be that I am wrong," said Iravati, with forced calmness, while her father became more and more excited; "but your representations cannot convince me. I have already heard them, and still more forcibly put, from the Prince, without being shaken in my resolution."

"Your resolution is, that you will resist your father. But it appears to me that hardly agrees with the principles to which you are so much devoted, and which teach that obedience from a child to a father is one of the first duties."

"Certainly; but not when this duty comes into conflict with a still higher one. However much it grieves me not to obey you, in this case I may not, and I cannot."

"Do you not know that a father has right over his daughter, and in cases of necessity forces her to obey?"

"I know it well, but also know that here compulsion would avail nothing. If I let myself be forced into a marriage with Salim, I should lose all value in his eyes, and so my influence over him would be as nothing. That he himself knows; but he will not think of force. If he did, he would not need your intervention. Akbar's heir is powerful enough to crush both your will and mine, if he chose."

Salhana clenched his hands, and impatiently bit his moustache. Beaten on all sides, and by whom? A simple girl, whom until now he had only known as the gentlest and most submissive of daughters. All his great plans and glittering prospects destroyed by this wilful and stubborn child. He who had dreamt not of a viceroyship alone, but to attain to the highest place next to the Emperor. He already saw himself in Agra, next to the throne as Grand Wazir, ruling Prince and land through his daughter; sovereign ruler over kingdoms and peoples—if not in name, at least in reality.

"Well," he cried at last, as he placed himself in a threatening attitude opposite Iravati; "you will not listen to reason, and you do not fear compulsion; but there may be something that you fear—the curse of a father!"

"The sorrow that is already laid upon me would be increased twofold," she answered; "but I would strive for courage to bear my burden without faltering. That must happen which is written by fate."

"You are courageous," said Salhana, coldly and sarcastically; "or you try to be so. But are you so sure that your obstinacy will not injure this Siddha, whom you acknowledge that you still love, and that the Prince may not avenge your refusal on him?"

The last blow seemed to reach its aim. Iravati, in despair, lifted her hands on high and then let them fall powerless at her side, while her head sank on her breast. With a hateful, triumphant smile, Salhana watched her. The victory at last was his, and the strength of the invincible one broken.

But the proud girl raised her head again, and looking Salhana full in the face, she said, first in a faltering voice, which soon became steady:

"What you have said, Father, is cruel, horribly cruel, and I can scarcely believe that you really mean it. But even should it be a threat in earnest, it has not the power to make me forsake the sacred duty that is laid upon me. If Siddha stood before us, and saw me hesitate, and violate my promise to save him from danger, he would despise me, and thrust me with good right from him. My life I will sacrifice for him, for it is his; but not my honour, that belongs also to him. His death will be mine; but what is fated we cannot avoid. Let vengeance strike the guiltless, but neither Salim nor you will gain anything by it. You will have lost a daughter and your brother a son, that would be all; and your ambition would in no way be advanced. But let us break off a conversation that may end in causing me to lose the respect I owe you. Think, my Father, that I am your daughter, and one of a noble and ancient race, who cannot but be alarmed where duty or honour are concerned,—or the man I love."

For a moment Salhana stood silently looking at Iravati, standing proudly and almost defiantly before him.

Their positions were changed; the hitherto submissive daughter now commanded, and forced the haughty father to subjection. Without a word, he turned and hurried away, with a fierce expression of foiled rage on his dark countenance.

1 See note at p. 62.

2 A goddess, the wife of Siva, named Kali, from her black complexion. The same as Durga.

Chapter XI.
"Tauhid-i-Ilahi."[1]

As usual, when evening closed in, a gaily coloured crowd thronged round the shops and houses of one of the smaller bazars of Agra, situated on the river. Here and there dice-players sat in open verandahs round their boards; and there passed drunken[2] soldiers armed with various weapons; a little retired from the crowd reposed solitary opium-eaters, lost in blissful dreams; and there also were grave Muhammadans deep in earnest conversation, and deigning for once to take a turn amongst the despised Hindus engaged in their social pleasures.

"Yes, Ali," said one of these to his companion, "with Akbar and his court things go from bad to worse. Evening after evening I know that these blasphemous meetings take place. Yesterday, about midnight, I passed by the palace, and what do you think I saw? All the Emperor's windows were brilliantly lit, sparkling with many lamps and wax tapers. But for what? For no feast such as a prince might celebrate. No; all was still as death, excepting a solemn song, or rather hymn. Akbar himself has, I have heard, composed several of them; and however well they sound, they have nothing to do with our religious service to the praise of the Great Prophet."

"And what does this betoken?" said Ali.

"What it really signified," was the answer, "I cannot exactly say; but there is no doubt but that the light and singing were in connection with the new teaching that Akbar is trying to introduce in the place of that of Islam, and into which he initiates his confidants—a kind of fire and sun worship, which in an evil hour he has taken from the ancient Parsees, and also from the unbelievers here. May Allah have mercy on them!"

"What kind of religion is it?" asked Ali. "Though I have heard of it more than once, yet I do not exactly know what it is."

"Nor do I very exactly," replied Yusuf; "but that it is very bad is proved by the opposition it meets with from all the faithful, especially from a man like Abdul Kadir, who is very learned and much esteemed by Akbar himself. From personal experience I have lately become acquainted with things still more disquieting than those of which I have already told you. Not long since I saw a man steal from the palace secretly, and as if afraid lest anyone should see him; a man whom you must know, but whom you cannot meet without a cold shudder of horror—Gorakh, the so-called Yogi. Now," continued he, sinking the whisper in which he spoke to a still lower tone, "do you know for what I hold that man? If not Shaitan himself, he is certainly his assistant; and with him Akbar has made a compact."

Yusuf was silent, regarding his comrade with horror. "Protect us, Allah!" he suddenly cried, pointing to a figure approaching by the river-side; "there he is in person! May the waters of the Jamuna swallow him up!"

And, in truth, there was the Durga priest, approaching a group of Hindus and Persians engaged in lively conversation.

"What I say," said one of these last, "is that we ought not, and we cannot, bear longer the scorn and ridicule which is openly and continually shown to our holy religion by Faizi and Abú-l Fazl, not to mention a still higher name; and I cannot understand how you people—although yours may be a different religion—how you can calmly look on at the destruction and overthrow of what you, as well as we, must hold sacred."

"But to that we have not yet come," said the Hindu. "It is well known that the Emperor and his followers do not think much of your Koran, and perhaps as much might be said of your religion. But so far I have heard nothing of destruction and overthrow; our temples are untouched, and no one interferes with our religious practices; while you Muhammadans in old days did nothing but torment and persecute us.

"As you well deserved, you sons of——"

"Come, men, no disputes," said a Persian soldier, interrupting them; "quarrels will not aid us." And he gave a sign to the angry Muhammadan.

"Let it be so," he answered, turning his back on the Hindu, and, accompanied by two friends, passed on his way.

Now Gorakh joined in the conversation: "It was well that you were present, Mubarak," said he; "open disputes may be dangerous. Most Hindus hold to the side of the Emperor; but if for the moment they are not to be won, when fortune changes they will come over to us. In the meantime what progress have you made?"

"The greater part of our mansabdars are already won," answered Mubarak; "and they will openly declare on our side directly the signal is given. Those that go with the army will turn round at the right moment, and those that remain here at Agra will do the same, and they can depend on their troopers."

This conversation had been listened to with eager interest by two men who had joined the group of speakers, and to whom, by the greeting they exchanged, they appeared to belong; but with still deeper interest they listened when Gorakh, in a low voice, replied:

"These last days have brought some changes in our plans; we must not wait to strike the blow until Akbar has reached the north, for it is always possible that in spite of the desertion of part of his troops he may gain a victory. Such reports from Kashmir would spread a panic, and we should find that there was little or nothing we could do here; so we must somewhat hasten matters, and put our plans into execution when Akbar is on the road, but too far off to return to Agra in a few days' marches on hearing that Salim is declared Emperor and has strengthened himself in the fortress; then there is no doubt that the malcontents in the army will turn against Akbar. Take care, then, Mubarak, and you others, that our people are warned in time, and hold themselves in readiness to carry out our plans, although the time is advanced."

After talking a little longer the conspirators separated, each going his own way, and leaving the last comers together.

"This is weighty news," said one.

"It is indeed," replied the other; "and if I am not mistaken it will make things easier for Akbar. How unfortunate that we cannot at once make our report to Abú-l Fazl; but we must wait till night, it may be dangerous to go to his palace before then; and also, I believe he is now with the Emperor, and we should not find him."

"I think," said the first, "that it will be wiser for us now to separate; we shall meet at midnight at the house of the Wazir." And greeting his companion, he turned up a side street, while the other continued along the river-side.

However fearful and profane the rites may have been that were supposed to have taken place in the private apartment of the Emperor—leading the pious Yusuf and his followers to believe that Akbar had concluded a compact with Shaitan—on that evening, at any rate, a right-thinking Mussulman would have seen nothing remarkable, though he might have taken fresh offence at the conversation if he had been able fully to understand and follow it.

Faizi, Abú-l Fazl, and the Brahman Kulluka, who had but lately returned from the north, were with the Emperor.

"No further report from your spies?" he asked his ministers.

"Not since yesterday," answered Abú-l Fazl; "but I expect them at midnight, and understand that they have news for me."

"Is it not sad," said Akbar, "that one must make use of such people? Oh! why are men thus forcing us to have recourse to such means?"

"It is," replied the Minister, "a necessary consequence of our present form of government, which cannot be altered. Malcontents, whether they are so with justice or not, have no means of redressing their wrongs when all the power is vested in one, and that one pronounces their complaints to be groundless. The ambitious and fortune-seekers make use of them as tools to attain their own ends, and they easily allow themselves to be so employed."

"But I never refuse to listen to the complaints of my subjects," said Akbar; "and if they are just, I redress them as far as lies in my power."

"If they are just!" repeated Abú-l Fazl. "Yes; but who decides that? The Emperor and his councillors?"

"But what would you have, then? We have heard of states and people in other parts of the world, where things are managed differently; but then, the condition of those people is very different from that of ours. How would it be possible among the many kingdoms and races subject to our rule to give any real share in the government to the people themselves, even if their character, their manners and customs, made it possible?"

"That is quite true," said Abú-l Fazl; "and I have already said that I regard further changes as neither desirable nor possible. When I alluded to the present state of affairs, it was only to show how unavoidable is the use of means that we are forced to adopt in order to avoid what is still worse. So far as these men are concerned whom we contemptuously call spies, they are less to be despised than one supposes; at least, the two I have now in my mind are honourable men, respected by others, and devoted to us heart and soul. It is true that they are well paid, still that is not necessary, they would be faithful to us without that; and they have indeed rendered us good service. They discovered Salhana's plot, and, what is not of less importance, the secret intrigues of Gorakh the Yogi."

"Yes," remarked Faizi, mischievously, "of that philosopher who for some time gloried in the favour of His Majesty, while he unfolded the mysteries of the Yogi teaching; but not much came of it, so far as I know."

Akbar coloured as the remembrance was brought back to him how with all his wisdom he had almost, though but for a moment, been entirely taken in by the cunning deceiver. But at the right moment Kulluka interposed, and continued the conversation by saying: "It is indeed to be regretted, but it is wiser to have little to do with this Gorakh. My former pupil, Siddha, has communicated to me things about him which show that caution is necessary. And yet he knows more, perhaps by tradition, of the ancient and now almost forgotten teaching than we shall ever discover."

"There you see," said Akbar, triumphantly, to Faizi, "that our friend Kulluka, who is so well acquainted with all the learning of the Brahmans, does not look upon the Yogi system as so utterly unimportant."

"I will willingly allow that it contains much that is valuable," said Faizi, "if our wise friend says so, from whom we have learnt so much that is worth knowing. But excuse me, Kulluka, if I ask what it is you expect from this system of days gone by? So far as I know, it is nothing but a foolish mysticism, promising an impossible absorption of the individual in the supreme, brought about by charms and enchantment, or, to speak more plainly, by clever feats of jugglery."

"I do not think so unfavourably of the system of Patanjali,"[3] answered Kulluka; "although I do not for a moment believe it can boast the possession of absolute truth. The union with, and resolution of the mortal into the immortal, of human existence into the spiritual, according to the Yogi view, is in itself not so great a folly. But no doubt this teaching is erroneous when it seeks, through absorption or union, to solve the mystery of the existence of the mind of man, by which in a kind of ecstasy the mortal is absorbed into the immortal. If this absorption were possible, it would in truth be self-annihilation. I do not think that the fundamental idea is to be so entirely rejected, or at least a part of it, of which all this is the result. Is it not a truth that, just because men find themselves so weighed down and bound within narrow limits, their spirits know no higher exaltation than that to which they rise in those rare moments when they lose the sense of their personality in nobler or higher and more comprehensive ideas? Provided the ideas remain no empty abstraction, but take their being from strong human life, from knowledge, art, and the contemplation of the social existence of men, what, I ask, can you place higher than so to lose the finite and self-seeking *I* in the universal good? From the place whence the individual drew the true spirit of life, to that place it should return if it in truth accomplished its destiny."

"These are words after my heart," said Akbar. "This same thought, that of self-denial, animates our own philosophical systems as well as the new doctrines that these missionaries from the West have come here to preach. But is there not another subject to which the thoughts of men should be directed, especially those of philosophers? However true and exalted this doctrine of self-abnegation is, what does it tell us of the eternal union of spirit and matter which pervades existence?"

"Indeed," answered the Brahman; "he would be unworthy the name of philosopher who did not take as a chief subject of philosophical thought the contemplation of life and morals proceeding from it. But who will ever solve for us the enigma of life?"

"No one, certainly," answered Faizi; "at least not at present. What future knowledge, in distant centuries may contribute to its solution we cannot even guess. But for the present should we not content ourselves with the conviction, shared by all wise men, both past and present, and expressed by many of them more or less clearly, that there is in the universe an eternal life without end and without beginning; a life and being through which everything is bound together or brought into union, of which the highest law is development—the development of the lower steps or forms of existence into those still higher. And what are we ourselves—we men? Always the same as that which surrounds us—a revelation of the universal being, each destined, in his own circle and according to his powers, to take his part in the general development. In proportion as we can clearly keep before our eyes the higher and more universal aims, so will narrow feelings of self-love retire to the background, making room for unselfish devotion to the good of our fellow-men, of society, and of the state."

"Very well put, my worthy Faizi," said Akbar; "but true as all that may be, does it content you? Do you not long for something else, something more?"

"Assuredly," was the answer. "That one idea, in its abstruse generalization, does not satisfy. We would understand it more clearly, and learn to apply it; we would strive after the knowledge of immortal life and of the original compact by observing their manifestations here; and to attain this knowledge all those strive who devote themselves to philosophy."

"You do not quite understand me," said the Emperor; "but I will allow all that you have said. What I meant was: has the universal being, of which you speak, its origin in itself, or in another still higher intelligence?"

"Intelligence and thought," was the answer, "are necessary attributes of this being, as well as that which we are accustomed to call matter or extension.4 Both declare themselves in infinite manifestations; and how is it possible that that which is an attribute of a thing can at the same time be its cause?"

For some moments a deep silence reigned. The Emperor sought for an answer, but shook his head and said nothing.

"My brother," at last said Abú-l Fazl to Faizi, "your reasoning is perfectly logical, yet it contents me as little as it does our venerated Emperor. What have you, and what have we, to do with this conception of soul and matter? What can it give us?"

"Well," answered Faizi, smiling, "it need give you nothing if it is true; and if it is true, you should own it, though it may neither content nor please you. I mean to show that my idea gives or possesses a value in life only in so far as it awakens in us devotion to all that we regard as good and true; and what can you ask for more than this?"

"You are right," answered Abú-l Fazl; "but I spoke not so much for myself and for us, as for those of less cultivation and enlightenment, who cannot comprehend all this, and yet seek for something more and higher than daily experience brings them. Would it not be possible so to dress up these abstract ideas as to make them more acceptable to the multitude?"

"Our friend Faizi," said Akbar, "now says what I myself have often thought. If it is not possible to discover new images or emblems for these conceptions or notions proclaimed by Faizi, can we not receive those of ancient days which were not peculiar to solitary and independent religious systems, but which sprang from the religious and poetical spirit of the people themselves?"

"I understand your meaning," replied Faizi, as Akbar was silent; "you allude, if I am not mistaken, to the new doctrine or teaching which the Emperor wishes to introduce, and with which some of his trusted friends are already acquainted. Is it not so?"

"In truth," answered Akbar, "you are not mistaken. But allow me to make use of this opportunity to say something further about it. To you Faizi, and you Kulluka, I am indebted for much elucidation, and the turn that our conversation has taken, which gives me the chance of expressing my meaning, is indeed welcome to me. Listen, then. For a long time I have sought for some form in which a rational religion might be expressed, and which would at the same time content philosophical thinkers and those of less enlightenment. At last in some measure I found what I sought in making acquaintance with the images of the ancient Persians, but above all, Kulluka, of those of your philosophical poets of old days. I mean those so well known to you—Sun and Fire. The contemplation of the most striking manifestations of light and warmth may at first appear empty and worthless; but more carefully regarded, they contain an exalted truth, which perchance the knowledge of coming centuries may, through its results, exalt to the highest place. See," continued Akbar, as he turned to the open gallery of the apartment, and pointed to the slowly-sinking sun, "there the glorious representation of all light and life in this world leaves us, to return to-morrow in sparkling glory. Earlier races regarded him as a god, and addressed prayers and adoration to him; while to the wise of old he was the exalted image of the principles of life, and the all-pervading force that is shown in endless manifestations. For are not light and warmth the givers of life, without which nothing could exist? In the light of the sun, moon, and stars, the flash of lightning, and the fire that we ourselves kindle on the hearth, we see the most common manifestations of this force—now beneficent, and now fearful and destructive. Everywhere is this force present—in the earth and planets, in man and animals, in light and water—though we may not always remark it. And if it is really thus, would it be considered as a mere poetical fancy if we chose this force as the emblem of the unity and the life of which, Faizi, you have just spoken? Our friend Abú-l Fazl is not only one with me in this, but is anxious that I should try my new teaching, or, if you will, the teaching I have borrowed from those of old days, among the people, and see if they would not accept it instead of the many superstitions that are now so general.

A name was necessary to distinguish this teaching from others; and though a name cannot express the full meaning, that of TAUHID-I-ILAHI, 'the unity of the Deity,' did not appear inappropriate. Ceremonies and public services are entirely excluded, unless you can call public service a simple symbolical adoration of the sun during the day and in the morning, and of light during the night, by means of appropriate hymns. Touching this," concluded the Emperor, "I have already imparted to you somewhat, but I have never before fully declared it to you. The time has now arrived: tell me frankly, what is your opinion?"

Neither of the friends appeared willing to comply with this request at once. At last Kulluka broke the silence.

"Wise Prince, pardon us if we are not at once ready with our answer; your important communication requires a moment's thought. In the plan declared by you there is much that is tempting, and also, according to my humble opinion, much that is serious. The justness and grandeur of your images, borrowed for the greater part from our old poets and philosophers, I shall be the first to admit; but, may I ask, is there not great danger? These symbols once introduced amongst the people and accepted by them, would soon lose their original meaning, and in the end would sink to nothing but an outward and mechanical religious service. We must well consider that this same teaching, which you wish to proclaim, once actually belonged in truth to the faith of more than one people; and what did it become? Not only in these later days, but in ancient times, to which you refer, doubt arose respecting the object of worship, and then, as now, many a pious mind asked: 'He who gives life, He who gives strength; Whose command all the bright gods revere; Whose shadow is immortality, Whose shadow is death; who is the God to whom we shall offer our sacrifice?'[5] Even then, Surya, the sun, and Agni, the fire, did not satisfy men as emblems of the representation of life and force; and shall a happier future await the *Tauhid-i-Ilahi* than that of the sun and fire worship of old days?"

Akbar gave no reply. "And you, Faizi," he asked, "what is your opinion?"

"I have little or nothing," he answered, "to add to what my worthy friend has already said. The doubt to which he alluded, as prevailing in the days of old, has been still more clearly expressed than in the passage quoted by him from the Vedas. Another poet puts it still more forcibly:

'Who knows,' he says, 'who knows the secret, who proclaimed it here?

Whence, whence this manifold creation sprang;

The gods themselves came later into being;

Who knows from whence this great creation sprang?

He from whom all this great creation came,

Whether His will created it or was mute?

The most High Seer that is in highest heaven,

He knows it, or perchance even He knows it not.'6

So it seems that doubt is as ancient as religion itself. But let us leave that on one side, and also the hate and opposition that a reformer must always expect from his contemporaries, the appearance of which we may already remark here and there where the new teaching has already been made known to the people. This an Akbar will not fear. But there is another danger that Kulluka referred to, which cannot be put so lightly on one side: the danger that a name once given, whether it be Allah or another, may become a personality to the uncultured, and be regarded as a personal representation, distinct from the Immortal Being; and then, naturally, all is at an end with your object—the unity of the Deity. And what will you have introduced, and what perhaps will you have made?"

"But, Faizi," asked Abú-l Fazl, "what would you do to make the people wiser and more reasonable? How would you bring about this reformation of ideas that the Emperor desires?"

"The great philosophers," was Faizi's answer, "of China, and all great civilisers have long ceased to profess any religion; but they have made a real beginning as regards the cultivation and the enlightenment of the people, and one which we have too much lost sight of. This is, above all things, the education of the people. There is the only, but perfectly certain means. It is true that the results do not soon appear; but those who put their hands to a great work seldom see the end, which surely comes at last; while each announcement of a new teaching, whether supported by the authority of revelation or not, though for a time it may flourish, in the end is sure to degenerate."

"There seems to be much truth in what you have said," was Akbar's answer; "and I will take it all into my most serious consideration. It may perhaps be best to restrict the new teaching to the circle of our own friends, in case we find its introduction among the people to be opposed by insurmountable difficulties. Still you will not expect that I should at once give up my favourite project. We will talk it over again. But enough for to-day; state affairs now call for our attention. I thank you, my friends, for all you have said: you, Abú-l Fazl, for the support you have lent me; and you, too, for your frank and well-meant opposition."

After having taken leave of the Emperor, Abú-l Fazl returned to his palace, accompanied by his friends, to receive in their presence the report of the two spies.

---

1 "The unity of God." The divine monotheism of Akbar.

2 Tobacco was introduced in the reign of Akbar. Before that time it was no uncommon thing for a Muhammadan prince to die of *delirium tremens*.

3 The founder of the Yoga philosophy.

4 *Uitgebreidheid* (D.); *Ausbreitung* (German).

5 Rig-Veda.

6 "Rig-Veda," x. 129.—H. S. Colebrooke. *See also* Max Muller, "Hist. Anc. Sansk. Lit.," p. 560.

Chapter XII.
Assassination.

It was on a bright fresh morning when Siddha, accompanied by two horsemen, took his way to Fathpúr, charged with the delivery of some letters, too important to be trusted to the hands of an ordinary messenger. The sun shone brightly, but its beams did not burn. In the trees sang many coloured birds, and squirrels and small monkeys sprang from bough to bough. All nature seemed awake and full of joy; and even the peasants met with on the road had exchanged their usual heavy tread for a lighter one, as if they also shared in the joy that reigned around.

But Siddha, once so full of mirth and hope, took no part in it. Sombre and lost in thought, he rode on silently, followed by his attendants. He seemed, indeed, another man from what he was when he first arrived in Agra and joked with Parviz and his friends, listening with sympathy to the confidence of the former about the noble daughter of the Treasurer. With surprise Parviz had remarked the change, though discretion withheld him from making any inquiries; and still more deeply did Siddha himself feel how different all with him now was. How different from the day when Kulluka had seen him spring forward gracefully on his steed, as though he would conquer the world, calling on the loved name of his future bride! How different when a single kiss from Iravati was bliss to him—before he had learned to long for the passionate embraces of a Rezia—when his conscience was pure, and he had no cause for shame in having made himself guilty of treachery, faithlessness, and ingratitude! Sombre indeed were his reflections, for now more than ever suspicion crossed his thoughts. Was Rezia really faithful to him, or did she only treat him as she did her husband, who, far more than he, deserved her love? In truth, did Salim only come to her for state reasons, or were there other motives for his visits? And then the conspiracy, in which Siddha had become more and more entangled. Now that he thought it over it began to assume quite another character; it was not entirely for the defence of his fatherland, but appeared to be directed to very different ends. And had not Rezia, on her own confession, deceived him more than once? and what reason had he now for believing that this time she indeed spoke the truth? Into what new entanglement had he now fallen? and for the perpetration of what crime did he allow himself to be used as a tool?

An exclamation from one of his troopers awoke him from his reflections, and looking in the direction to which the soldier pointed with his lance, he saw in the distance a group of horsemen engaged in combat.

"Forward!" cried Siddha, putting spurs to his horse; and followed by his companions at full gallop, he turned towards the combatants. As he approached, to his astonishment and alarm, he recognised Abú-l Fazl, and in the man who sought to cut him down with his sabre Nara Singh, a Raja whom he had met more than once with Prince Salim. Directly the Raja's followers caught sight of the new comers, a detachment rode to encounter them. Siddha attacked the leading man of the troop, who soon lay with his horse on the ground, pierced by Siddha's lance. He then drew his sword, and with one blow emptied another saddle. He had harder work with the third, who was an accomplished soldier, and well acquainted with the use of the sword; and while the two troopers were busy with their opponents, others came riding up to the assistance of their comrades. The affair began to look very critical for our three, when Siddha by a fortunate blow placed his enemy *hors de combat*, and was just ready to receive the new comer, when the retreat was sounded, and they at once turned bridle; but at the same moment that he had felled his opponent and seen the others hurrying up, Siddha beheld Abú-l Fazl throw up his arms into the air, letting his sabre fall, and then sink from his horse to the ground. The next moment Nara Singh had called off his soldiers and retreated at a gallop over the plain. Siddha's first impulse was to pursue the murderers; but on second thoughts he saw that he, with his two men, one of whom was wounded, could do little, while the Minister's four servants lay stretched out dead on the field, and Abú-l Fazl, above all, required his aid.

Springing from his horse, and flinging the reins to one of his followers, he knelt by the side of the wounded man, and loosing his clothes, sought to staunch the blood that flowed from a deep wound in his chest. To his joy Abú-l Fazl opened his eyes, and recognised him; but his joy was of short duration.

"Your help, my brave Siddha, comes too late," he said, in a faint voice; "my work for the Emperor and his kingdom is over. One last command I give you: if you suspect who the murderer is, keep his name from Akbar."

"Nara Singh," answered Siddha, "was, I see clearly, only a hireling; the real murderer is—" and here he hesitated to say the name.

"Salim," continued Abú-l Fazl; "I had already been warned against him."

Exhausted, the dying man sank back in Siddha's arms; but shortly after, consciousness returned, and he found the strength, though his voice was scarcely audible, to send a last greeting to his imperial friend, whom he had so faithfully served all his life. "Say to Akbar that my last thought was of him, and tell him I die in the firm conviction of the truth of those principles of which we have so often spoken, and so lately as yesterday. The glory of the sun I shall hardly see more, though I feel that the light still lives in me, but that also will be soon extinguished. I do not complain; I believe that I have been in a position to do some good to my fellow-men, though less than I wished, and so I die content. Strive, my young friend, so to live, that you may one day say the same. And now farewell," whispered the Wazir, after a short pause, gently pressing Siddha's hand. His head sank on his breast, and Siddha soon felt that his arm only supported a corpse.1

At about the same time, but far away from this spot, another drama was being played, which, though in some respects different from the tragedy of the Wazir, in others resembled it closely. Among the mountains of the Himálayas, especially near Badari-natha, a burning heat had for some time reigned. At evening, the beneficent heavenly time, dark rain-clouds appeared, promising drink to the thirsty earth, but they were again driven away by the evil Vritra, the dark demon; and the next day the burning rays of the sun returned to dry up and parch all vegetation. At last the mighty Indra, monarch of the heavens, rose up and prepared himself for the strife. Again at evening the clouds gathered, and again the demon strove to disperse them; then Indra seized his lightning, and flung it among the mountains with so mighty a blow that it re-echoed, rattling and thundering from all sides. Vritra felt the stroke, but would not at once abandon the combat, and only a few heavy rain-drops fell here and there on languishing nature. Again fell the mighty blow, while the mountain tops and valleys were lighted by one dazzling blaze; gigantic trees were cleft in two, and heavy masses of rock were flung down into the ravines. Then the rain fell heavily, and brooks and mountain streams began to swell and rush downwards to the valleys. At last the fearful battle was over, rain ceased to fall, lightning flickered through the twilight, and no sound broke the silence except the rushing of waters.

Then Gurupada, the hermit, left his dwelling, to enjoy the fresh air laden with fragrance. He seated himself beneath his verandah, overgrown with roses and jasmine. He sat there enjoying the peace of nature and the new life which the refreshing rain had called forth; while he thought of the ancient epic of the clouds, with Indra the slayer of Vritra2 as its hero, which floated before his mind, as if it had been a poem of yesterday. Then sombre and disquieting thoughts forced themselves upon him. The accounts that Kulluka had lately brought from Kashmir and Agra filled him with anxiety respecting the future of his dearly-loved country. "And so," said he to himself, "it must in the end come to what I have so long feared, and hoped to have averted by many years of self-inflicted banishment. A strange ruler is on the point of seizing on our unhappy country, and the road is smoothed to him by our own fatal disunion. He is right from his point of view: he must restore order in a neighbouring State when the anarchy continually causes disturbances in his own empire; and if this cannot be accomplished while the independence of that country is respected, then must it be forced to subjection. But is there in truth nothing that can be done? No, no," continued he. "Kulluka's proposal that I should return, and, perhaps supported by Akbar, take the government from the hands of my weak brother—no, that would not do. My return would only be a temporary remedy, even if it were that. And I have become too old and unpractised in the art of ruling again to reign, and, above all, there, where youth and energy are required. Life cannot last much longer; I am weary and long for rest; I have long sighed for union with the immortal Brahma, whence we take our short independent existence, and to which we shall return again." And Gurupada slowly closed his eyes as he stretched himself upon a soft bed of fresh moss. A flash of lightning, that for a moment lit up the valley and all around, awoke and called him back for a few moments to his reflections.

"And perhaps it is as well that things should indeed go as they seem fated to do. A renewed party warfare, of which the end can never be foreseen, would impoverish our people, and bring our country to ruin. But should it be subjected to a wise and just government, its industries and commerce would revive, and its former prosperity return. Akbar is a prince who knows how to make his subjects happy; and to-day many people bless him who formerly resisted his rule. Yet it is hard for a country to see itself deprived of a liberty which has been its boast for centuries. Ah, that it might be spared me to see this happen to my own country!" So saying, he laid his head down again, with a sigh, and, half listening to the rushing of the brook, fell into a light slumber. All seemed in the deepest rest far and near; there was nothing to disturb the old man's sleep, except that every now and then he became aware of the humming of an insect, and felt it brush his cheek gently; and then a strange, unaccountable feeling crossed him that he was not alone. Again he looked up, but could see nothing, and even the insect seemed to be driven away by his sudden movement. In a short time it returned, then flew away, and again returned, until the sleeping man took no further notice of it, and gave himself up entirely to slumber. This was not so heavy but that the slightest cause would again awaken him. Suddenly he put one hand to his neck and seized a cord that had been flung round it; with the other he felt around him, and touched a cold, slippery body that had been rubbed with oil. Having freed himself from the cord, he seized his assailant with both hands, but in vain; he slipped through his fingers and appeared to escape. The stillness of night was broken by a sharp cry, answered by a growl, and close by Gurupada saw two fiery balls gleam. In another moment a flash of lightning showed him his tiger Hara, with its powerful claws fixed in the body of a man who lay stretched on the ground.

At the sound of this cry the servant hurried from the house with a torch, the light of which showed Gurupada that his sight had not deceived him; and he at once understood what had happened. The man that lay there had attempted to strangle him; but, just in time, he had felt the cord; and the tiger, driven by some instinct, had followed the Thug as unobserved as he himself had approached the hermit.

"Back! Hara," cried Gurupada, springing forward and seizing the tiger by the neck; "back, I say."

At first the animal would not move, and then, slowly and unwillingly obeying the voice of its master, it drew out its claws, and retreated growling, for a few paces, and laid itself down.

With the help of the servant, the hermit lifted the fallen man from the ground, where a blow from the tiger's paw had laid him; and finding that life still lingered, they placed him carefully on the moss.

"I know this man," said Gurupada, after having closely examined him. "In the days of my power I showed him many favours and benefits. What could have driven him to this treacherous attack?"

On hearing these words, the wounded man looked up, and gazed attentively and earnestly at the hermit; then murmured, with astonishment, "Nandigupta! is it possible!"

"Nandigupta, in truth," was the answer. "What induced you to seek my life?"

"My lord and prince," said the Thug, with a firm voice, "I swear to you by Siva and his holy consort that I knew not who you were, and had long thought you dead. Had I known it, I should never have had the strength or courage to fulfil the behest of Durga, however great the punishment of her anger might have been. But, happily, she herself did not desire your death, and sent this tiger to take my life in the place of yours. Blessed be her name!"

Exhaustion prevented his saying more. With the servant's help, Gurupada washed and bound, as well as was possible, the terrible wound caused by the tiger's claws, and having given him drink, and seeing he began to recover a little, Gurupada asked further, "What drove you to this deed? and if you did not know who I was, who told you that Durga desired my death?"

"Gorakh the Yogi," was the reply.

"Ha! the villain!" murmured Gurupada; "then there must be more behind. So you have become a Thug," he continued. "I am sorry to see you so led away and blinded. Was I the only one pointed out to you by Gorakh as a chosen sacrifice?"

Pain for a few minutes hindered the wounded man from replying, though his countenance betrayed nothing of what he was suffering. At last he answered and spoke very steadily, with pauses between his words, "The First Minister of Kashmir, Salhana's brother, is also chosen; but his death is entrusted to my brother, who is also well known to you. Should he fail, then I am to carry it out."

"And has your brother started for Kashmir?"

"He left me yesterday a little distance from here, and took his way towards the north."

"On foot?"

"Yes."

"Are any others acquainted with these orders respecting the Minister and me?"

"No one else knows. Only when it is known that we have failed will the task be entrusted to others."

Gurupada signed to his servant, and went on one side with him.

"Go," he said, "and saddle your horse at once. You must instantly set off on a journey."

A low, suppressed groan called him back to the side of the wounded man.

"My lord," he murmured, "I have only a few minutes to live; and I ask you to add one more favour to the many I have enjoyed at your hands: say that you forgive me."

"I forgive you, unhappy man," answered Gurupada; "I know you were nothing but a tool in the hands of others."

"Then I die happy, and with a foretaste of bliss enter into immortal life, assured of the grace of the goddess both to you and me, through the wonder she has worked in receiving me as a sacrifice in your place. Holy Trinity, holy Durga!" cried he, in a louder voice, and stretching out his arms as though animated with fresh strength; "receive me into the temple of your glory! I come!" With these words he fell back motionless, and the faithful follower of the Goddess of Destruction was no more.

For some time the hermit remained gazing at the lifeless body, to which, in the wavering light, its emaciation, dark colour, and forehead marked with the red and white symbols of Siva, gave a ghostly aspect.

"To what," he muttered, "cannot religion or fanaticism lead! it turns otherwise good and quiet people into criminals, murderers, and mad-men. Still this man is in no way to be pitied; he died as a martyr, in the full conviction of being received into endless happiness. But the hypocrites, the shameless villains, such as Gorakh, who make use of such simple souls as tools wherewith to execute their accursed plans, what of them? What do they deserve but a war of destruction? Yet no," he continued, shaking his head, "that would not be right. No mercy where a crime has been committed or attempted; but no persecution when it is only threatened. Who can place the limit where a religious sect becomes dangerous, and where it is not?" Here the return of the servant interrupted his thoughts.

"Help me," he said, "to carry this man who lies here. He is dead, but I do not wish that Hara should devour him, which otherwise he certainly will do; and when we have finished, then to horse. Hasten you to Kashmir, to warn the Minister of what we have learnt; and endeavour to trace out the brother of this man, whom you well know. Seek to hinder him in his undertaking, and to prevent his communicating with any of his associates. If you can, also discover where Gorakh is; do not spare him for a moment: the wretch doubly deserves the cord he prepares for the necks of others."

"But, honoured master," asked the servant, with hesitation, "must I leave you entirely alone here in the wilderness? It seems that your place of refuge is now discovered, and there may be fresh attempts on your life. Must I leave you, just at this moment when I might be of service?"

"My best friend," answered Gurupada, smiling, "do not disturb yourself about me. What is my life in comparison with the greater interests that depend on the speedy execution of your mission? I am here as safe as with you for my guard, at least as long as Hara lives. You have seen how brave a guard he is. I would not advise any more of these marauders to show themselves in the neighbourhood. Hara now knows those kind of people, and is not inclined to allow them to come here in peace. Is your horse ready?"

"Yes, lord."

"Well, quickly away. First, help me with our work here."

---

1 Abú-l Fazl, in 1598, was sent by Akbar to the Dakhin. Salim broke out in rebellion; and the Emperor, in his trouble, sent for his trusty Minister. Abú-l Fazl hastened to rejoin his master. But Salim, who had always hated the Minister, instigated a Rajpút chief of Bandalkhand, named Bir Singh of Urchah, to waylay him. Abú-l Fazl was murdered near Narwar, on the 12th of August 1602, and Bir Singh fled from the wrath of Akbar, leading the life of an outlaw in the jungle until the death of the great Emperor.

2 A favourite allegory in the Rig-Veda, connected with Indra's power over the elements, is his war with the demon Vritra. "With his vast destroying thunderbolt Indra struck the darkling mutilated Vritra. As the trunks of the trees are felled by the axe, so lies Vritra prostrate on the earth. The waters

carry off the nameless body of Vritra, tossed into the midst of the never-stopping, never-resting currents. The foe of Indra has slept a long darkness."—"Rig-Veda," Sukta xxxii.

Chapter XIII.
Parting.

The tidings of Abú-l Fazl's death had made an overwhelming impression on the Emperor. It seemed to him as if everything that had until now been his support was suddenly failing him. He who had been so strong, who had never known faint-heartedness when threatened by the fiercest storms, who had braved the greatest dangers, and had always come back victor from the strife, now felt his strength crippled, and as though he were almost powerless among the many disturbances that were again breaking out in his empire. All he was capable of in those first days was to order the arrest of Nara Singh, the murderer; but this order it was impossible to carry out, as the Raja had fled and found a safe refuge far away, to await the time when Salim should ascend the throne and load him with favours. However, it was not possible that a man of Akbar's character could remain bowed down under the burden of sorrow, however heavy it might be. For some days he shut himself up entirely, and admitted no one except Faizi and some of his most trusted friends; but with time courage returned to him to receive others who sought audience either respecting their own affairs or those of the state. Among these was Padre Aquaviva, who, before his departure, wished to take a personal leave of the Emperor.

"So you are going to leave us again, worthy Father?" said Akbar, as the Jesuit was ushered into his presence.

"I must do so, Sire," answered Aquaviva; "our Provincial summons me back to Goa. But I cannot depart without expressing to your Majesty my heartiest thanks for the honour and favours that have here been shown us, though I hesitated to ask an audience after your serious and bitter loss. A worthy man, a true friend, and a faithful servant was Abú-l Fazl, and the memory of such a man is certainly a comfort in the midst of the sorrow that his loss causes. But," added he, after a moment's pause, "this would not be to me a sufficient consolation."

"Not enough!" repeated Akbar in surprise. "What more would you demand?"

"I should wish for the certainty that he died with a purer soul, and with happier expectations than was possible."

"Abú-l Fazl," answered the Emperor, in an earnest but calm voice,—"Abú-l Fazl was as pure of soul as any of yours can be, without saying more, and he died as I would wish to die."

The Jesuit waited, expecting Akbar would add something more, but he was silent; and the tone of his reply clearly showed that to ask for further explanation would be imprudent.

"Do you expect to return soon?" asked Akbar, after a few minutes silence.

"That will depend on the orders I receive," answered Aquaviva. "So far as I am myself concerned, with sorrow I am compelled to confess that my mission here has been a failure."

"How a failure? Have you not received here the fullest protection, and been shown all respect and fitting honour? and have you not enjoyed the most complete liberty to preach what you will, and to convert whom you can? Do you reckon that as nothing? Here, where a few years ago, under my predecessors, any preaching of your doctrines would have met with the punishment of death."

"Sire," answered the Padre, "we should indeed be ungrateful did we reckon such important privileges as nothing. Yet I must repeat that our mission is a failure as respects its principal object. You know well with what glorious hopes we came to Agra; the reverent interest you took in our holy writings, and in the ceremonials of our Church, had filled us with hope that in the end the light of truth would sink into your noble heart and deep-thinking mind; we had hoped, and almost expected with certainty, that the Church of Christ would greet in Shah Akbar one of, if not the most famous of her sons. These hopes and expectations we cannot now flatter ourselves were anything but idle; so, cannot we say with truth that our mission has failed in its highest aim? Still, it may be that here and there in our teaching there are difficulties which your philosophers cannot now solve, which closer study and research will throw light upon. I think of the great benefits that the Church has showered upon the West, and which would not here be wanting did she possess like power."

"With reason," said Akbar, "you now leave on one side the real dogmatical questions, for about them we shall never agree, and for the moment I feel no inclination for their discussion. You speak of benefits; I believe, willingly and with reason, that your Christian doctrines have done much for the world—more, perhaps, than any other religion—in the application of the principles of universal love of our fellow-men, and self-sacrifice; however, as we have already shown you, this is not exclusively taught by your doctrines, which, if they have done much good, have also done much that is evil. Have you not introduced the greatest intolerance that the world has ever known? Have not you, you priests, in the West exalted yourselves to tyrannize over the consciences of your fellow-men? Have you not doomed hundreds and thousands to the stake because they differed from you on some point of faith? And you call these benefits! Then, indeed, you have strange ideas of doing good; and your love for your fellow-men is of a strange kind. Tell me," he continued, turning a penetrating look on Aquaviva, "tell me, how would you treat me, Akbar, whom you now honour so highly, were I a Christian subject of one of the princes who obey your commands? Would you not thrust me into a dungeon, and, if I remained hardened in my unbelief, deliver me to a judge to be condemned to the fire and stake?"

Perplexed, the Jesuit drew back. Such a question he had not expected; and what could he reply? Certainly it could not be denied that in all probability Akbar would be so treated were he in the situation he imagined.

"Sire," at last he stammered, "that is not the case; and how can Akbar, the mighty Emperor of Hindustan, think of himself as the subject of one of our princes?"

"Certainly it is not so, fortunately for me! but your answer shows that my hypothesis was well grounded. Now another question: what would you do with me, Emperor of Hindustan, as I am? You wish me to be as one of your princes, who are submissive to your orders, and to use me as a tool for the maintenance of your clerical tyranny. Naturally you are very anxious for my conversion. Well, I tell you, once for all, you will never see it; not even if I entirely accepted your Evangelists, and were really publicly or privately to embrace them. I could have nothing to do with your present Church, well knowing what fatal consequences to a State would follow on its monarch taking such a step."

"Then," said Aquaviva, "nothing remains to us but to pray to our Lord that He by a miracle will bring about that which our zealous and feeble efforts have been unable to accomplish. And this prayer, I feel certain, will not remain unanswered. Reflect, O powerful ruler, that against Him the great of the earth are as nothing, and that He can punish those who withstand Him. He, and He alone, will triumph, and the gates of hell will avail nothing against the rock of Peter, while Christ and His Church will endure until the end of the world."

"That may be your affair," cried Akbar, losing a little of his usual patience; "mine is to watch over the liberty and rights of my people, and to defend them against you, as against the mullahs or priests of any other creeds. Remain here, or go, as it best pleases you; preach as seems good to you, and build churches. You shall enjoy the same privileges as Muhammadans in their mosques and Hindus in their temples. There is, however, one warning which I must give you: the moment I find you attempt to introduce any persecution amongst your converts or others, as already has been the case on the coast of Malabar, that moment shall you be banished from my kingdom, never to set your foot within it again."

With suppressed wrath Loyola's follower listened to these proud words; but what could he do, what could he say? He had no complaint to bring against this invariably tolerant prince, and to defy the formidable monarch would have been sheer madness. Nor would there have been a martyr's crown to gain by doing so. If he, a helpless missionary, were to use threatening and injurious language, the Emperor would not harm a hair of his head,—only send him and his to Surat,[1] and from thence in a ship to Goa, where he would be landed with the utmost courtesy. Perhaps he would not even take that trouble, but simply laugh, "I have the door, show it him." Miserable and ignominious situation for a member of that order elsewhere so powerful and so feared, before whom the people trembled, and princes and popes were forced to bow their heads in submission!

Akbar interrupted the reflections of the disappointed and silent missionary. "Worthy Father," he said, in his usual friendly tone, "it indeed grieves me to be obliged to speak with so much frankness and harshness in maintaining my authority in the combat you have yourself invited; and I do not wish to see you depart in anger. I have learnt much from you and yours, the knowledge of which was very welcome to me, and for that I am grateful. If I cannot fulfil your wishes, believe that it grieves me; and if on some points we differ from each other, do not imagine that causes me to respect you less highly. If you will leave us, so be it; but let us part in friendship. Let our parting be in the spirit of the noble Founder of your religion, who said well, that He came not to bring peace but a sword, and yet strove to lay the foundation of a kingdom of peace and love amongst men."

If Aquaviva a few moments before had bent his head before the might of the Emperor, another power now subdued him, that of Akbar's moral greatness. The religious fanatic, the passionate zealot, himself felt this, and it was with a trembling voice that the defiant, fearless apostle spoke a few words of farewell to him who stood there obdurate of heart, his eye blinded to the light of truth, and his ear deaf to the warnings of the one Holy Church.

"Forgive us, noble prince," he said, moved in spite of himself, "if we have said what was displeasing to you, and seemed ungrateful for the many benefits we have received in your kingdom, or at your hands. Ascribe it to the fervour for our faith which animates us, and which is certainly not less strong than the enthusiasm which leads you to devote your life to the welfare of your people. Though you may yourself set no value on our prayers, yet be assured wherever we may go they will always be offered up for you."

Silently Akbar returned the reverent greeting of the Padre, as he slowly left the room, his fingers moving nervously, as if he were telling his beads.

In one of the passages of the palace, where a single lamp shed a dim, uncertain light, he suddenly stumbled against a man, who answered his excuses by a suppressed curse. "Cursed Christian dog," he muttered, as he hurried on. It was Abdul Kadir Badaoni, who was on his way to the Emperor, into whose presence he was ushered by servants, and who greeted him by saying, "You see I am always ready to speak with you. I made no difficulty about receiving you when this morning you requested an audience, although the sad circumstances in which I am placed have caused me to see but little of my friends in these last days."

"Sire," began Abdul Kadir, with apparent respect, but in a tone of unmistakable anger, and without paying the least attention to the friendly manner in which the Emperor had received him, "I come to bid you farewell; the time of my departure draws near."

"You also, my worthy friend?" asked Akbar. "And what obliges you to leave us so suddenly?"

"Unwillingness," was the reply, "to remain here and witness what is to me a daily scandal, and grieves me to the soul; and unwillingness, also, to take part in the treachery and conspiracies with which I see you surrounded, and in which, against my own wishes, I must share were I to linger here. Akbar, your empire approaches its fall! I warned you, when yet there was time, to save yourself; now, perhaps, that time is passed. I know not what is decided on, and I do not wish to know. The resistance you have aroused by your foolish and criminal scorn of our holy religion is, I consider, too powerful to be turned aside. Think of the ambition of Salim your son, and the secret alliance of other and not less ambitious people, who know how to lead him away, so that they may become masters of the rank and appointments now withheld from them. Think of all this, and you will agree with me that the state of affairs is at best extremely threatening to the continuance of your reign; but, as I said," he continued, not remarking the slight smiles that his dark forebodings had called forth on the lips of the Emperor, "I will not remain to be a daily witness of what here occurs, and is talked of far and wide. The holy Koran you have scorned and trampled under foot; you deride the great Prophet; you indulge in godless practices, learned from impious fire-worshippers; you receive openly at court, and privately in your own apartments, our bitterest foes—the Jews and Christians—you treat them with honour and load them with favours—such a one I have just seen leaving your palace; you receive Indian charmers and magicians, and all such people as Shaitan himself has sent here. In truth, Jalalu-dín Muhammad, you do honour to your name! Jalalu-dín, the glory of faith! Bitter irony of destiny that gave you such a title, which you were destined to insult in so shameful a manner. And now, again, as if all that were not enough, as if you would fill up the full measure, see, see the exaggerated honours paid to the memory of this Abú-l Fazl, this arch enemy of the true faith! He, with his brother Faizi, the denier of God, tempted you to this injustice and to the desertion of our holy religion; and this is the man whom you publicly honour and exalt above all. If his life was no warning to you, then may his death be so before it is too late. You have been told, doubtless, all that was beautiful about his last moments; but believe me that the truth has been withheld from you. I, however much it may cost me, will draw back the veil, and tell you how Abú-l Fazl died. Hear, and shudder at the terrible account which is known to everyone excepting yourself. As long as speech was left to him, Abú-l Fazl did not cease to blaspheme his God in a manner to awaken horror in all who heard him; then he began to yelp or bark like a dog; his features were contorted and his lips blue, as though he already felt the first pangs of that eternal punishment that awaited him."

"Those are lies, shameful lies!" cried Akbar, suddenly awakening from the composure with which, until now, he had listened to the fanatic's ravings. "Shameful scandal, of which you religious zealots are alone capable, when you leave reason in the lurch and seek to throw blemishes on a noble character. How Abú-l Fazl died, and what were his dying words, I know from one I can trust; therefore spare me your idle inventions. I will not hear them. I have listened patiently to the insolent words you have dared to use towards me; I have shown you an indulgence that perhaps no prince in my place would have done, and you have misused it, which I will not suffer. Attack me, insult my dearest convictions, revile me, Akbar your Emperor,—it is well; all that I will pardon. But do not calumniate my truest and treacherously murdered friend, or I will make use of my power to silence for ever the tongue that has attacked in so cowardly a manner a hated opponent who can no longer defend himself."

"Take my head," said Abdul Kadir, as, undismayed, he looked the Emperor in the face. "You know that I have ever desired to give my life for you. If my death can do you no service, it may at least appease your unjust wrath. I have said what I believed to be the truth, whether you believe it or not. I did my duty, and you can do yours, or what you are pleased to consider as such."

"Enough," said Akbar, recovering from his indignation; "I desire your life as little as your death. Go hence unharmed, but do not dare ever again to come into my presence."

Without a word of greeting, Abdul Kadir turned round, and with a proud and defiant look strode towards the door; but as he laid his hand on the curtain that hung before it, the Emperor called him by his name, and the proud Muhammadan turned round in surprise.

"Abdul Kadir," he said, "do not let us part so. We have known each other too long, and learnt to respect each other too highly, to part in such a manner. For I know, in spite of our difference, your respect and esteem are mine—even your vehemence proves it; and I, on my side, do not only look upon you as a learned and wise, but as a brave and honourable man, which in these days is of far greater value. I would not willingly see any one leave me in anger, and you least of all. Go; I understand that it is necessary you should do so, and that it cannot be otherwise; but do not go with wrath in your heart: think on the long years that we have passed together in peace and friendship, and forget the cause that makes our parting unavoidable."

As Akbar began to speak, Abdul Kadir's countenance still retained its defiant expression; but by degrees this softened at the generous words of the forgiving prince, and though he said nothing, his whole bearing spoke, as Akbar held out his hand. He grasped it warmly, and a tear fell on it as he bent his head. Then he turned and went, never to return, for he also was one of those whom the Emperor would see no more. Akbar remained for some time gazing towards the curtain that had closed behind his friend of former years. At last, with faltering step he approached the open gallery, and gazed out on the gardens, with their softly falling fountains, lying in profound peace under the silvery moonlight. Then, wearied out, he sank on one of the marble seats, and covered his face with his hands.

Thus, they all forsook him one after another: Abú-l Fazl cruelly torn from him, the Christian missionaries departing in anger, and now Abdul Kadir bade him farewell for ever; and all this happened in the moment when, above all, he needed the support of true friends—in the midst of dangers and difficulties, when even his own son rose against him, and strove to wrench from his hands the sceptre he had so long wielded for the prosperity and welfare of his subjects. And all this for the sake of religion! For that Salim took up arms in the name of the true faith was certain; and it was generally believed that Nara Singh had been a tool in the hands of religious fanatics.

"Religion," said Akbar to himself, "what is it, then? Is it a blessing bringing peace and joy to the soul of man, showing him his utter nothingness, leading him to humility and adoration, and awakening in him the love of his fellow-man, and the desire to live for the good of others? Or is it a fatal thing, making man prouder, more overbearing to others, the deeper his convictions are rooted; a madness that at times masters the greatest and noblest, forcing them to hate and curse, and that brings crime, murder, and bloody strife amongst the people? Would it be fortunate, or unfortunate, should the human race with one consent cease to possess any religion? Unanswerable question! Full of the greatest contradiction, and yet to which every one would be ready to reply without thought. Without religious worship all are agreed that there can be no salvation for man, no order in society. But when the question of the choice of a religion arises, at once the flames of conflict break out; and each man cries 'Mine, and mine alone!' Swords leap from their scabbards, and steel and violence are to decide what is truth. Is it possible that some day a religious system may arise that will content all, and unite the human race in one bond of love? Were they idle and foolish dreams with which I flattered myself when I believed that I had found it? Alas! it is hard to lose friends, but harder to lose cherished illusions that are dearer still."

A hand laid gently on his shoulder made Akbar look up. By his side stood Faizi, to whom was allowed the privilege of approaching the Emperor unannounced.

"Akbar," said Faizi, "awaken from your sad and useless musing. Must I be the one to say to you, be a man!—I, who, in comparison with you, am so weak? But it is necessary that I should so speak. I do not feel less keenly the loss of my dear brother, than you the loss of a true councillor and a much-loved friend. It is necessary that we should both rouse ourselves, and not allow grief so to overwhelm us as to make us weak in the face of dangers that still threaten the kingdom; therefore I dare to say to you, show yourself again a man. To be so cast down is unworthy of you; and if Abú-l Fazl could know it, he might perchance acknowledge for the first time in his life that Akbar is not faultless."

"My true and noble friend," said Akbar, "I thank you from my heart for your frank words. To exchange thought for action is indeed now necessary. However, you perhaps are mistaken as to the nature of the thoughts in which you found me sunk; the memory of your brother had only a share in them." And then Akbar recounted the farewells of Aquaviva and Abdul Kadir, and the reflections to which they had given rise.

"In all that," said Faizi, after a moment's reflection, "I recognise my magnanimous Emperor, and my philosophical and idealistic friend. You know what are my feelings on the subject you have touched upon. I do not set much store by what men are wont to call religious worship, when by that they mean an unlimited mystical feeling devoid of all reality, and still less when it depends on unproved propositions and dogmas that take their rise in imagination. However right men may be when they call me atheist, they are not so when they deem me an unbeliever. On the contrary, I believe much; but my faith rests on firm ground, on that of experience itself. Among other things, I believe, as I have said more than once, in the law of gradual development, not in material life alone, but especially in the soul and mind of man. In this development I see the solution of the great problem that you, like all other reformers and founders of religions, most wish to discover. Think where we men began, and how far we have already progressed, and think at what point we may yet arrive! We were nothing better than animals, and after the lapse of some thousand years we are reasonable beings; and when thousands and thousands of years have rolled by, where shall we be? Shall we not—not only some of us, but all, perchance—have attained a clear insight into the immortal and necessary union of things (or union of spirit and matter) through continued search and through the development of knowledge. Then, content and resting on this knowledge, should we not dispense with the dreams that we now accept under the well-sounding name of religious worship, which, well-considered, is only a means to satisfy our self-love, by assuring us of salvation in a future state, which no mortal can put on one side."

"Your spirit soars high," said Akbar, "and your eye sees far—to me it seems too far and too high. I think of the present; the future brings me but little consolation."

"But," asked Faizi, "do I lose sight of the present? Does it not belong to the first maxim of my faith—or, if you prefer it, to my philosophy—that men should fulfil to the uttermost the duties laid upon them? Truly, contemplation and knowledge are idle when for their sake reality is thrust on one side. If philosophy did not teach us to devote our powers to the living present, then were it nothing but a phantasy and an idle delusion of the soul. To work with zeal and energy for the end we propose to ourselves, is a very different thing from wishing for impossibilities, and falling back discouraged at our want of success. And so it is with religion, or, in a more limited sense, with the religion of the people, or the conviction of the people respecting the invisible world. This does not develop suddenly at a sign from some inspired reformer, but slowly in the course of ages; and in all cases it must be preceded by an indispensable condition, that of the cultivation and enlightenment of the people, and this is not possible unless they possess the means—not possible without prosperity. And in that which concerns the first foundation of enlightenment and cultivation, has Akbar just cause for self-reproach and discouragement? Can he say that he has not done enough, or at least much, for the welfare of the people entrusted to his rule? Look back, my Emperor, on what you have accomplished, and, leaving your theological contemplations on one side, judge if the consequences of what you have done are not the best encouragement to continue with energy the work that is already begun."

Faizi was right, it was no flattering speech of a courtier, when he praised the social reforms that the Emperor had introduced and continued with success. The experience of following centuries bear out his words. Of Akbar's religious dreams scarcely a trace was left after his death, but his land system has remained the foundation on which the successive rulers of Hindustan have built, and at one time it was proposed, by an able and intelligent Englishman, to introduce this system into our Dutch Indian possessions, where it would have borne good fruit. This, however, fell to the ground through the dulness and want of knowledge of our Governors."

"You are right, Faizi," said the Emperor, rising to his feet and lifting up his head as though animated with new life; "we must work, not dream, work as long as the day remains, unwearied, and without pausing. You must stand by me now that I have lost my greatest support; and I think I may promise that you will be as content with Akbar as he with you. But now for one more emblem; averse to them as you are, this will find grace in your eyes. See yonder faltering, mighty apparition! in that I recognise the condition in which for days my soul has been bowed. But to-morrow the sun again rises, and I will once more show myself, not as I am, but as I should be. That is the duty of a prince. So long as the impulse does not come from the people, the prince, with his councillors, should be the fountain of light and life in the State. If at times I forget this,—then, Faizi, call, as Abú-l Fazl did, the holy duty of a prince before my spirit, and speak to me as you have done this night."

---

1 Akbar came into possession of Surat in 1572.

Chapter XIV.
The Discovery.

The Emperor, at the head of his troops, had set out for the north, and all accounts reported that he was already at some distance from Agra. Siddha was still waiting for orders to join his detachment, which had marched among the first; what wonder, then, if he had sought to shorten the time of waiting by repeated visits to Rezia Gulbadan! One evening he turned his steps towards her dwelling, although he could not flatter himself it was with the same eagerness as formerly. He had begun more and more to distrust her; and these repeated visits were partly to obtain more knowledge of her secrets and of the conspiracy. He little suspected that that evening would disclose to him more than he cared to know. Arriving at the little gate in the wall, he found, to his astonishment, that it was not shut as usual, and, in all probability through carelessness, the key had been left in the lock. He could therefore enter without giving the usual signal. Carefully closing the door behind him, he ascended the path with rapid steps. As he drew near the verandah he found fresh reason for surprise. Just at that moment a man entered, whom, at first, he did not recognise, but, as he withdrew into the thick shadow of the many plants, the lamplight showed his uncle Salhana, who, scarcely greeting Gulbadan, cried in the utmost excitement, "We are betrayed, shamefully betrayed! The Emperor," he continued, as Gulbadan listened in terror, "is acquainted with all our plans. How, I know not, but it is too true. I have positive information from Gorakh, who, as you know, accompanies the army in disguise. Akbar not only knows of our undertaking from the beginning, but his spies have informed him of all the changes that have taken place in our plans. Cunning as he is, he let it come to our ears that he had seen through our first plan, without letting us know that he was also acquainted with the second; allowing us to think that he had fallen into the trap. Now he and his army have marched as though really for Kashmir. That is all very well, but he will suddenly turn round, and by forced marches surprise us here at Agra, when we believe ourselves to be in safety. I am only just warned in time to prevent Salim, on the settled day, from being proclaimed Emperor; but that will not avail us much. When Akbar knows all, he will not spare us, although he may not catch Salim in the act; and nothing now remains for us but to have recourse to the most extreme measures."

"And what are they?" asked Gulbadan.

"Gorakh and his followers," answered Salhana, "can aid us, and they must. Before the Emperor has time to reach Agra his life must be taken."

At these words a shudder ran through Siddha, and he laid his hand on the hilt of his dagger, and was about to step forward, but restrained himself in time.

"Salim must know nothing of this," continued Salhana; "nor must we tell him when the deed is accomplished. He may, indeed, have his suspicions, but he will conduct himself as though he knew nothing; nor will he hold us in less honour. To-morrow I go to the army to arrange all with Gorakh, who has told me how I may recognise him in his disguise; and in the meantime you must take care that Salim is warned. I myself will not visit him, for fear of rousing suspicions. Tell me, on what footing are you now with him?"

"I have not seen him here for a long time," answered Gulbadan; "and the reasons for his continued absence are unknown to me. However, I am not uneasy: I know, cost what it may, he will have me for his Sultana; and that shall be when he is Emperor, not before."

"And while waiting, you occupy your time with that nephew of mine I entrusted to your care, is it not so? A brave young man, and one in whom you seem to find pleasure."

"For a time; but now he begins rather to weary me; and, well considered, he is not of much use. Without ceasing, one has to discuss with him over and over again all kinds of ideas of honour and duty. When he has served our turn, I shall show him the door, and all the more, as he may stand in the way of my plans with Salim."

"What is that?" suddenly asked Salhana, turning towards the garden side of the verandah: "I think I hear a movement; is it possible that some uninvited guest may have found his way in?"

"Impossible," answered Gulbadan; "the door in the garden wall is locked, is it not?"—Salhana had forgotten that in his haste he had left it open.—" And from the other side there is no danger, for Faizi started this morning to join the army. Go by this path, it will be more prudent, as you might meet Siddha in the neighbourhood of the garden wall."

"All, then, is settled, is it not?" said Salhana. "You undertake Salim and those here in Agra, and I charge myself with Akbar; and if I am fortunate, we and his people will shortly be freed from his rule."

With a slight greeting Salhana then disappeared behind a curtain, taking a side path unknown to Siddha, so that to follow him, according to his first impulse, was impossible.

The best course now was to return at once, and ensure the failure of the plot by warning the Emperor before the conspirators suspected anything. But his longing to show Gulbadan that he had ceased to be her despised tool was too great to be resisted, and with one bound he was in the verandah and standing before her.

"Cursed snake!" he cried, "you caused me to become a traitor; but do not flatter yourself that your accursed plot and that of yonder ruffian will succeed. I, who begin to weary you, will hinder it."

"Ha! you have been listening, then," said Gulbadan, an expression of hate and malice crossing her hitherto gentle face, depriving it of all its beauty; "and now you intend to betray us,—but that shall never be." Before Siddha could guess her intention, she flew towards him, aiming a blow at his heart with a dagger. He half-mechanically sought to ward off the blow, but his arm fell helpless to his side at the sight of a figure that appeared to rise from the ground behind Gulbadan, and who seized the murderess' hand in an iron grasp.

Gulbadan turned round hastily, and sank with a cry of horror to the earth. Behind her stood Faizi, and behind him two servants with drawn swords.

"Mercy!" she implored, returning to her senses, while Siddha stood motionless, gazing at the scene before him.

"Mercy, my lord and master!" And with her head bowed down so that her dark locks swept the ground, she crept on her knees towards Faizi, who stepped back as she strove to approach him more closely.

"Back!" he cried; "do not touch me. Bind that woman," he said, turning to his followers, "and take her to my castle of Mathura. There let her be closely watched; and should she ever make an attempt, however slight, to enter into communication with the outer world, then carry out the sentence from which to-day I spare her. Never again will I see her, nor a single hair of her guilty head." Then he turned and spoke to the fallen one who knelt at his feet; but his words were not such as to lighten her punishment. "Hope gives life," he said; "and you, whose name will never more pass my lips, perhaps flatter yourself with a vain expectation. You think you can reckon on the protection of one more powerful than I, or who will one day be so. You think that Salim will stand by you, and release you from your imprisonment. This is a vain hope. He whom you have also deceived imparted to me your connection with yonder man; and this was Salim himself, whom you imagined safe in your toils."

As he spoke, Gulbadan had raised her head, and listened with attention; but at his last words, with a cry she sank senseless to the ground, her arms stretched out in front of her.

"Do your duty," said Faizi to his followers. And she was hastily conveyed from the apartment. "And now you," said he, approaching Siddha, as he drew his sword from the scabbard.

"I have forfeited my life," replied Siddha. "Strike! I ask nothing better than death from your hands."

"That I understand," said Faizi, thoughtfully, and letting the sword sink slowly back into its sheath; "and I am not inclined to fulfil your wishes. Others in the same case would think differently. A Musalman would lay your head before his feet; a Hindu would have you strangled; and a Frank, most foolish of all, would challenge you to fight. But I choose none of these. You may live, and depart unharmed from hence. Live, with the remembrance of the ill you have done, and of the manner in which you, who call yourself a nobleman, have repaid a true friendship. The remembrance of this shall never leave you, though you may become famous and rise high in rank; and however highly you may be honoured and respected, yet you will always cast down your eyes before any honourable man, remembering how in your youth you treated a friend. This is the punishment I lay upon you! Now go."

Obeying an imperious sign from Faizi, and bowed down with shame, Siddha turned, and with faltering step took his way through the garden and still open door. For a time he wandered on unconscious of all around him. In spite of the lateness of the hour, he saw some labourers busy lading a boat; and as though it were his own affair, he stood narrowly watching their every movement, now wondering how they would manage to convey in safety some heavy bale over the plank that connected the vessel with the shore, and now shaking his head at their awkwardness. Then some soldiers attracted his attention, who sat drinking and playing dice by the wavering light of a torch, and he began to wish to join them in drinking and playing. But at that moment one thought drove out all others, the remembrance of the plot to murder the Emperor. Had Faizi heard all, so that he could warn Akbar? But these questions he was unable to answer. Then why not go himself, without a moment's further waste of time? Salhana was to start the following morning, and another starting at once could easily precede him.

Siddha wasted no more time in thought, but hurried to the quarter of the city where his detachment was; and giving over the command to another officer, he turned to his own dwelling, and ordered Vatsa to saddle the bay—the bay given him by Faizi, and which, after discovering Rezia's true name, he had never dared either to ride or return, though now, in the service of the Emperor and empire, he mounted it.

"Prepare to follow me to the army," he said to Vatsa, as he led the horse out, "but at some distance. Start in an hour's time, ride hard, and if necessary deliver the message with which I entrust you." He then imparted to him as much as was necessary touching the plot against the Emperor, and ordered him to seek Akbar at once if he should not find his master with the army. Having said this, he struck spurs to his horse, and set off at a gallop.

A hurried journey, neither allowing himself nor his horse necessary repose, soon brought him to the army; and no sooner had he reached the camp than he sought an audience with the Emperor, which, after a short delay, was granted him.

"What do you do here?" asked Akbar, in a stern voice. "Who has given you leave to desert your post in Agra? It may go hardly with you if you cannot answer to my satisfaction."

"Sire," replied Siddha, "if I had nothing worse than this to answer for, I might call myself happy; but I come to accuse myself of the greatest crime a soldier can be guilty of against his prince—that of treason."

"I suspected as much," said the Emperor, "and therefore gave you orders not to leave your post; and now you yourself come to assure me of your treachery. Good; speak further."

As shortly as possible, without withholding anything, Siddha recounted how, led away by Gulbadan, he had deceived his friend and benefactor, and become a traitor to his Emperor. During this recital Akbar paced up and down with slow steps, his countenance expressing nothing of what his feelings might be; but as Siddha ceased, he stopped before him, and said, sternly, "Your crimes deserve death."

"That I know well," was the answer; "and I come to receive my punishment at the hands of your Majesty,"

"Why did you not seek safety in flight, when you suspected that your treason was discovered?"

"Crimes demand their penalty; and how can I go forth into the world while it remains unpaid, an object of contempt to myself and others?"

"But how is it that you have come so suddenly to this determination? For this there must be some cause. I suspect you have not told me all; something is still wanting to your story."

"You are right; but what I have still to tell could not be said until my doom was pronounced. Now I can proceed. The power which, in spite of myself, that woman so long had over me was suddenly broken. The bandage fell from my eyes, and at last I saw clearly what I was, of what I had been guilty, and what punishment I deserved." And now followed more in detail the description of the scene that had taken place on the last evening he had seen Gulbadan, and of the plot he had overheard.

Still no expression was visible on the Emperor's countenance; but, as he again walked up and down, his step was more hurried. When the story was ended he remained for some time silent, and then said, "With reason you seem to have thought that your last communication might have some influence over the sentence that I had to pronounce on you. You have rendered a great service to me and to my kingdom, and you are mistaken if you imagine that the sentence I pronounced was an irrevocable one. To say that a crime deserves death, is not to say that no mercy can be shown to him who is guilty of it; and yours is a case in point. Without your further communication, I might have recalled what I said, and shown you mercy. You have sinned deeply, Siddha, against me, and certainly not less against my friend. You are not a criminal, you have been the victim of an overwhelming temptation, and I know myself what it is to be so tried. But your feeling of honour was not destroyed, and sprang again into life as soon as you awoke from your dream. I do not in the least palliate what you have done, nor consider your fault a light one; but I am of opinion that you do not belong to the class incapable of improvement, and who, for the sake of society, cannot be allowed to live. I believe that your future actions will wipe away the memory of your misdeeds, and your conduct of to-day assures me that you will never again be guilty of treachery towards me. I therefore give you your life, and leave you in possession of your rank. Do not let me be deceived in you a second time."

For some moments Siddha found it impossible to reply, but knelt before the Emperor and kissed respectfully the hem of his robe.

"I thank you, Sire," he said at last, as the Emperor signed to him to rise, "not for life, that was no longer of any value in my eyes, but for the opportunity granted me in some measure to make up for the ill I have done. And if I may ask another favour, it is that I may at once be allowed to take part in the war that is now being waged in the north against the robber bands."

"This favour I will also grant," said the Emperor; "but first I will entrust you with another task. Some of the most faithful of my own life-guards shall be placed under your orders; go with them to meet Salhana, seize him, and bring him here in the greatest secresy, so that Gorakh may know nothing of his arrest."

At a sign from the Emperor the audience was at an end; and no sooner had Siddha received the command of his troop of guards than he was again on the road. Sooner than he had expected, he met his uncle, who appeared to have travelled in great haste, and was accompanied by two followers. These were soon disarmed and prisoners. Salhana defended himself for some time, but was at last overpowered, and, to his anger, pinioned by order of his nephew, whom until that moment he had held in such contempt. A veil was flung around his head, so that no passers-by might recognise him, and he was hurried by his captors to the camp.

In the Emperor's tent his bonds were loosened, and he was left alone with Akbar and Siddha.

"Your treachery, Salhana," said the Emperor, "and your latest plans are known to me; your nephew has told me all. Prepare to die,—the executioners await you."

Flinging a glance of rage and hatred towards Siddha, Salhana threw himself at Akbar's feet, touching the ground with his forehead. "Spare my life," he implored. "Punish me, gracious Prince, as you will; but let me live, and I will confess all, and tell all that I know."

"Salhana," replied the Emperor, contemptuously, "I knew that you were a traitor and a villain; but I had still to learn that you were also a coward. As for your confessions, they are worthless; I already know all that you can tell me excepting one thing, where and how is Gorakh to be found?"

"This I can tell you," cried Salhana, welcoming with joy this ray of hope; "I can tell you exactly how to find him, and then——"

"I will grant you a shameful life; but should your information prove false, then, you understand, the sword awaits you."

Salhana now eagerly gave all particulars by which Gorakh might be recognised in his disguise.

"Have this man closely watched," commanded the Emperor, turning to Siddha; "and you yourself, with your men, go in search of Gorakh, and when you have found him, hang him on the nearest tree."

This order was executed without delay. They were soon on the track of the Durga priest, and before long he was their prisoner.

"Ha! my young friend," said he, with his hateful laugh, recognising Siddha; "and is this the way you repay the interest that I have shown in you? However, let it be; but show me one courtesy, that can cost you nothing. Tell me, who is my betrayer? It can only be Salhana; am I not right?"

"You are," answered Siddha; and then, turning to his followers, he said, "Forward! take this man outside the camp, and carry out the sentence pronounced by the Emperor."

"And what is the sentence?" asked Gorakh.

"The halter," was the reply.

"Good," he said; "that is in my line."

It was needless to bind him, for, without the slightest attempt at escape, he calmly walked between two soldiers.

For some time Siddha did not turn to look at him, nor did his guards observe his actions very closely. But as they left the camp, and Siddha turned to give some orders to his followers, he saw the Yogi busied in marking characters on a long leaf that he held in his left hand, and must either have picked up on the road, or have had concealed in his clothes. In another moment he held it high in the air, waving it as though it were a fan.

"Come," cried Siddha, impatiently, "leave that juggling alone, it can help you no further, and throw that leaf away; we have had enough of your magic."

Gorakh obeyed, but not before he had laughingly made two more signs in the air. He then threw it on the ground, and they proceeded on their way. A few moments later the lifeless body of the priest hung from the bough of a tree.

In the meantime two men, from their appearance the servants of some nobleman, had witnessed the arrest, and, unnoticed, had followed at some little distance the troop that was conducting the doomed man to his place of punishment. As soon as the soldiers had passed the place where Gorakh had flung away the leaf, the two men sought eagerly in the sand, and soon found the object of their search. It was a dry leaf, on which were hastily written a few words with some sharp-pointed instrument. After reading it together, one concealed it carefully in his garment, and they hurried back to the camp.

There, as soon as the news of Gorakh's death reached the Emperor, Salhana received the promise of his life; but was given in charge to some soldiers, who were to guard him closely. When the war was ended, then should it be decided what was to be done with him. Imprisonment in some fortress or other, he understood well, would be his lot so long as Akbar reigned. But when Salim ascended the throne, without doubt he would be set free; and then, perhaps, too, he would have an opportunity of wreaking his vengeance on Siddha.

He was not so closely watched but that it was possible to approach him; and one evening it happened that the servant of a splendidly dressed person that passed by, slipt a rolled-up leaf into his hand. What could it be? A secret communication from one of his friends, from Gulbadan perhaps, pointing out some means of flight. "Salhana," ran the hastily written note, "the Emperor who has doomed me shall not die to serve you; Durga chooses for her victim you, who have betrayed me."

With a cry of terror, Salhana's arms fell helpless to his side, and the leaf dropped to the ground. He knew but too well the meaning of those few words, and he knew that his sentence was irrevocable. The last order of the

Durga priest would not be neglected; rather hundreds of his followers would be sacrificed than leave that command unfulfilled. Was there indeed no hope, no chance for him? In truth, as good as none. If he were but in Agra or in some fortress! where it might not be so easy to penetrate to him as here in the open field. But he was in the rear of the army, which only progressed slowly. He implored his guards to keep good watch by him, as his life was threatened by assassins; but they only laughed at him, and he heard them say to each other, "That would be no great loss." Then he prayed to be allowed to have a light at night, and this request was only met with ridicule at his cowardice. He had not another peaceful moment. During the march he imagined that behind every bush he saw some dark figure lurking, that watched and followed in his footsteps. When they halted to rest he remained on his guard, keeping his eyes on the jungle and trees around. And then the night—the long, frightful, endless night! He did his best to remain awake, listening to every sound, and feeling around him in the dark; but at times sleep overcame him, and he awoke with a start of terror, and felt his throat, thinking he could not breathe. Sometimes he fancied the cord was round his neck, and about to be drawn tight; then he had to convince himself, by feeling with his fingers, that it was only imagination; and at last to put his hand to his throat became quite an involuntary movement. Then the question rose before him, whether he should not take his own life, and so end his martyrdom; but he dared not, his courage was not sufficient to plunge a dagger into his own heart; and then there was still the hope, however slight, that he might arrive safely at Agra. But slowly and still more slowly marched the army. At last the Thugs took upon themselves the task Salhana dared not perform, and freed him from his suffering. Early one morning his guard found him lying dead in the tent that had been pitched for his shelter during the night.

Chapter XV.
Amendment.

In the meantime affairs at Agra followed the course which Akbar and his councillors had foreseen, especially after having received Siddha's communication. It had been feared that Salim might be warned in time of the return of the army, and would not be caught in the act, in which case great difficulty would have arisen in convicting the Prince of treason; but now that the message from Gorakh, the chief of the conspirators in the army, had been intercepted; and that Gulbadan had been deprived of the means of warning Salim, the chance had greatly improved. In truth, though reports did reach the ears of the conspirators of the return of the Emperor and his army, yet as they were not confirmed by any tidings from their accomplices, these reports were considered as an attempt on the part of Akbar's friends to prevent the conspiracy from being carried out.

On the appointed day, Salim took possession of the imperial palace, and caused himself to be openly proclaimed Emperor. At the same time he dismissed many of the principal officers, appointing others in their places. Alarm and surprise became general throughout the town. Rich people closed their houses, and tradesmen their shops, and Agra, so populous and full of life, appeared a city of the dead. The reports of Akbar's return had found more belief among the people than among the conspirators, and they feared a terrible struggle when Salim, having strengthened himself in the fortress, should be able to offer a formidable opposition to his father. But when the Prince demanded admission to the fortress, to his no small astonishment the governor refused compliance, shut the gate, and directed his artillery on the town. The governor, faithful to Akbar, had, with his knowledge, chosen the side of Salim, so that the latter had thought himself certain of the fort. And now the reports of the movement of the army gained strength, and it was said that it was within an easy day's march. Placed, as it were, between two fires, and finding himself deserted by others who had aided his rebellion, Salim saw that his only hope was instant flight. But it was too late; the advanced troops had already closed all the entrances to the town, and as Salim attempted with a few followers to leave it, he was taken prisoner by a division of cavalry, and, though treated with respect, carried back to the palace where he had been proclaimed Emperor. A few days later he received an invitation to appear before Akbar, who had then returned to Agra—his prince, his father, and his judge! Salim was brave, still he felt his courage sink, being fully conscious of his guilt. He knew that Akbar could be generous, but still that he could be severe in inflicting punishment when it was necessary for the welfare of his kingdom. His well-grounded fear gave way to surprise, when, left alone with the Emperor, he found him stretched on a divan, supporting his head on his hand, the other hand hanging wearily over the side. He did not alter his position as the guilty one entered.

"I have long delayed seeing you, Salim," began Akbar at last, throwing a hasty glance at his son, who stood covered with shame before him. "I dreaded this interview, and wished that it might be spared me." For a few moments he was silent, then half raising himself, and holding his arm up in the air, he burst into a passionate and bitter complaint. "My son, my son," he cried, "that I should have lived to see this! To what have false friends and a false ambition led you? You knew how dear you were to me, and how, when it was possible, I sought to forestall your slightest wishes, and how I loaded you with honours and treasure; you know, too, you have heard more than once, both from your mother and myself, how I, then childless, prayed for the gift of a son, and how, when the prayer was granted, I celebrated it by the foundation of Fathpúr, where I had so often offered my prayers to Allah. But had I known what awaited me at your hands, my prayers had not been so earnest, nor my joy so great when they were granted. Ah! was it impossible that for once you should place some restraint on yourself, and wait with patience for your father's death before you ascended your throne? was it impossible to return in the slightest degree the love that I had always cherished for you, and which had surrounded you with benefits?"

Salim knew not how to reply, as his father for a moment ceased to speak. He felt this reception deeply, so different from what he had expected, and the loving though melancholy words addressed to him, in spite of his errors; for Salim was not bad, nor hard-hearted, but weak and easily led; and on him rested the curse of despotism that Akbar had escaped,—the curse of the despot, and of him who is to become one,—that of placing his own will in the way of right and duty.

"But no," continued the Emperor, "you would not, or rather you could not. You have never possessed the power of restraining yourself in anything; how, then, should you in this? For a time I saw with joy that you had given up your drinking, but for how short a time did this improvement last! You, who in my place wish to rule over others, cannot rule yourself. Had you only better understood your position, then your own interest would have shown you the right path. You would have seen that the straightforward fulfilment of duty would gain the respect and love of your future subjects; while actions such as those you were guilty of, only rendered you contemptible in their eyes, and when you had gained your wish and were their ruler, their obedience would be due to fear or self-interest, so foolishly and blameably have you lost their respect, and covered yourself and me with shame. If I could but have prevented this! I attempted it, when, following the counsel of Faizi, who was always well inclined towards you, I sent you to Allahabad, not suspecting that Salhana was a false traitor and one of the most dangerous of the party that was seeking to mislead you. Enough; the attempt to save you from your evil companions failed, and things continued their course. Then it became necessary to prove publicly that neither craft nor force could avail against Akbar, and that the reins of government remained in the Emperor's hands. You have forced me to it, and on your head rests the blame of what has happened to-day. You have done yourself much injury, and grieved me deeply, more deeply than you can comprehend. May you never learn from experience what a father feels when, sword in hand, he is forced to meet his son as an enemy."

This sad experience was not spared Salim, and in his old age the day came when the words of his father returned to his mind, and when Shah Jahan, his dearly-loved son, not only opposed him in the field, but defeated him more than once. When his father ceased speaking, his conscience awoke from its long sleep, and he recognised that crime to its fullest extent, which false councillors had palliated and made light of. Overcome by his feelings he flung himself on his knees before his father.

"Rise up," said the Emperor, at last, after having for some time silently regarded his son; "and listen. That I possess full right to inflict punishment upon you, you less than anyone can dispute. But I require from you no further humiliation than that which you have already undergone. I do not wish it, because it would damage your future rule, shaking that respect which men will owe to you when you succeed me on the throne. If I punished you further publicly, I might as well declare you disinherited, and choose one of your brothers as my successor; but that I neither will nor can do. I hold you too dear to take such a course, so long as it can be avoided; nevertheless all depends on you. Tell me frankly, do you wish to work with me for the good of my kingdom, or do you feel no inclination and no strength for it? In the one case I will charge you with an honourable, though it may be laborious share; in the other, you can remain at my court, and there endeavour to learn as much of the art of government as is indispensable for your future. I leave the choice to you."

"My father," replied Salim, "I feel that I deserve neither of the generous offers you make me, and I should not complain if my last deed excluded me from the succession to the throne; but if indeed you leave me the choice, then, without hesitation, I choose the first. However difficult and dangerous may be the task entrusted to me, I will strive my utmost to fulfil it. You have indeed laden me with favours and honours, perhaps too many; my time has been thrown away in idleness, while you spent every day, from morning to evening, labouring for the good of the State; and then miserable idleness led me away to listen to the temptation of traitors, who pictured to me the fame that would be mine when power was once in my hands. Now, give me some work, however lowly, and I may perhaps be able to make up for the evil I have done."

"You judge yourself justly," said Akbar, "and to know oneself is the first step in the right path. I acknowledge that I am not myself free from blame for leaving you without employment, in the midst of luxury and self-indulgence. But enough of this. The rich and fruitful Bengal has not long been subject to my rule, and does not yet enjoy the privileges of a settled government. Go, and help me to carry out my principles of government there also. You shall reign under me, but almost as an independent king, until the day when, after having won the respect and love of your people, you shall in peace succeed to the empire of the whole of Hindustan."

Tears of joy and gratitude sprang to Salim's eyes, as he respectfully kissed the Emperor's hand before leaving him, full of fresh courage and a new love of life. The reconciliation between father and son was sincere, and Akbar foresaw that the peace and friendship between them would never again be disturbed.

Though joy reigned in Agra as the time passed by, in Allahabad there was sorrow, at least in Iravati's heart; for the new governor, in a few words, had imparted to her the news of her father's death, but withheld from her all particulars, while he begged that she would remain in the castle as long as she pleased. She had never been aware of the crime of which Salhana had been guilty; and though she had not loved her father very dearly, still she had always held him in the highest respect, and, forgetting his recent treatment, she mourned him truly. In the midst of her grief another event happened, which gave her a fresh shock. Not long after the tidings of Salhana'a death had reached her, Kulluka the Brahman was announced. His faithful servant had been his only companion on his perilous journey from the north.

"Noble lady," he said, when admitted to Iravati's presence, "I accepted a sad task when I undertook to deliver a message, sad both for you and me. I bring you a token that you know well": and feeling in his girdle, he drew out a finely-woven veil, and laid it in her hands. It was the same she had thrown to Siddha when for the last time she had seen him beneath her balcony.

"I understand all," she cried, turning deadly white; "he is no more."

"When I left him," answered Kulluka, "he was still alive, but I fear the worst, and I doubt whether I shall ever more see my former pupil in life."

"But say, what has happened?" asked Iravati. "See, I am quite composed, and can listen calmly to all you have to tell."

Then Kulluka recounted all that he knew of Siddha's last encounter. The Emperor had granted his earnest wish, and allowed him to march with his

Rajpúts against the rebels in the north. There for some time, among the mountains so well known to him, he carried on a war which was both successful and glorious; he sought rather than avoided dangers, and had been victor in many a daring adventure, from which even the bravest of his followers had shrunk. At last, however, the insurgent bands, as he was traversing a mountain pass, managed to cut him off from the main body of his troop. After a long and hard struggle, in which many of the enemy fell before his sword, covered with wounds, he sank from his horse to the earth, while most of his followers lay either wounded or dead around him. Vatsa, who had never left his side, instead of attempting useless revenge, let himself slip from his horse, and lay motionless as though dead. A few moments later the troop arrived and drove back the enemy, and Vatsa sprang to his feet and found to his joy that his master still lived. With the help of some of the soldiers the wounded man was laid on a rude, hastily constructed litter, and carried to a Buddhist cloister in the neighbourhood. "At that moment," continued Kulluka, "I was myself in the cloister, when the soldiers arrived with their sorely wounded leader. The good monks gladly afforded him all the help in their power. Among them was one learned in medicine, who assured me that neither skill nor care should be spared to bring him back to life. After a time Siddha regained consciousness, and seeing me, made a sign of recognition; but it was some minutes before he gained strength to speak. 'Friend,' he said, 'I am going to leave you, I feel that I cannot recover. Do me a service.' I looked inquiringly to the monk learned in healing, but he shook his head. He also seemed to have little or no hope. He strove to enjoin silence on Siddha, but Siddha heeded not. 'I must speak,' he said; 'Kulluka, take the veil that you will find there with my armour, take it as quickly as possible to Iravati, and tell her that she was never so dear to me as now that death is near. Go at once, and do not wait for my death; let me die knowing that she has received this token from your hands.' He then shut his eyes and spoke no more. I did not hesitate to fulfil his last wish; and taking the veil, and leaving Siddha to the faithful care of the monks and Vatsa, I at once set out."

"I thank you," said Iravati, "for the service you have rendered us both. But Siddha still lived, he was not dead when you left him? Then I know what I have to do."

"To do?" asked the Brahman. "What can you do?"

"I shall go with you to Siddha," answered Iravati calmly.

"You!" cried Kulluka in astonishment; "a weak, helpless woman attempt to pass through mountains and forests swarming with bands of insurgents and robbers, without a strong escort!"

"You did not fear," was the answer, "to expose yourself to these dangers to fulfil Siddha's wishes, and I fear them as little. Do not be afraid that you will find me a hindrance; I am not so weak, and am well accustomed to mountains and forests. No," continued Iravati, as Kulluka made fresh objections, "do not attempt to shake my resolution, you will not succeed; and if you will not take me, then I will travel, accompanied by a servant. Do you think that I have come hastily to this determination, and that I shall draw back? I have more than once thought of the possibility of such an event as has now happened. I have often compared my life to that of Damayanti, and have determined that she should be my example. And what is my self-sacrifice to hers? Alone and despoiled of everything, she wandered through the wilderness, seeking her faithless consort. I, at least if you allow it, go under the protection of a man of tried courage, and where he can force his way I can follow."

"His arm will never fail when you need his protection," cried Kulluka; "and though his arm may be stiff, it still has strength enough to wield a sword. I both honour and respect the resolution to which you have come. Now prepare for the journey, and you will find me ready to undertake it with you."

Without delay Iravati gave orders to her servant to hasten all the necessary preparations for the journey, while in a few words she told her the reason for undertaking it. The faithful Nipunika was not a little shocked when she heard the recital, but as she made an attempt to dissuade her dearly loved mistress from the undertaking, Iravati insisted on silence.

"Let me go with you," entreated she.

"No," replied Iravati, "that is impossible; to protect one woman is enough for Kulluka and his servant. I have told you of my plan, which for the present must be a secret, in order that, in case I should not return, some one may know where I am, and what I am doing in Kashmir."

"But would it not be better to ask the Governor for an escort?"

"No, for a few armed men would awaken suspicion; and the Governor cannot spare a strong detachment. We three alone have a far better chance of accomplishing our journey in safety."

It was not, however, possible to depart at once, for Kulluka's horses were so fatigued by the distance they had come, that rest was necessary until the following day. Iravati found the hours of waiting long and wearisome: she sat, still dreaming over the one subject that was master of all her thoughts. Suddenly, with a terror which she could not explain to herself, she looked up as she heard the step of some one approaching, and in the next moment the man whom of all others she least expected to see, stood before her—Salim.

"You here!" she cried.

"I am on my way to Bengal," answered the Prince, "and have arrived at a fortunate moment, to hinder you from carrying out a plan too wild and foolish ever to have found place in the mind of a sensible woman. Through love to you your servant has disobeyed your orders, and begged me to interfere, which I have promised to do."

"Do not trouble yourself, my lord, with my plans, I entreat," said Iravati. "I am no longer a child that knows not what it does; and in any case, it is not your duty to watch over me."

"But I shall do so, for the sake of your welfare, and also—why should I not say it frankly?—because I cannot bear to see you go to my hated rival, who is himself untrue to you. I cannot bear the idea of your showering caresses on this man, if you find him living, when you have rejected me; and therefore I shall make use of my power, and force you to remain here against your will."

"You can do so, Salim," answered Iravati, "but you will not. You know well that instead of gaining by so cowardly an exercise of your power you would only lose; you would not win me, nor hasten Siddha's death by one moment; and this action would draw down upon you my deepest contempt instead of the respect which, until now, I have felt for you, although I could not give you my love. Do you desire this? And not my contempt alone, but also your own. Will you behave as a weak woman who is not master of her own heart, and give way to unreasonable passion? or do you wish to behave as a man who knows how to rule himself, and who, by so doing, shows me he is worthy to reign over others? Choose for yourself; I ask no favour."

With hasty step Salim paced up and down, while within his breast there was a bitter struggle between duty and passion, honour and self-will. To allow her, whom he had vainly striven to win, to go to his accursed rival was hard, almost beyond his powers. Still she was right; the exercise of his might would avail him nothing, only cause him to lose her respect, which he prized above everything. And then her last words, recalling his noble, generous father's exhortation, which he had so deeply felt! Self-control, self-denial, the first duties and virtues indispensable to a prince—never before had he considered them seriously; and after his promises to lead a new life, should his first action be one which Iravati, with justice, called a cowardly exercise of power?

"Iravati," he said, at last, "I submit, as I did before, to your will. What it costs me I need not say. Enough, I obey. Alas! as I said before, why did I not know you earlier? You would have made a different man of me; but this is all over, and I will endeavour to submit to the inevitable. Go, then; though I cannot but consider your resolution as rash, still I admit it to be courageous and noble. One thing more. It is not impossible that you may still find Siddha living, and then I understand only too well that you will be reconciled, and keep the faith you have sworn to him. I shall look upon this with envy, but neither seek vengeance on you nor on him whom you hold dear. Let it be said that the weak and selfish Salim controlled himself, and that the future ruler of Hindustan can rule his own heart. If, sooner or later, you or Siddha Rama have need of my protection, I give my princely word that it shall not fail you. Only one favour I ask of you, though you will receive none from me. Although it may be that we shall never meet again, do not refuse me your friendship, and do not think with anger and contempt of a man whose crimes towards you were caused by the deep love he felt for you."

He awaited no answer, but hurried away. "My father!" he murmured, "for once at least you have cause to be content with your son."

Chapter XVI.
Faizi's Curse.

In a Buddhist monastery among the mountains, Siddha lay stretched on his sick bed, while Iravati watched by his side. Her joy had been great at finding him still alive when, after her long and dangerous journey, she at length arrived; but this joy had been tempered by the doctor's assurance that his state was a most critical one. When she was admitted to his room, she found him still senseless; and who could say whether he would ever regain consciousness, or recognise her before his death?

After a long time of anxious watching, a slight improvement gave rise to hope, and Iravati was warned that if she would continue to tend the wounded man, she must allow herself more rest. Kulluka and the monks persuaded her to take short walks; and it was not without pleasure that she at times visited the little temple belonging to the monastery when the bell called the believers to prayer. With earnest attention she listened to the words of the chief priest when he spoke of the gradations of human life, and how sorrow fell on all, and how rare were the visits of happiness, and how the greatest bliss for man was to be freed from all human ties and to attain Nirvána.1 In these teachings Kulluka found much with which he could not agree, and, in other circumstances, would perhaps have remarked to the priest that to live for the good of others was a nobler aim of life than to remain sunk in idle contemplation. But opposition was perhaps superfluous. The practice of these Buddhists was better than their teaching; for though they took no part in the turbulent life and sorrows of the world, still they did not spend their time in idleness. Unwearily they wandered amongst the mountains, visiting all the poor inhabitants, scattering their good deeds and consolation wherever misery was to be found, without respect of nationality, religion, or caste.

One evening Iravati was seated by Siddha's couch, while the doctor watched him from the other side, when he slowly opened his eyes, and, throwing a hasty glance around him, seemed to recognise Iravati. He softly murmured her name, and again closed his eyes. The doctor made a sign to Iravati to withdraw, which she unwillingly obeyed, and hastened, with a heart full of joy, to seek Kulluka, and to impart to him the glad news. The next day the improvement still continued, and the patient could even speak. But Siddha made but little use of this power even when Iravati was with him; and though he knew her and his friend, he did not seem to remember any of the events that had happened,—a mist seemed to hang over his mind. Almost without consciousness he would sit, gazing before him, and only Iravati's voice could arouse him from this stupefaction. This still continued, even after his bodily strength returned and he was again able to take exercise.

Once it happened, as he strolled with Iravati in the neighbourhood of the monastery, that some word of hers, or some object on which his eye fell—she herself could not tell which—seemed to awaken memory in him. Suddenly he stood still, gazing with wonder around him, and passed his hand over his face. Then shaking his head, he walked on, and then again stood still, gazing inquiringly at the high mountain tops, then at the blue sky, and at the valleys and woods that lay around. A deadly pallor crept over his face, and with a wild look he turned to Iravati. Memory had returned in its full strength, but how? and, perchance, was not forgetfulness both better and happier?

"Go, go!" he cried, at last. "What are you doing here, unhappy one, with me? How can you bear that I should approach you—I, the faithless traitor, laden with the heaviest curse that was ever laid on man?"

Iravati listened in breathless terror. She did not understand all, though more than enough. She attempted to speak, but her voice failed her, and overcome with sorrow, she sank at his feet.

"The curse!" repeated Siddha, wildly; "the curse of Faizi—'Live with the memory of what you have done; and though you may attain all your heart desires, yet shall you always cast down your eyes before an honourable man.' And should I dare to raise them to you, pure and innocent, whom I betrayed as basely as I did my noble friend! Go, I say, far from here. A figure stands between you and me. It is that of Faizi. He stands there, threatening as when he spoke my doom."

As Iravati raised her head, she saw him cover his face with his hands, as though he dared not look at her. "Come," she said, "let us go in; you have done too much, and so false visions torment you. Come, then."

"Visions," answered Siddha, bitterly; "would that they were! But, no. I am now again myself; my strength has returned, and with it the recollection, the terrible recollection, more real than ever. I never yet felt the full meaning of Faizi's words; but now that I again see you, I comprehend them. Before the Emperor, and even before the meanest of my soldiers, have I cast down my eyes with shame; but never as now. Vainly I sought an honourable death. Iravati," he continued, "you do not know with whom you speak; you do not know my last crimes."

"I do know," she answered, "though perhaps not exactly what happened between Faizi and yourself; but I have gathered sufficient from the words you have let fall."

"And yet you still speak to me," cried Siddha. "You do not turn from me; you even come to tend my last days."

"Did I not give you my word, Siddha? and was I not bound to keep it until you yourself gave it to me back? and that you have never done. Did you not send me by Kulluka the token that told your last thought was mine? and I felt that I had taken duties on me, although no marriage ties bound us."

"Then I now release you from your promise," said Siddha. "It is true that no sooner did I awaken from that miserable blindness than my love for you returned with a strength that until then I did not know. You, you can be true to me, and fulfil all your duties. But you can love me no more."

"I love you now, as I always did," replied Iravati.

"You seek to convince yourself that you do, from an exaggerated feeling of honour; but it is not possible that you should do so, and the day would come when you would regret that you had not known yourself better. There can be no love where there is no respect. The woman must look up to the man, and unhappy is the union where he is the weaker. Go, and forget me; I am not even worthy of your remembrance."

"Then you thrust me away?"

"I have no right to thrust you away, nor to release you from your word. I only do so in order to give you rest, and to spare you any self-reproach that you might feel at leaving me of your own free will."

"Listen to my prayer, Siddha," said she, entreatingly, and laying her hand on his arm. "I will not dispute what you say, I will not wish or require anything as my right. I only implore you to listen to the wish that is dearest to my heart. I do not ask any promise for the future. I give you the fullest liberty; but let me remain with you for the present, even if it is for a short time. It is impossible for me to part with you now."

"No, and never!" answered Siddha, sternly. "No hesitation, no weakness; once for all, leave me and forget me." And pushing Iravati, who went on before him, he prepared to hurry away, so that he might never again see her whom until this moment he had never loved so tenderly.

"Let it be so," said Iravati, rising up, with an injured feeling of self-respect, and speaking with a firm voice; "let it be so, you are perhaps right. You make yourself unworthy of my love. Once, in spite of your promises, you have been unfaithful to me, but that I had forgotten and forgiven; for I knew you had been led away by temptation unknown to me. But now you drive me from you, not because I have committed any fault, but because you are too proud to confess to your wife that you have once been weak and unable to withstand temptation. Leave me, then. Without you my life is without value; but a forced love no woman can seek, not even from the man she loves. And now, to the memory of the crime you have been guilty of against a friend, add the memory of a woman whom you loved, yet sacrificed to your selfish pride."

Siddha hesitated. Should he go, or stay? The latter he would gladly do, but how could he reconcile it with honour? "Who shall decide?" he said, striking his forehead with his hand. "There is truth in what you say, though it is in conflict with what I consider right. Yet," continued he, "another, who is wiser than either of us, shall decide between us."

"You mean Kulluka?"

"No, not him. Highly as I prize his opinion, I know beforehand that he would only try to secure our happiness, and, to do so, would decide that you are right. He would not be impartial in his judgment. There is another; but do not ask me further. He alone can I trust to decide between us; and he will advise me. Listen, then, Iravati; let me depart hence as speedily as possible. Perhaps I shall return soon, perhaps never. Should I return, then my life shall henceforth be devoted to you. If not, then understand that you will never see me more, and that you are freed from all ties that bind you to me. Do not raise objections, but have patience with me, such as, till now, you have always shown."

Before Iravati could reply to this new and unexpected proposal, Siddha had disappeared to seek his servant, and to order his horse to be saddled, so as to set out on their journey, his destination being unknown to her.

Iravati hastened to Kulluka, and told him all that had passed, and Siddha's extraordinary determination; but the guru, seeing that it was better to let Siddha take his own way and not to oppose him, tried to console Iravati with the hope that she would soon see him again. In the meantime Siddha had taken leave of the Buddhist priest, giving him a rich present for the benefit of the monastery, and then, followed by Vatsa, had ridden away.

Again the last rays of the setting sun fell on the slopes of the Himálayas, and again Siddha, accompanied by Vatsa, followed the path that led to the valley where the habitation of Gurupada was situated. He was received by the old servant, who quickly recognised him, and without delay led him to his master.

The hermit welcomed his young friend with pleasure, but saw with concern the change that had taken place in his appearance. His face, once so full of joy and life, was now pale, and had assumed a sad and dark expression; and his whole bearing had lost its former elasticity. In but a short time the youth had become a man, and not one full of life and strength, but one bowed down under the weight of sorrow, which Gurupada's sharp sight told him was the heaviest that falls to the lot of man, that of self-reproach.

"Most revered," said Siddha, after the first greetings; "or let me rather say, most gracious prince——"

"No," interrupted the hermit; "continue to call me Gurupada, for I am nothing more."

"I obey," said Siddha, "and I see with joy that you have not forgotten me. Perhaps you still remember the last words you said to me, when, after a short visit to your hospitable dwelling, we took our leave."

"I made you promise," replied Gurupada, "to seek me again if it should ever chance in your life that you should need the counsel of a true friend; and I understand that this is the reason which now brings you here. If I may judge from your looks, the cause of your coming is a very bitter one."

"You are right," said Siddha; "and when you have heard all, you will wonder that my appearance does not more clearly proclaim my feelings."

"Come now," said Gurupada, "to the other side of the house; there we will seat ourselves, and talk quietly of all that has happened."

Siddha gladly accepted the invitation, and after having, at the earnest request of the hermit, partaken of some refreshment, he began to recount all that had happened until the moment of his parting with Iravati in the cloister.

Gurupada listened with the deepest attention and interest; and when the tale was finished he remained for some moments silent, sunk in thought; but at last, looking at Siddha, he said: "In truth you have laden yourself with a heavy burthen, but not so heavy as that a man cannot bear it. That you allowed yourself to be led away by Gulbadan is not to be defended, although it may be excusable; but that you did not part from her, after discovering who she was, was an inexcusable offence against your friendship with Faizi. Your original faithlessness towards the Emperor was partly the result of an error; but to remain in his service and to conspire against him was a crime. I do not judge your conduct more leniently than you do yourself; on the contrary, I judge it still more harshly. You believe that the tale of your faults was closed when you confessed your crimes to the Emperor. But you deceive yourself, you began to commit another, which may be just as unfortunate as those which preceded it, although you were led into it by an error. The greater part of mankind imagine with you that repentance is a virtue, and that by penance and self-punishment alone can sin be washed away. But few errors are so ruinous in their result as this, when penance consists in the penitent's withdrawal from the circle in which he can labour usefully, and when also he punishes others as well as himself. And this is what you would do. First, you sought death on the field of battle, which was the simplest place, as you would not lay violent hands on your own life. But what good would your death have produced, or how could it undo the ill you have done? Unable to find an honourable death, you declare your intention of living a solitary life in the jungle, devoted to prayer and penance; but for what? How could this serve yourself or others? And then Iravati, your bride! you desert her, not because she is faithless to you, but because you have cause to feel shame in her presence. Thus you punish her more than yourself. Do you call that duty and virtue? No, my friend, such a course would end in being worse than an error. You look at me with astonishment; but the course you propose would be one of pride and defiance, because you know that you have lowered yourself. Iravati was right; you were too proud to bind yourself to a woman who knew all your weaknesses, and who had nothing to reproach herself with; and it is indeed pride that prompts you to fly the world. You fear to meet some one acquainted with your former evil deeds. You dare not look a man in the face, for fear of what he may know of you. Is that, I ask, virtue and courage? is it not, rather, a cowardly weakness?"

"But Faizi's last words," said Siddha.

"I foresaw that objection," continued Gurupada; "and I do not deny that it has a certain weight. But let us beware of exaggeration. That Faizi should have acted and spoken as he did is easily to be understood in his place. You probably would have done the same; and he, were he in my place, and had to decide impartially, would doubtless say as I do. A man need not spend his life bowed down in humiliation because in an evil hour he has been guilty of a shameful deed, when his after life has been spent so as to gain the respect of his fellow-men. Now listen to the counsel you ask of me, which I willingly give. You have arrived at the full consciousness of the wickedness of your conduct, and you have accused yourself before the Emperor, before Iravati, and before me. That was well done; but the knowledge and clear insight of your evil-doing must not be the last step, but the first, in the right path. It should restrain you from all errors, not only those of the same class that have already led you astray, but also from others. It should teach you to keep better watch over yourself, your impressions, your passions. You should have greater dread of deeds which you could not confess to others without shame; and in the end you should attain to a state of mind which will make it impossible for you to act against duty or honour. But this cannot be if you seek to avoid temptation by flying from it. Resist temptation, and begin in the first place by conquering your own pride. Therefore take Iravati for your wife, and render yourself worthy of her. Go to the Emperor, and pray him to entrust you with some work by which you may serve your country; I doubt not but that he will willingly grant your request. I understand that you desire to avoid Faizi, and that is well; you owe it to him to spare him any meeting, and Hindustan is large enough to keep two men apart. In Kashmir, or in other places, you may render as good service as in Agra itself. Think over this, and, after reflection, let me know what your decision is.—No, no, do not answer me at once," said Gurupada, seeing Siddha ready with his reply; "take the repose of which I see you have need, and to-morrow, when you have thoroughly weighed all I have said, tell me if you still see difficulties in following the advice I have given." And with a friendly greeting the hermit left Siddha to his own thoughts.

The next day Siddha was ready to take farewell of Gurupada, perhaps for the last time. For a long while the two men stood in earnest conversation, and as at last the traveller turned to mount his horse, he warmly pressed his host's hand, saying, with a trembling voice, but with a countenance cleared from all trouble, "I thank you, Gurupada, for the manly advice you have given me; I owe you a new life, and I hope to bear myself in it very differently from what I have done in the past, which I shall never forget. You have taught me what true repentance is; may I never give you reason to think that your good counsel has been given to one who is unworthy of it."

1 There have been many discussions on the true meaning of Nirvána. The best essay on the subject will be found in the "Pali Dictionary" of Mr. Childers.

Chapter XVII.
The Tomb.

In the neighbourhood of the village of Sikandra rises that magnificent building, the tasteful splendour of which is the pride of Hindustan, while it awakens the admiration of all travellers, and is one of the last memorials of the departed greatness of the Mughals. A wall with many towers gave entrance, through a broad gateway of red marble, to a path lined with shady trees, above which rose a building of majestic height and of great circumference. This building excited admiration, not alone by the stern beauty of its outline, but also by the richly-wrought gateways, minarets, cupolas both high and low, and open galleries, by which it was surrounded, giving it more the appearance of a number of palaces and pleasure-houses than of a monument. However, it was not destined for the abode of the living, but to preserve the memory of the illustrious dead,—of Akbar himself.1

A few years after the occurrences already narrated, a silent pair stood in this park: a powerful man, in rich attire, one hand resting on the hilt of his sword, while the right was thrown round a lovely woman who stood beside him, looking like the graceful ivy that clings to the oak. It was Siddha Rama, accompanied by Iravati. They stood lost in admiration before the tomb, and thought of the man of whom they had so often spoken with the greatest reverence.

Much had happened in these few years. Akbar was no more, and in his place reigned his son Salim, who, in accordance with the wish of his father as he lay on his dying bed, had girded on the sword the Emperor had always worn, and who was now, under the name of Jahangir, the Emperor of Hindustan.2 That he was not to be compared to Akbar was to be expected, still his reign was not bad; and it fell to the lot of his successors—to Shah Jahan3 and Aurangzíb4—so to corrupt the formerly powerful empire, as that it fell an easy prey into the hands of British conquerors.

Salim had not entirely laid aside his evil habits, and Sir Thomas Roe, the English ambassador, had an opportunity of seeing him in much the same situation as Siddha had done, at the banquet given in his palace. Still he was not the hopeless drunkard that he had appeared to be.5 To Iravati he had kept his word, and in spite of his disappointment, found himself happy in his marriage with the wise and beautiful Mahal, whose influence over him was great, and always for good.

That Kashmir must in the end submit, had long been foreseen; and after the failure of Salim's conspiracy, it cost Akbar but little trouble to penetrate through the ruined country and force it to come under his rule. The weak king died, his unworthy sons were banished, and Siddha's father was made Vice-King, Siddha receiving an important appointment, with the understanding that he should succeed to the Viceroyship; while Kulluka, faithful as ever, was always ready with counsel and advice. It was not long before the people began to appreciate the blessing and prosperity of a wise and settled rule.

The hermit of Badari-Natha did not long survive the subjection of his country. Once, when Kulluka went to visit him, he found the servant alone. His master had become suddenly unwell. He died in a few days, and was buried on the heights overlooking Kashmir. Hara, the tiger, laid himself down on the grave, and growled fiercely when the servant sought to entice him back to the house. He refused the food and water brought to him, and in a few days was lying dead on the grave of his friend and master.

Parviz knew nothing of the affair with Gulbadan, and Siddha occasionally received good news from him. He was happy in his marriage with the daughter of the Treasurer, and though in high office, was busy in arranging the literary and diplomatic papers of Abú-l Fazl, his deeply lamented uncle.

Abdul Kadir held himself aloof from public life, and though wiser, was still an earnest enthusiast for the true faith. He sought consolation for his many disappointments in writing his history,[6] in which he complained bitterly of Akbar, and railed at Abú-l Fazl and Faizi, although they had never harmed him.

Padre Aquaviva did not return to Agra, but others came to continue his work, with as little success. Though three centuries have passed, the conversion of Hindustan remains the dream of western zealots.

Whether the faithful Vatsa espoused the talkative but good-hearted Nipunika, history says not; but it is very probable that they followed the example of their master and mistress. The happiness of these two was unbroken, though dark memories often arose in Siddha's mind. But by degrees he had learnt not to allow himself to be weighed down by them, and to hide his regrets from Iravati. He had remarked how deeply it grieved her when his countenance was clouded with gloomy thoughts of the past, the cause of which she well understood, for he had confessed all to her. Soon after their marriage she had given him a son, whom he loved nearly as much as herself. He understood how great a treasure he had won, when he heard of Salim's wishes, and what her answer had been; but when he expressed his admiration, she only replied that in her place every woman would have acted in the same manner.

Siddha remained long lost in thought before Akbar's tomb, when his attention was roused by an approaching footstep. In dismay he stepped back as he recognised who drew near; and the exclamation which broke from him told Iravati what an unhappy meeting had chanced.

"Faizi!" he cried.

He who, lost in thought, was passing them, suddenly stood still, and then drew back, as he recognised the man who had so deeply injured him. But, changing his mind, he slowly advanced, and as he saw Siddha preparing hastily to withdraw, he said:

"Remain, and listen to me. Here, by the tomb of the prince who ever more willingly forgave than punished his enemies, and who did not know what hate was, I should feel no anger. I have often striven to follow his noble example, and to forgive the wrong you have done me. I could not, I had not the strength; but now, on this holy spot, where accident has brought us together, I have found strength to do what Akbar in my place would have done. I forgive you, Siddha."

Deeply touched, and with bowed head, Siddha stood before his noble enemy, while Iravati gazed with admiration on the man who in such a strife had been victor over himself.

"Look up," continued Faizi; "no longer avoid the sight of your former friend. The words that I addressed to you in my anger were not undeserved, but to a man of your character they were a fearful and perhaps too severe a punishment; and I know from Kulluka what an influence they have had on you, and to what wild actions they nearly drove you. From our friend I learnt that in the first place you were not the tempter, nor in the beginning did you know who the tempter was. Her great influence and power I know well myself; but she is no longer to be feared. In her captivity she herself made an end to her guilty life. Enough of the past, especially in the presence of her whom I must greet as your noble consort. Let the past, then, be forgotten by us. What I have since heard of you, has made you again worthy of the respect and friendship of a man of honour. Take, then, my hand, as of old."

It was Iravati who clasped it, while Siddha could scarcely conquer his emotion.

"I thank you," she said, "from my heart, for your generosity. What you have said has lifted the dark cloud that overshadowed our married happiness, and the leaden weight is at last removed which for so long has weighed my Siddha down."

"I seek for words," at last said Siddha; "but words to express what at this moment I feel are not to be found. Once I thought myself comforted and strengthened by the words of a wise man, and as though I were born to a new life; but now I feel the new birth for the first time. Your friendship,

Faizi, was always most deeply prized by me, and all the bitterer was my self-reproach, and the harder my punishment, to lose it so shamefully, and through my own fault. The friendship that you give me back so nobly, I esteem as the highest gift I could receive."

"Our present accidental meeting," replied Faizi, "must be of short duration, and in all probability it will be our last. That I have withdrawn from the service of the State is already known to you. Salim, or, as he likes better to be called by his proud title, Jahangir, never looked upon me or my brother with a favourable eye; besides, I should find it hard to serve him, for reasons which you need not that I should explain, and so I withdrew myself from public life, and lived retired at Agra. But now Shah Abbas, King of Persia, has invited me to his capital, and to occupy myself there with literary studies.7 This invitation I have accepted. I start for Ispahan to-morrow, and I may remain there. But I could not leave this country without a farewell visit to the last resting-place of my princely friend—the friend who was everything to me, Siddha, more than life or happiness; and had you sinned against him, I do not believe that I could ever have pardoned it. But you have shown that you honoured and prized him, though you never had the opportunity of knowing him intimately, as but few did, both in his greatness and his weaknesses, which were still loveable."

"It is true," rejoined Siddha, "I never learnt to know him closely, but I have known enough to awaken my deepest admiration and reverence. I knew another prince whose life has ended, to whom I owed a debt of gratitude, and his memory is dear to me; but if I was asked which was the greatest, I am now convinced that the secluded philosopher, who had said farewell to all worldly joys, was surpassed by the philosopher on his throne, who in the midst of the wildest divisions and disturbances knew how to preserve the same evenness of character and uprightness of mind. In truth Akbar deserves his name."

"And that shall be said by all coming generations," replied Faizi, "both in the East and West. The title of 'the Great' has been given by favourites and flatterers to many a prince, but with little right. To be truly great means that a ruler knows how to govern himself as well as others, and to give up his life to sorrow and trouble for the welfare of his fellow-men; and it was in this that he who rests yonder was great. There have been princes, and there still may be more, whose names in the world's history will be better known than his; and it is possible that there may be those who will win still higher fame, but seldom in history can one point to the name of a ruler who, in the midst of his greatness, knew, like Akbar, how to remain a man in the most beautiful and noblest meaning of the word. And now," concluded Faizi, clasping the hands of Siddha and Iravati, "farewell. Think of me sometimes, when I am far from here. You can do so now without bitterness; and this also takes from me a burden which I have often found hard to bear."

For some time after Faizi had left them, Siddha and Iravati remained in the park. At last they left the spot where they had come to render a last silent homage to the memory of the Great Emperor.

"So they all pass away," said Siddha, musingly, as they turned towards home; "all we have learnt to know and reverence. He who has just left us, in all probability we shall see no more. But such men as Akbar, Faizi, and Abú-l Fazl do not die when death ends their lives here; they live in the memory they leave us, and in their works. The thought of them animates those who come after them; and is not that true immortality?"

1 Akbar died in October 1605, aged sixty-three. There is grave suspicion that he was poisoned at the instigation of his son Salim, who ascended the throne under the name of Jahangir. He was buried at Sikandra, about four miles from Agra, and a splendid mausoleum was erected over his grave. The building was commenced by himself; and Mr. Fergusson says that it is quite unlike any other tomb built in India either before or since, and of a design borrowed from a Hindu or Buddhist model. It stands in an extensive garden, and is approached by one noble gateway. In the centre of the garden, on a raised platform, stands the tomb, of a pyramidal form. The lower storey measures 320 feet each way, exclusive of the angle towers. It is thirty feet high, and is pierced by ten great arches on each face, with a larger entrance in the centre. On this terrace stands another far more ornate, measuring 186 feet on each side, and fourteen feet nine inches in height. A third and fourth of similar design stand on this, all being of red sandstone. Within and above the last is a white marble enclosure, its outer wall entirely composed of marble trellis work of the most beautiful patterns. Inside is the tombstone, a splendid piece of arabesque tracery. But the mortal remains repose under a plainer stone in a vaulted chamber in the basement.—Fergusson's "Indian Architecture," p. 583.

The Earl of Northbrook, when Viceroy of India, presented a rich carpet to the tomb at Sikandra, to be placed over the stone which covers the remains of the greatest ruler of India.

2 Salim, under the name of Jahangir, reigned from 1605 to 1627. His mother was a Rajpút. He was cruel, avaricious, and debauched. He suppressed the rebellion of his son Khusru with the most horrible cruelties. In 1608 Captain William Hawkins landed at Surat, and was received with great favour by Jahangir at Agra. But, after two years, he failed in securing trading privileges for the East India Company, and left Agra in 1611. The influence of Nur

Mahal, his favourite wife, was paramount over Jahangir; but he had no children by her. Of his four sons, he kept the eldest, Khusru, in prison for rebellion. Parwiz, the second, was a drunkard. Khurram, afterwards known as Shah Jahan, succeeded his father. Shahryar was the youngest. In 1615 Sir Thomas Roe arrived at the court of Jahangir, as ambassador from James I., and remained until 1618. Jahangir died on October 12th, 1627, and was succeeded by his rebellious son as Shah Jahan.

3 Shah Jahan reigned from 1628 to 1658.

4 Aurangzíb reigned from 1658 to 1707.

5 It was Nur Mahal who induced Jahangir to be more moderate in his cups.

6 Best known as the "Tarikh-i-Badauni."

7 This invitation is, of course, not historical. Our author, as he tells us in his Introduction, has prolonged the life of Faizi for the purposes of his story. In reality, Faizi died before the murder of his brother Abú-l Fazl.